ADVANCE PRAISE

"Nhi Aronheim has lived many lives: the privileged daughter of a physician in Vietnam, frightened child who escapes barefoot through the jungles of Cambodia, refugee in Thailand with only two pieces of clothing to her name, adopted daughter of an American family in the South, and now wife, mother, and writer. In *Soles of a Survivor*, she writes beautifully about war and its aftermath, adversities and misfortunes to be overcome, the vicissitudes of religion and fate, and, ultimately, resilience, endurance, and gratitude. Her life and her words are an inspiration."

—**Lisa See**, *New York Times* bestselling author of *Snow Flower and the Secret Fan, The Tea Girl of Hummingbird Lane, Peony in Love, Shanghai Girls, Dreams of Joy,* and *China Dolls*

"Using candid and courageous language, Nhi Aronheim weaves a tale of perseverance and fortitude against the backdrop of a country torn apart by war and a mother's desire to seek the best for her children. Part coming of age, part personal and family saga, *Soles of a Survivor* tells the story of a resilient, exceptional girl growing up, growing away, and becoming the woman she was destined to be."

—**Cynthia Swanson**, *New York Times* bestselling author of *The Bookseller* and *The Glass Forest*

"*Soles of a Survivor* is a story of awe-inspiring bravery, grit and love. Nhi Aronheim has navigated worlds within worlds—from the jungles of Cambodia to the suburbs of Kentucky and more—and she brings each one to life with cinematic clarity. *Soles of a Survivor* is an astounding book, one I will never forget."

—**Domenica Ruta**, *New York Times* bestselling author of
With or Without You and *Last Day*

"It's said that refugees lead three lives: their life before being driven from their home; their life on the move, seeking refuge; and, if they survive, a new life adapting to a foreign land. Nhi Aronheim lives all those lives and more in this memoir of persistence, hope, and healing."

—**Alan Gratz**, *New York Times* bestselling author of *Refugee*

"Aronheim's indomitable spirit and determination to survive what many cannot bear to even imagine is truly extraordinary. Her astounding survival, astonishing grace, and radiant gratitude are a triumph of the human spirit and tribute to the incredible strength of this extraordinary woman. Her message of strength and positivity is needed now more than ever. We must never forget the horrors that humans can exact on each other so as to learn from the past and do better in the future. Aronheim's courageous tell-all is a vital first-person preservation of a part of history that is too-often overlooked, and a powerful reminder of the vital and wonderful part that immigrants play in American life. *Soles of a Survivor* is a must-read for memoir-lovers, survival-lovers, and those who believe in the power of women's voices, and women's stories."

—**Sara DiVello**, author of *Where in the OM Am I?*

"Nhi Aronheim's *Soles of a Survivor* is a powerful, uplifting memoir. The story traces the harrowing journey of a young girl from her life as a political refugee on the run to the pinnacle of the American Dream. The book is a beacon of light for dark and trying times."

—**Tiffany Reisz**, *USA Today* bestselling author

"Nhi Aronheim overcame almost unimaginable odds escaping her homeland as a twelve-year-old in 1987. This inspiring story of her harrowing escape through the jungles of Cambodia, surviving the squalid refugee camps in Thailand, and then thriving in the United States is a valuable addition to the expanding literature of the post-American war Vietnamese diaspora."

—**Marc Leepson**, arts editor and columnist,
The VVA Veteran magazine

"Every spring, as the world itself reveals the possibility of renewal, the Jewish People gather around their Passover tables and retell the story of a miraculous journey from degradation to liberation. Our Haggadah is the guide for this annual telling. In her riveting narrative, *Soles of a Survivor*, Nhi Aronheim has penned a version of her own Haggadah detailing a stunning and unlikely path from the war-torn streets and jungles of Vietnam to a new life in America. As her story unfolds we learn of good people she encountered whose kindness and goodness ultimately love her into a sturdy belief in herself, even when merging the two worlds of her personal history proves complicated. Nhi's is a story of redemption pulled from her most intimate memories. It is at once a personal and universal journal in which we learn how the author ultimately finds a home for her heart with her beloved, and a home for her soul within the Jewish community, a community she makes stronger and kinder. In its pages, the reader cannot help but feel that renewal is ever a possibility."

—**Rabbi B. Elka Abrahamson**, president,
The Wexner Foundation

"Nhi has shown all of the characteristics that define her life—toughness, resilience, compassion, and hope. Those traits come through in this record of an extraordinary young woman's continuing journey. Vietnam and the United States will be linked in many ways for generations to come—most powerfully in the lives of people like Nhi. *Soles of a Survivor* is an important addition to our continuing exploration of that relationship. Even more, it is a story that should inspire us all."

—**Clarence R. Wyatt**, author of *Paper Soldiers: The American Press and the Vietnam War* and president, Monmouth College

"High talent alongside high energy and strong values are a tough combination to beat …. amazing and inspiring story."

—**Dr. John Roush**, president emeritus, Centre College

SOLES *of a* SURVIVOR

Dear Deb,

Best wishes to you,

Nhi A

SOLES *of a* SURVIVOR

A MEMOIR

NHI ARONHEIM

Skyhorse Publishing

Skyhorse Publishing books may be purchased in bulk at special discounts for sales promotion, corporate gifts, fund-raising, or educational purposes. Special editions can also be created to specifications. For details, contact the Special Sales Department, Skyhorse Publishing, 307 West 36th Street, 11th Floor, New York, NY 10018 or info@skyhorsepublishing.com.

Skyhorse® and Skyhorse Publishing® are registered trademarks of Skyhorse Publishing, Inc.®, a Delaware corporation.

Visit our website at www.skyhorsepublishing.com.

10 9 8 7 6 5 4 3 2

Library of Congress Cataloging-in-Publication Data is available on file.

Cover design by Brian Peterson

Print ISBN: 978-1-5107-6028-8
Ebook ISBN: 978-1-5107-6029-5

Printed in the United States of America

CONTENTS

To my beloved husband, Jeff, and children, Max and Sarah, and to all my families and friends who always believed in me and helped me become who I am today.

AUTHOR'S NOTE

In writing this book, I relied on my memory and have strived to be as accurate as possible by turning to photo albums and articles, and by interviewing family members and some characters in the story.

For events where I could not substantiate detail, I've reconstructed some dialogue based on my memory, knowing that each time we remember something, we alter our perspective slightly.

The stories in these pages are recollections and interpretations of events that shaped my life over many years. I understand that other people may recall things differently and have their own perspective of certain events.

For privacy, the following names are pseudonyms in the book: Sister Second, Brother Fourth, Sister Fifth, Koi, and Jamie.

INTRODUCTION

I've been told that, though I'm only 4'9", my story is immense—so I'm now sharing it with the world. With *you*. Several anthologies and a documentary that aired on PBS have profiled my harrowing journey as a child refugee who went on to live the American Dream.

But I've only told part of my story. Until now.

I've written my memoir because the world desperately needs more stories about tolerance, unity, and how to work together for a common good.

I've also written my memoir because my story isn't much different than the story of the many millions of *other* refugees who've fled, or are fleeing, their countries for safety and opportunity.

The soles of my feet still bear the scars of my horrific escape from Vietnam—where I trudged through the jungles of Cambodia as a child with a group of strangers seeking the land of opportunity: America. My only possessions at the time were two pieces of clothing and a heart filled with hope.

My physician father worked for the US government, and the Communists imprisoned him for doing so when the war ended. To avoid the rest of our family meeting the same fate, my quick-witted mother bribed a driver to put us on a bus headed for Saigon.

At the age of ten, I struggled to survive on the streets of the fallen city until I escaped, not knowing if I'd ever see my family again. My harrowing trip through the Cambodian jungle, and eventually on a boat to Thailand, led me to an orphanage where I lived for two years until I qualified for refugee status in the United States.

Soles of a Survivor isn't just another inspirational survival story, however. It's about the lessons I've learned about humanity and diversity since arriving in the United States. After I met my Jewish beau, we married.

I now have a deeper appreciation for the parallels between the Jewish and Vietnamese cultures, and others. I eventually converted to Judaism, though the process of conversion was challenging. It's difficult for most people, but it was particularly difficult for me, an Asian woman adopted into a Christian household.

Now I relish being a Vietnamese Jew.

Soles of a Survivor shows it matters less what religion we're part of, as long as we radiate goodness to those we meet. For example, I honor and greatly admire the Christian family in Kentucky that adopted me, when I had nothing to offer them but love. Thanks to their support and devotion, despite overwhelming barriers, I graduated high school as class valedictorian in just three years.

While in college, I had the opportunity to return to Vietnam with a film crew and reunite with the family I never thought I'd see again. A second trip to Vietnam with my legal guardian brought my two mothers face-to-face.

It wasn't a storybook ending.

Life isn't like that, at least not most of the time.

When we went to Vietnam, my birth mom—who at one time only wanted the best for me—showed signs of jealousy during the visit and considered me "too Americanized."

Maybe she's right.

I'll leave that for you to decide.

As I'm writing this, I'm reminded of one of the five toilets in my current home. It has fancy features such as a heated seat, automatic lid opener and closer, sprayer, and dryer. I am awed and deeply grateful regarding how far I've come, from the days I had to immerse myself chest deep in a pool of sewage trying to hide from soldiers.

I can also now afford to cover my scarred feet with any shoes I desire.

But my shoes aren't who I am.

Neither are my scars.

My *heart* is.

This book is an invitation, from my heart to yours.

I'm filled with gratitude for all I've been fortunate to accomplish and become in this great country. I hope my story inspires and empowers you. And I hope that, like me, through your challenges, you, too, will find healing and joy.

There is light at the end of *every* tunnel.

PART ONE
REMEMBERING

CHAPTER ONE
BEGINNINGS

"Mom, I told you, you can't serve pork. I'm marrying a Jewish man and serving pork will offend him and his family!" I shrieked, my Vietnamese accent hardly noticeable anymore. "Jews don't eat pork because it's considered unclean."

"You can't have a southern wedding without a roasted pig!" my Christian, Georgia peach adoptive mother replied.

I adored my adoptive mother and was more than grateful that she offered to plan my wedding in just four months and host it on her eight-hundred-acre farm in the Virginia boonies. I knew my mother meant well and for somebody raised in the South, tradition was everything, but pork was out of the question. It would offend my new Jewish family and friends who came down from the New England area—not the way I wanted to start my married life.

"No pig and no pork! That's final!" It was probably hard for her to understand how a beloved tradition could be construed as "offensive," but she finally relented, albeit under protest, and pig was off the menu.

Back in 2000, not only were Asian-Jewish marriages extremely uncommon, but most of the one hundred and forty farm folks she invited to our wedding had likely never met a person of Jewish descent—or somebody who was Vietnamese, for that matter. All of them were coming to our wedding as a show of support for my parents. They would bring homemade pies and other wonderful desserts, no doubt all looking forward to seeing our out-of-town guests' reactions on the hayrides that my parents organized around the property.

We weren't going to have a preacher or a rabbi perform the ceremony. At the time, a reform rabbi would not even consider marrying an interfaith couple like us. I, however, did agree to the Jewish tradition of breaking the glass, signifying "our breaking down the barriers between people of different cultures and faiths." This tradition also implied that our marriage was as fragile as glass and we should treasure every single day together as if it were our last. That was a tradition I could be in total agreement with.

My soon-to-be husband never pressured me into converting to Judaism and I loved him for it—he knew using that tactic with me had no chance for success and would probably push me away. He did request that I agree to teach our children about Judaism and the Jewish faith and traditions.

"Yes," I said. "Under one condition—it must be Jewish *and* Vietnamese!"

It wasn't that I opposed the idea of converting to Judaism; rather, conversion had to be real, from the heart. Otherwise, it would be empty and meaningless. My husband-to-be completely understood.

Within months after our wedding, I honored my commitment to learn as much about Judaism as I could so I'd know how to raise our family when the time came. I read many books about

Judaism and asked my newlywed husband about his faith, culture, and tradition. His typical reply was, "I'm sorry I don't know the answers. Growing up, I often skipped religious school to go to 7-Eleven to buy snacks and candies. I know I am a bad Jew."

"You are such an idiot when it comes to knowing about your heritage! I guess I'll have to learn from someone else and you can join me if you like," I replied after getting frustrated with his regular responses.

I signed up to take the "Intro to Judaism" class and my husband agreed to attend with me, which I really appreciated. And then something amazing happened. As I got deeper and deeper into the teachings, I was amazed—astounded, really—that there were so many similarities between what the Jewish people had gone through and what the Vietnamese people had to endure. It seemed that in addition to dealing with continuous oppression, prejudice, and tyranny, the Jewish people had also developed a great work ethic despite all their trials and tribulations. They dedicated themselves to the education and nurturing of their families no matter what the cost, and they stuck together as a people, never forgetting where they came from. They were also immigrants who endured the worst persecution and suffering imaginable, people who wandered endlessly for years in the wilderness—never giving up hope that someday they would enter the Promised Land and begin their new and better life. Their history is one of loss, hope, resilience, and survival against all the odds.

And so is mine.

* * *

Imagine not knowing what year you were born, or how many brothers and sisters you actually had. That was the reality of life in Vietnam in the early seventies.

My birth certificate claimed I was born on February 24, 1975, but my mother was adamant that I was actually born two years earlier, in 1973. I have sixty-six first cousins on my father's side of the family, many of them old enough to be my parents. Many of them I never met. Large families were common, and often, instead of being creative with names, parents would call their kids by numbers based on their birth order. It might be out of superstition, but families would always call the firstborn "Second" and continue from there. So my dad, whose real name was Tao, was called Tenth, being the second youngest of ten children. For many parents with numerous kids, having their children's birth recorded was not high on the priority list, which was why it took my mother almost two years to get around to doing it.

My earliest memories take me all the way back to when I was about two years old. My family and I lived in a beautiful countryside house in a prestigious area of a town known as Ha Lam, located in Central Vietnam, near Da Nang. I can vividly recall the beautiful lake that surrounded our entire compound. It was a jewel, and colorful water lilies and lotus flowers in full bloom gently floated on the lake's tranquil surface. While I had no concept of what heaven looked like back then, I was certain that it couldn't compare to the fairy tale setting I saw every morning when I awoke.

We had no television, radio, or telephone to keep us entertained, so we would run out to the rice paddy fields each morning to gather up mud to create clay toys to play with that day. When that got old, we would cut down baby bamboo stakes and create flutes out of them. My siblings and I would spend our afternoons playing around those beautiful big evergreens that surrounded the lake like a protective fence, shielding us from the realities of a country being torn apart by death, despair, and war.

We were taught at an early age that whenever we heard the sound of airplanes, no matter how distant the sound might be, we were to race home and hurry into our bomb shelters. Ours was located next to our pharmacy. It was a dark, damp place, with its thick concrete walls and low ceilings. But it was also perfect for playing hide and seek, something my siblings and I did often. Still, we were mindful to run to the shelter whenever we heard the distant whir of an airplane; if you didn't, you could be blown to bits by American bombs. Even in fairy tales, there was always a dark side that could appear at any moment.

* * *

We were the most prominent family in the region. My father, a well-respected physician, worked in private practice. He was also employed by the American military, taking care of the injured American soldiers. His private medical practice and pharmacy sat on our property right next to the main house. My beautiful, petite mother, with her long dark hair, pretty smile, and flawless skin, was ten years younger than my father and worked beside him as his nurse.

I had two older brothers and two older sisters—and maybe more. My mother had suffered three miscarriages, and I would occasionally wonder about these other lost siblings I could have had. During this time, Vietnam had a polygamy system whereby men could have multiple wives to show off their social status. Father had two official wives and numerous mistresses, who also bore him children.

My siblings and I sometimes asked why Mother would marry Father, knowing she would be his second wife.

"I had two choices," she replied. "Either marry a farmer and work long hard days on a rice paddy field for the rest of my life, or marry a handsome, successful doctor who I not only learn from but also have a higher social status. I have so much more freedom and opportunities than I would if I had been a farmer's wife." She shrugged. "So being wife number two to a doctor is far better than being wife number one to a farmer." It was not, perhaps, the fairy tale response one might expect, but I understood her reasoning.

When my parents got married, Mother didn't want to share a house with Father's first wife and kids. She wanted her own home and her own kids. So, Father shuttled between the two houses and set up his medical practices in the towns where the two wives lived. He spent one week with us and one week with his first wife, which made it challenging for patients to know when he was available. Back then, there were no telephones, so if you needed a doctor, you just headed out to his office, hoping he would be in. Father was the only doctor in the region, so sometimes people trudged long distances to get his help at our home only to realize that he was with wife number one that week. In that case, they had to travel again to another town, waiting to see him. Eventually, nearby towns developed a system to inform each other what town Father was in that week.

* * *

Patients came from all around and by the first light of day were already lined up outside our property, waiting for Father to treat them. Sometimes, it was something relatively simple, like a bad cold, and the patient would make a stop at the pharmacy for some cough syrup after being examined by Father. Other times, though, it was more serious, and in some cases, fatal. One afternoon, a woman showed up at the clinic, begging Father to rescue her dying son, who had been struck by lightning. He was a few years older than I was at the time, and his mother kept pleading through her tears, "Save him! Please save him!"

But there was nothing Father could do.

"I'm sorry, I can't save your son," he told the boy's hysterical mother. In her grief, she seemed unable to hear him, and instead kept repeating her unanswerable plea. "I'm sorry. His entire body is fried," Father said again.

The boy's mother bowed in front of Father, wailing, as if she were able to express her anguish fully enough, it might somehow bring her son back. Father had no choice other than to just walk away because there truly was nothing he could do for the boy.

More often than not, though, Father was able to help the many patients that came to see him. I found this fascinating, and sometimes I would climb the large shade tree outside of Father's office and watch through the window as he performed surgery or delivered a baby. Some of the things I witnessed seemed quite strange, like when he stuck needles in certain places on a patient's body. I didn't know what acupuncture was and found it incredible that no one ever seemed in pain when he did this. Even more shocking was when I once saw him remove a woman's breast—I knew nothing about cancer and had no idea why he would do such a thing.

Later, I would learn that if his female patients couldn't afford his services, he'd tell them about "other ways to pay him," which explains why, in addition to his five children with my mom, and ten with his first wife, he sired so many others out of wedlock.

* * *

In spite of the raging war, my family lived fairly well considering what was going on all around us. I was fortunate enough to have a live-in nanny named Chieu, who fed, bathed, cooked, and took care of me whenever my parents weren't around. She was such a kind, loving woman, and I completely adored her. She was probably around forty, and she had thick, dark hair she would often wear in a bun. She played with me when my sisters and brothers wouldn't, and kept me occupied when my parents were busy tending to patients well into the night.

Our home was always a bustling, busy place, not just because people were ill and needed care from my father, but because we had the only water well in our village. The well was located in the front yard, outside of the main house. It was about six feet in diameter and had a circular wall, about three feet high, surrounding it. So, not very tall, and it is quite fortunate and rather incredible that a child never fell in. A cat did once, and the well had to be drained, which meant the entire town had to come help. Using nothing more than a piece of rope to secure themselves, some of the braver adults formed a chain of people and handed up bucket after bucket of water until it was empty and the well could be cleaned. Quite a bit of work, but it's what needed to be done if people wanted clean water.

There was no electricity in our village, so at night, many people would often sit outside, the adults talking while the kids ran in packs, playing games in the dark of night. By far, my favorite time of year was the Mid-Autumn Festival, or *Tết Trung Thu*. A celebration of the rice harvest in the middle of the eighth lunar month, this festival also celebrated the children. For us, *Tết Trung Thu* meant staying up past our bedtime, carrying carp-shaped lanterns under the glow of a full moon, and eating as many mooncakes as we could. These soft, sticky treats were filled with sweet-bean paste or lotus-curd paste, and were sometimes made in the shape of animals. The mooncakes the adults feasted on were usually round and baked in molds with elegant, intricate patterns, making each cake look like its own piece of art.

These were happy, idyllic times, and they were about to come to devastating halt.

* * *

On April 30, 1975, the communists finally took control of the entire country. Decades of war had ended, but there was no peace to be found. Soldiers went door-to-door, demanding to see anyone who worked for, or had ties with, the American military. It was truly a scary time, though they tried to present it as the opposite.

"We want you to come forward, and ask for forgiveness," the soldiers proclaimed. "We will forgive you." Empty promises—no one really believed it.

Father knew he couldn't hide. Too many people knew him. When the soldiers pounded on our door, Father turned himself in and asked for forgiveness, hoping that the soldiers would keep their word. To nobody's surprise, they did not.

Instead, they dragged him away. There was nothing any of us could do, except stand there and watch. The tears streamed down my face, but it didn't matter how loudly I screamed his name—he was not coming back. Our whole family was traumatized and even the family dog sat by Father's shoes in mourning and refused to move or eat—he would die soon afterward.

The soldiers took Father to a reeducation camp that was more like a prison. Here he found himself among military officers, religious leaders, government workers, and other people, like himself, who had helped the Americans. The conditions at these camps were horrendous. Detainees were beaten and tortured physically and mentally. Food and water were regularly withheld, pushing most to the brink of starvation. Days were spent being reeducated through "productive labor," which might include planting crops or sweeping minefields. At night, they slept on filthy concrete floors, only to awaken the next morning for another day of hard physical labor.

The detainees were severely malnourished and disease was rampant. Many people died. Those who fell sick or became too weak to work any longer were kicked out and sent home to their families, though in many cases, this was not the sort of happy homecoming you might imagine. Many of the detainees who returned home would die soon after.

We were only able to visit Father a few times, and before we were allowed to see him, the guards would force us children to sing a song about how much we loved Ho Chi Minh. Even now,

many years later, that song haunts my memories and makes my
heart ache:

Who loves Uncle Ho Chi Minh more than teens, children.
Who loves Uncle Ho Chi Minh more than teens, children.
Who loves Uncle Ho Chi Minh more than teens, children.
Who loves Uncle Ho Chi Minh more than Vietnamese children.
Our high-altitude, bar,
Uncle us, eyes like a star, long beard.
Uncle us, brown skin because of dew wind.
Uncle us, vow vigorously vengeance home.
Ho Chi Minh respectfully loved us love Uncle Ho Chi Minh whole
    life.
Ho Chi Minh beloved Uncle Ho for three years because of race.

Uncle but now old, old but still cheerful.
Day by day we wish.
Hope Uncle lives forever to lead children into human beings,
And build the house by people.
Ho Chi Minh respectfully loved us love Uncle Ho Chi Minh whole
    life.
Ho Chi Minh loves us we wish that Uncle Ho Chi Minh lived
    forever.

Contact visits weren't allowed in prison. It didn't matter how
badly I wanted to give my father a hug, none of us were able
to touch him. The guards instructed us to stand outside the
gate to talk to Father through a barbed wire fence. I barely
recognized him. The man who had been taken away had been
vigorous and confident—the man who stood before me now

was a frail, weak shell of the man he used to be. We were only allowed to visit for about fifteen minutes, and then we were forced to leave.

Back at home, things were not much better; our peaceful existence was completely shattered. Communist agents, called Viet Cong, ordered us to get rid of my nanny, whom I had become so attached to—she was like my second mother. I was inconsolable for hours after she left, unable to understand why the adults I loved were being taken away from me. Our idyllic, fairy tale life seemed a distant memory, though little did I know that things were about to get unimaginably worse.

* * *

I woke up one morning to the sound of heavy footsteps and shouting, loud male voices that I didn't recognize. I slipped out of bed and found my older brother, Cu, who I sat huddled next to in the living room as a dozen or more soldiers traipsed through the house, looking at our belongings. The soldiers carried big guns and what looked like enough ammo to start another war. They roamed the house like they owned it. By now, the rest of my siblings had also woken up and we sat, with Mother, in the living room.

"We're placing you under house arrest," one of the soldiers told Mother while the others began to file out of the house. There were so many of them, and they walked so heavily, I could feel the vibration through the floor. I just wanted them to leave. I wanted Father to return, I wanted nanny Chieu to play with me down by the lake, and I wanted our old life back.

The soldier, a man who did not appear much older than my own father, eyed us. "We'll be monitoring your every move. You don't go anywhere unless you have permission."

The soldiers left our house, but didn't go far. For the next several months, if we wanted to go anywhere, we had to get permission from the soldiers, who camped out on our property. Even going to school had become a big production because we had to get permission from the soldiers just to do that.

And then one day, the soldiers were gone. They didn't tell us they were leaving, or if they'd be back, but it was a relief to regain even some of our freedom back. It was around this time that Mother started hearing rumors that the communists were going to come back and would seize people's assets. She began hiding penicillin and other expensive medications we still had in the pharmacy. She became quite inventive when finding places to stash gold—an old rice pot would do just fine, and even our backpacks were used.

"Go to your uncle's home on your way to school," she'd whisper. "Give him the backpack."

Sometimes she'd hide gold in a relative's home without even telling them, so they could avoid arrest from knowingly harboring our wealth.

One day, the soldiers returned. Mother wasn't home, so they talked to my brother Cu. "Where did your mother hide her valuables?" they demanded. Cu said nothing. The soldiers, these grown men, beat up a ten-year-old boy until he couldn't take it anymore.

"I'll show you!" he shrieked. "Just stop hurting me." He limped around the house, blood flowing freely from his nose, a shiny bruise already starting to form on his cheekbone. Cu showed them the rice pot. Behind the large silk painting that hung in our living room. Under a loose floorboard in the pharmacy's back corner. The soldiers greedily took the gold, and anything else of value. But still, it was not enough.

"Show us who your parents talked to and where they were hiding things," they insisted.

Fearful of another beating, Cu grudgingly obeyed. He would tell me when he returned later how our aunts and uncles acted as if they had no idea what he was talking about and demanded that he leave immediately.

"Why would they say that to you?" I asked. "They're our family."

He shook his head. The bruise on his cheek had swollen like an egg, was as purple as the water lilies floating on the lake. "I could tell they felt bad," he said, "but they're afraid, too. They don't want to get arrested."

"But why are they taking all of our things?"

"The new government says that under communism, everybody should be equal. They think our family has too much wealth. They're going to give our things to the poor."

But I could tell from the look on my brother's face that he didn't really believe that, and after seeing the way the soldiers behaved, I didn't either. Later, I would learn that our gold and other valuables were really distributed to family members of the communist party.

The prison released Father early from his sentence, thanks to his older brother in the communist party who sponsored his freedom. Uncle Ninth had been on the side of the Viet Cong, fighting against the Americans, while Father had been working for them. After the war, Uncle Ninth became a high-ranking member within the communist party, which enabled him to get Father released from the reeducation camp early.

At first, this was great news—finally, some good news for our family. But the Father who returned to us was not the same Father who had left. With his place to practice medicine gone, Father was unable to continue to work as a doctor. Even if our home had not been destroyed, I don't think he would have been able to work in the capacity he had before. He had been tortured and severely brainwashed in the reeducation camp. Not only did it seem he had forgotten how to be a doctor but also how to be a father. He yelled at Mother that she needed to take care of him and demanded she give him any money she managed to earn. He would hit her if she answered in a way he didn't like. We kids didn't fare much better, and he'd even beat up Cu the times my brother tried to step in and protect Mother.

I didn't want to be around him, and would try to make myself invisible when he was around. *Who was this man?* I'd often wonder sadly. What had happened to him at that camp to make him like this? Would he ever change back?

Mother didn't seem to think so, and not long after Father returned, he was gone again. He couldn't take being looked down upon like just another poor person, when in his old life he had been one of the most distinguished members of the community. He left to go live with his first wife and family. He would never be the same person again, and Mother didn't want us to be around him.

Over the next three years, we would lose more than just all of our assets to the communists. The soldiers marched on us again, this time demanding that we leave our home. We were forced to leave in a whirlwind of chaos, so quickly that we were not able to bring anything with us. Not that there was much left to take, anyway.

We were to board a bus to go to a reeducation camp, though not the same one my father was at. My sisters were crying. Mother's face was hard to read, but I knew she hated leaving our home as much as I did. I looked over my shoulder as I boarded the bus, and saw the house, where I had lived so happily, one last time. Years after we left, the house, my father's office, and the pharmacy were demolished, and a police station was constructed in its place.

"I heard what these kinds of camps are like," Mother whispered to us as the bus started off. "It's all propaganda. Brainwashing. They want to get our allegiance to the party by showing you images of Americans killing children, or when they carry a dead baby's body." She shook her head.

As we boarded the bus headed for the camp, Mother said, "I don't want you to grow up in that kind of environment."

I knew the kind of environment she wanted us to grow up in. Ever since the fall of Saigon, she had one dream: for her children to have a better life in America. "It is the greatest place in the world," she would say. "One day I will get you there— whatever it takes." Even amid tragedy, Mother remained doggedly insistent on having her way. I wasn't sure how she would manage to pull that off now, with us on a bus on our way to the reeducation camp.

Yet I should not have doubted her resourcefulness. A few hours into the bus ride, the driver pulled into a rest stop. There were several other buses there, and I wondered if they were also on their way to a camp. We were allowed to get off and use the bathroom, or buy some food if we had the money.

Mother wasn't interested in using the bathroom or getting food though—instead, she took some of the gold she had managed to hide from the soldiers and bribed our driver with it. He would keep the gold and say nothing when we boarded a different bus full of merchants. Despite the risk and potential danger ahead, we headed south into the belly of the beast that was Saigon.

* * *

It was 1980 and the communist party ruled the entire country, but Saigon—renamed Ho Chi Minh City—still enjoyed some freedoms—but not many.

Fear, anxiety, and depression became chronic states of being. We had only the clothes on our backs and were fortunate to have them. In order to go from one town to another during this time, you needed to show the correct paperwork—sort of like needing a passport to travel between the United States and Mexico. Without the proper papers, we were considered illegal residents and limited in what we could do or say.

Once we arrived, Mother contacted my older half-sister, Dung, who I had never met before.

"Can you find us a place?" Mother pleaded, then handed Dung some gold that she'd sewn into the hem of her clothes.

My half-sister found a small one-room place for the six of us in the slum—worlds apart from the sprawling lake-view home we'd grown up in. It was a ramshackle building made out of two concrete walls and an old tin metal roof, looking like all it would take was one strong gust of wind to blow away the roof. Threadbare clothing flapped on lines strung under the roof. There was no electricity, and we got our water from a small hose. If we wanted to drink the water, we had to boil it first to kill any germs. The tin roof had so many holes in it that when it rained, water leaked all over us as we slept—huddled together, side by side—on the cold concrete floor. Lizards, rats, and cockroaches seemed more at home in our little room than we would ever feel. Yet despite the deplorable conditions, I actually found our leaky roof to be comforting, as cool rain from the sky tumbled down, enveloping me, the water providing a much-needed sense of calm.

One thing that did not provide a sense of calm was our bathroom, if you could call it that. I called it the "Helly Hole" because really, that's exactly what it was: a large, deep hole in the floor you had to squat over whenever you had to go. The hole was above a shallow, muddy creek, as was common in Vietnam, since there was no central sewage system at this time. The hole could easily swallow a grown adult, so I was convinced if I were to fall in, I'd be lost in the river of festering sewage. But we had to be under the radar because we were living there illegally. Getting caught meant being arrested and sent to a remote reeducation camp, which we knew would be unimaginably worse than our current situation.

Even though I found using the Helly Hole disgusting, we still had it better than some. It wasn't uncommon to be going to the bathroom and look down and see a person below, walking along the creek, among the sewage, hoping to find some fish or bottles that they could recycle.

Being without a resident card also meant we couldn't purchase rationed meat or rice from the government, so we never had enough to eat. Buying "black market" food was too costly, so many nights, our family of six sat on the floor and had to share two boiled eggs and a bowl of plain rice. Sometimes, Mother would add a spoonful of fish sauce, often with a healthy dose of squirming maggots.

"Just avoid the maggots when you scoop the sauce," Mother would tell us. "And if you accidentally eat some, it's okay—they're good protein." I didn't care how badly my stomach twisted and cramped in hunger—just thinking about having a white maggot wriggling around my mouth could send me into convulsions. Still, I ate the food since we did not have other choices.

Mother refused to let her spirit be dampened, no matter how wretched our living situation was. She decided she wanted to cook a special meal for us to celebrate the biggest holiday in Vietnam, the Vietnamese New Year, or Tet.

"Just because we live somewhere different doesn't mean we can't still celebrate."

Her enthusiasm was contagious, and my siblings and I immediately found ourselves awash in memories of the good old days. We all agreed that we wanted a special dish from central Vietnam: rice pancakes with shrimp and pork. Such a meal had always been a big family production, and this time it would be no different.

To make the dish, we had to soak the rice for a few days and then bring it to the miller's so it could be grated into liquid flour. It took us about an hour to get there on bicycle, me riding on the back of the bike while my oldest sister, Second, pedaled. The streets were crowded with people, many also on bikes, and some walking. Motorbikes zipped by and commercial trucks trundled down the road, leaving big clouds of exhaust in their wake. Riding through the slums, the air was heavy with the stench of sewage and rotting trash. But we were going to be making one of our favorite meals. I clung to this thought as we navigated the chaotic streets.

"This is going to taste so good," Sister Second said while we waited. I closed my eyes, imagining biting into the warm, freshly made pancake, wrapped around a piece of perfectly cooked shrimp. To have something to eat that wasn't rice crawling with maggots seemed almost too good to be true, but I knew we'd all be enjoying it soon enough.

We started back on our journey home, with a bucket of liquid rice flour this time, instead of a container of dry rice. I balanced the bucket of liquid flour the best I could on the bike's rear rack, but I knew the moment my sister pushed off that getting home was going to be a challenge. The bucket would start to lean and I'd grip it more tightly, trying to straighten it. No sooner did that happen and Sister Second would have to steer around someone, or we'd hit a pothole, sending a jolt through the bike and straight up my spine. My arms ached and my fingers were numb, but I refused to let go.

Almost there.

I was about to relax, knowing we were about five minutes away, when someone ran into us. I didn't even see who it was; one moment I was perched on the back of the bike, hugging the bucket of rice flour, the next the bike was no longer under me and the bucket was no longer in my arms. Sister Second and I hit the ground hard, but I didn't have time to register the pain because the bucket exploded, bathing my sister and I in the precious liquid. The bike lay on its side, rear wheel still spinning.

My sister and I looked at each other. There was nothing to be done, no way to correct this or collect what we could; the liquid that hadn't soaked us was a swampy puddle on the filthy street. We burst into tears and didn't stop crying when we got back to the house, Mother hurrying over to us, believing we were hurt. We had a few minor scrapes, but it was the pain of being so close to having something comforting, something familiar, only to have it ripped away, that hurt so badly. Although we were covered in white liquid flour, thankfully we were not injured.

That particular Tet, we had no special food for the holiday.

* * *

It's true that we were dirt poor, yet Mother still wanted us to get the best education we could. Because we lived in Ho Chi Minh City illegally, we were not allowed to go to school the way the other kids were. Mother ended up bribing the school so we could attend class for a few hours in the morning. The school was small—there were six classrooms surrounding a courtyard, which was little more than a concrete slab, that we were allowed to mill around in during break.

At first, I was excited to go back to school, but that excitement evaporated my very first day.

"Are you a beggar?" a girl asked me.

"No," I said.

She narrowed her eyes. "You sure dress like one."

The few pieces of clothing I owned had holes, loose threads, stains. Nothing matched and nothing quite fit right, either—an article of clothing would either be comically large, like a T-shirt down to my knees, or a little too small. I ignored the girl, and her friend who chimed in. It was the first day, after all, and I figured they would forget about me.

But they didn't. They kept right at it, whispering to each other when we were supposed to be writing in our workbooks. There were six of us at a table, and though I tried to remain focused on my schoolwork, their giggles and snide comments got to be too much.

During our break, I jumped up on the table and kicked those two girls as hard as I could with my bare feet. I didn't even care that the whole world could see me butt naked under the cheap ragged skirt I was wearing—if they bothered to ask or make fun of me for it, I'd tell them it was more important for Mother to spend money on food and education than to buy underwear for me. I only got in a couple kicks before the teacher yanked me off the table. The two girls were both crying, but they weren't injured. After my big fight, word spread quickly about the undisciplined poor girl. None of the kids bothered me much after that.

* * *

At least at school they didn't. Kids in the neighborhood had no problem making fun of my siblings and me for being so poor. There was one family in particular, who lived next door, who vehemently despised us, mainly for being poor, but also for not having a father. They were also poor, but still in a much better situation than we were. They had a larger space with a private bathroom and did not have to bathe outside with a dribbling hose. That was our only source of water, so when we wanted to clean ourselves, we had a choice: strip down and stand naked in the street or bathe yourself while still clothed. Mother and my siblings would wait until dark and keep their clothes on, but I didn't care who saw me, and would "shower" whenever I wanted to.

One night, close to New Year, Cu asked me if I wanted to get back at them. "Look what I have," he said, and he opened his hand. Firecrackers. My other brother, Fourth, stepped outside.

"I found these on the street on my way home," he said, showing us an armful of tin cans.

Cu nodded, a mischievous grin on his face. "Perfect."

We walked onto the sidewalk between our home and the next-door neighbor, and I helped my brothers arrange the fire-crackers underneath the tin cans, aimed right at their door. My brothers lit the firecrackers and we stepped back into the shadows, watching as sparks shot off and the cans flew right into the front door, like little missiles. We laughed until we cried, and when the door was flung open, we ran into our home, cracking up the whole way.

* * *

Mother expected all of us to pitch in to help scrape together what little money we could. For me, this meant waking up at three in the morning most days to sell gasoline in liter bottles for the motor vehicles and motorcycles. Mother purchased the gasoline in large plastic containers that she would then divvy up into liter bottles. She would mix in some lower-quality gasoline to make it stretch further, and then instructed us to sell it as high quality.

The earlier we woke up, the less competition we had. Having once had a nanny who did everything for me, I, now at only ten years old, was reduced to dodging the chaos and fearless drivers on the road so I could sell anything that could put food on our table. I was certainly not alone out there on the streets of Saigon. There were many other vendors, all of us just trying to make what little money we could. To pass the time, I would sometimes strike up a conversation, hoping some of the more experienced vendors might clue me in on a way to make better money.

One of the things I quickly learned was that working together would be beneficial for everyone. If one of us had a customer that was looking for something we didn't sell, instead of turning them away, I'd find a vendor who had the desired item. The vendor would give me a small commission fee after I sold the item to my customer. In this way, we never had to turn anyone away, and sometimes, as a vendor, you could make a little extra money without having to hustle.

This was how I started selling counterfeit cigarettes.

It seemed more people were interested in buying cigarettes from me as opposed to gasoline, so I began to sell those. But selling cigarettes on the street corner didn't bring in much profit, and I was certain I could come up with something better to earn more money so that we could eat.

I should find out where my dealer gets his cigarettes, I thought to myself. *And I will bypass him and go straight to the source.* It was a good plan, but it did have its challenges: Even if I went to the source, who would be willing to deal with a ten-year-old kid? And how the heck was I going to get the money to pay for it? I knew who might have some answers.

Mother looked at me for a long moment after I told her my idea. "You've become very street smart and can clearly talk your way into anything," she said. "If you can get to the source,

I'll use some of our saved money to fund your business. But remember, what you're doing is illegal and you'll have to talk yourself out of trouble if you get caught. And make sure you never mention to anybody that I know what you're doing. If a young child gets arrested, in most cases, the police will release you shortly after. But if an adult gets arrested, the punishment is much more severe."

With Mother's approval, I secretly followed my dealer for days. I followed him through the busy streets, dodging pedestrians and motorbikes and people being pushed on cyclos, the three-wheeled bike taxis. I passed vendors parked right on the sidewalk, sitting on dilapidated lawn chairs or short-legged wooden stools, selling cold soda or fruit. It was easy to blend into the crowd and my dealer had no idea he was being tailed.

I followed him into Chinatown. Chinatown in Ho Chi Minh City was the largest in Vietnam, called *Cho Lon*, which means "Large Market." It was home to an enormous Chinese population because China had occupied Vietnam for over a thousand years. After the war ended, many Chinese chose to remain in this part of Vietnam, so the communist government often left them alone to run business in their own area of town.

It was a descent into a dizzying, colorful sort of chaos, the main roads hectic with traffic of all types, sidewalk vendors hawking everything imaginable, from cooking utensils to spices to dried seafood. The alleyways snaked this way and that, like a maze you could lose yourself in if you weren't careful.

The Chinese wholesale merchants were, for the most part, quite nice to me, and once I started coming around regularly and they recognized me, they almost became like friends. They were all older, middle-aged men and women who might have had a daughter my age; perhaps I reminded some of them of their own kids and that's why they were kind. They all spoke fluent Vietnamese, with a Chinese accent. By asking around, I later got referrals for new connections that allowed me to buy tobacco, cigarette buds, paper, and packages at wholesale prices. The Chinese in Cho Lon had a great reputation for being straightforward and honest business people, so that made things much easier for me.

Initially, I had planned to approach the merchant my dealer got his supply from, but I didn't want to get beaten up for going directly to my dealer's source, and now that I was more familiar with Chinatown and its people, I had options. I decided to approach another merchant a few booths over. He was probably fifty years old, and he listened intently when I explained to him what I wanted to do.

"I have an adult-handler who wants to know how we can set up a new connection for counterfeit cigarettes. He doesn't want to get himself into any trouble, so he sent me, a kid. He's already trained me to keep secrets under any circumstances," I said, lying through my teeth.

"It costs money," he said.

"I know." I showed him the money I had with me. After seeing that, he was more than helpful.

With my new source, and with Mother's funding, I was able to purchase all the ingredients I needed. The merchant also told me about a small attic space above his friend's home in Chinatown that I could rent out; it was already equipped with everything I'd need to make the cigarettes, all I needed to do was pay the fee. The tool I used to make the cigarettes was a wooden box with a metal bar and two handles; it was about twelve inches long, six inches wide, and four inches deep. The merchant also taught me how to roll tobacco, attach cigarette butts, cut, package, and seal them in fancy 555 cigarette packs (the most expensive cigarettes at the time).

I was in awe of my final product. Now that I was getting the supplies directly and making the cigarettes myself, my profit quadrupled. As always, I gave all of the money to Mother, though sometimes she would give me a little so I could treat myself to a dessert. Mother knew my activities were illegal, but I was bringing in more money than I ever could selling gasoline.

"I see something in you," she said. "I trust you, even though you're young." But she would always follow that praise with an admonition.

"Even though you sell cigarettes, I don't want you smoking because it's quite addictive." I was shocked by her hypocrisy at times. I found it unbelievable that Mother would let me produce and sell illegal counterfeit cigarettes, but ironically would forbid me to smoke them.

I remember one day when Mother beat up my two older brothers because they were sneaking around and smoking cigarettes.

"I might be small, but I have no problem beating you up. And if you ever smoke again, I'd rather kill you before the cigarettes do," she threatened as she screamed and lashed out at them. I was petrified whenever I saw Mother's reaction over cigarettes.

"And if I get arrested for beating you up, then you all will become orphans and homeless," she continued. After that beating experience, my two older brothers never tried smoking again.

Because of my new *operation,* every time I saw the police walking toward me, my heart raced and my palms began to sweat. I would scamper the other direction. I knew my behavior was wrong, but when faced with being wrong versus putting food on the table for my family and myself, I did what I had to do at the time to survive.

* * *

During this time, the Vietnamese government kept changing and releasing new currency called *dong.* This method continuously de-valued the money. One hundred dong on any given day could become one dong, or just be rendered worthless the next day. Citizens wouldn't deposit money in the bank because they didn't trust the government-run financial system. Mother kept all our money hidden under the floor of our home. And somehow, intuitively, she was able to suspect the timeframe of the currency change and always knew when to have me transport a huge bag of cash into Chinatown to buy various products.

"Take all this money to Cho Lon and buy any products we can sell," she would order.

I was freaked out carrying around so much money and was always concerned about being robbed.

"What's wrong?" she asked one morning. "Get down there quickly and buy whatever you can."

"I don't like traveling with so much money." I was tough and scrappy, yes, but I knew there would be little I could do to fight off someone who might try to snatch my overstuffed backpack.

"You have nothing to worry about," she said. "You look like a homeless kid and nobody would ever suspect that you would be carrying this much money. It's the perfect cover. Just buy whatever products you can with all this money while it's still worth something!"

I followed Mother's instructions and bought many different products with the money, often things like wholesale fabric that we could resell, or dried food like shrimp and fish. It really paid off because a few days later the government released new currency and we made a huge profit selling those same products in such a chaotic economy.

This type of new currency release happened several times, and Mother's timing was spot on every time. It was like she just *knew*, though I think she was very good at observing people's behaviors and spending patterns. Even though her smart money moves with my Chinese merchants was incredible, after a while, my connections started telling me that I was screwing them and they no longer felt good about doing business with me. I was adamant that I was only eleven years old and didn't know anything about the release of new money. I would explain that I was only doing what my handler instructed. But in my heart, I did feel guilty about the whole thing because they were right.

Upon seeing my "success" at lying and talking my way out of anything, Mother gave me all the freedom I wanted. Of course, there were limits, but not many.

"You must not steal, and you can never sell your body." She would say this often, and in such a tone that suggested she felt even more strongly about this than us not smoking cigarettes.

"You are on the streets of Saigon. Everything will be available to you. When you get hungry, you'll be tempted to sell your body or to steal, but I never want you to do that—ever.

And no alcohol and no gambling. You see the homeless families living on the streets. Do you know why that happens? Because of the father's gambling. Or alcohol addiction. Or both. And you see how miserable those families look. The poor wives. Many men become quite abusive in those sorts of situations. Do you want to end up living on the streets, sweaty and convulsing because you're going through alcohol or drug withdrawal?"

"No, of course I don't want that. I won't do any of that, I promise." Though I couldn't help but think it a little ironic that apparently, lying and deceit were acceptable to her.

Mother looked on me favorably because of my street smarts and the fact I was bringing in more money and had more responsibility. My siblings would also sell the cigarettes I made, but Mother did not trust them to go to the Chinese merchants with the bag of money to buy more supplies.

"Your brothers and sisters are too honest," she would say before handing me the bag of money. "You're the only one I trust to do this." And so, handling all that money and procuring the new supplies was my responsibility, and mine only. I suppose it's understandable that my older siblings began to dislike that Mother seemed to trust me more. They couldn't understand what Mother saw in me and why I appeared to be her favorite. They especially hated to hear Mother tell them they all could learn a thing or two from me even though I was the youngest. I was the opposite of everything that a traditional Asian girl or woman was supposed to be. My free spirit and undisciplined behavior irritated them whenever I was around.

But the thing was, I didn't really like who I was becoming either, drawn toward a darkness I couldn't seem to get out of.

I became depressed. I didn't want to go to Chinatown anymore; I didn't want to be part of this daily hustle. I hated feeling like I was cheating my newfound friends in Chinatown.

"Nhi, what is wrong?" Mother asked me one morning. I didn't want to stay in our tiny one room, but I also couldn't seem to summon the strength to get up. "Are you sick?"

"No." Well, at least not in the way she was referring to. I felt homesick, I realized, and my yearning for our old way of life settled on me like a dark cloud, seemed to infect every cell in my body. "I want to go home," I said.

"This is our home."

"No, our home where I grew up." We still had family living in the area. It didn't seem like such an impossible dream to go back there.

But Mother was shaking her head. "It's over six hundred kilometers away. The train ride is slow, long, and takes up to five days. We don't have money for a train ticket. Besides, you are only eleven years old and don't even know how to take a train yet."

"I'll ask for help about which train to take and when to get off," I said quickly. "If you give me just enough money to buy cheap food along the way, then I'll figure out the train ticket situation. I'll jump the train if needed."

"I don't think that's a good idea."

"But why not?" I pushed myself up from the thin mat I used to sleep on, suddenly energized with the possibility of returning home. "It'll be fine. You're always telling me how much you trust me. How street smart I am. If I can handle the streets in Saigon, catching a train will be no problem."

And what could she say to that? She herself had told me how much faith she had in my ability to handle a situation, and she also knew how stubborn I could be. She finally threw up her hands.

"Fine! Just make sure you stay in crowded areas so you don't get kidnapped."

The next morning, I made my way to the train station. I asked an older woman which train I should take.

"Are you traveling alone?" she asked. "Where are your parents?"

"They're just getting our luggage," I said. "I just wanted to make sure that we were going to take the right train." This answer seemed to satisfy her and she told me that the next arriving train would get me to the center of the country, Da Nang; she knew this because she was going further north, to the city of Hue. I thanked her and then stood near this family while we waited for the train. As we boarded, I stayed right behind the mother, making it appear as if I, too, were part of the family. I found a seat and kept my head down.

It was a four-day journey by train, but I was afraid to let myself fall asleep because I was afraid of a conductor coming through to check for tickets. Whenever I saw the conductor making his way through, I would sneak off into the bathroom, or into a different car. It was like a game of cat and mouse, except as the hours wore on, my eyelids began to get heavier. I rested my head against the window and told myself I'd shut my eyes for just a moment . . .

Someone was tapping my shoulder. I opened my eyes, a crick in my neck.

The conductor stood in the aisle, an annoyed look on his face. "Your ticket?" he said. I tried to clear the layers of fog from my brain.

I looked around, as if I were trying to locate someone. "Hmm," I said, after a moment. "I'm with my parents and they must have walked to a different compartment to get their blood moving. Let me go and find them." Once I was out of sight, I took off and avoided any future encounter with that particular conductor whenever I saw him coming.

The train made numerous stops as we traveled north along the coast. Occasionally, I would get off in the new station and walk around, just to stretch my legs and buy food. The first time I did this, I was easily able to get back onto the train, but the second time, the conductor was right there at the door and checking for tickets as people boarded. I hurried down to the next car, only to find another conductor at the door, doing the same thing.

I stood there on the platform, still trying to figure out how I was going to get back on, when the train started to move. The doors had been shut, and the train began to pick up speed. If I didn't do something soon, it would be gone, and I would be stuck. So, without even thinking about what might happen if I was not successful, I ran and jumped onto the train. I held onto the exterior hand railing and stayed perched on the narrow steps as the train began to move faster. I could see through the window, and when the conductor's back was turned, I forced the door open and slipped in. I never even considered the possibility of getting hurt or killed jumping onto a moving train because I was too excited about seeing my old neighborhood.

I made it to my hometown safely and found my uncle's home. They were surprised to see me, to say the least, but happy to hear that we were doing the best we could in Ho Chi Minh

City. Unlike that city's chaos and noise, my childhood home-town was quaint, still calm and peaceful.

"Your mother let you take the train here all by yourself?" Uncle Hong asked, raising his eyebrows.

"She didn't want me to," I said. "But I told her I'd be able to make the trip alone. And she trusts me. I just missed it here so much." The claustrophobic, dirty feel of the city seemed like a distant memory, and one that I had no desire to revisit any time soon. "I would really like to see my childhood home."

Uncle Hong looked down. "I don't think you would."

"But that was the whole reason I made the trip."

"It's not your home anymore, Nhi. The government seized your family's property." Uncle Hong tried to convince me, but I insisted I was going to go back there, with or without him. He relented and took me, along with a few of my cousins. The lake was still there, though there were fewer water lilies than I remembered. But the house was gone. In its place stood a police station, painted a lurid yellow. There was a massive photo of Ho Chi Minh right out front with the Vietnamese flag, bright red with a yellow star in the middle.

I stood there, tears spilling down the sides of my face. What had I been expecting? I wasn't sure, but it wasn't this. Except for the lake, nothing was recognizable; it was almost as if I had imagined those early years, those happy times, living here. Any shred of hope I might have been clinging to that we would eventually get to go back to the way things were dissolved. Perhaps that was why Mother had allowed me to come; she knew I needed to see it with my own eyes. My old life was gone forever.

I stayed with Uncle Hong for a week. During that week I played with my cousins and got to act like a regular kid. My spirit was lifted and I felt revitalized. But then Uncle Hong said it was time for me to go back to Ho Chi Minh City to be with my mother.

"Your mother will start worrying about you, if she isn't already," he said.

"But I don't want to go!" I gave him a pleading look and tried to swallow the lump in my throat. "I want to stay here."

"That's just not possible," Uncle Hong said. "Your mother wouldn't want that, anyway. Think about how much she would miss you." The thing was, I knew he was right—if I didn't return on my own, Mother would find her way up here to get me and bring me back. My stubbornness would not win out this time.

My older cousin, Nguyet, put me in a bamboo basket, balancing me along with another fruit basket over her shoulder like some carnival act, as we headed toward the train stop, so that I could catch my ride back to my mother.

* * *

Not long after I returned from my trip, we were awakened one night when soldiers burst into our room. It was dark and they were shouting about us living there illegally. They mostly ignored the five of us kids huddled on the floor and instead arrested Mother and ransacked our room, taking the little money we had.

"We heard that you listen to American news on the radio," they said to Mother as they walked her out of the room. "So now we arrest you."

The government and its police force framed people all the time and put them in jail whenever, and for whatever reason they chose. Sometimes they'd plant a piece of paper with scribbling on it and then say, "We are arresting you because you have this piece of paper showing you're scheming against the government. We will put you in jail."

The first time Mother was arrested, she was back the next morning. "I bribed them to let me go," she told us. "But this doesn't mean they won't come back. And their real motive isn't really to be throwing people in jail; they want to come in and take whatever valuables we have. Which isn't much!"

Mother was right, and it felt like the soldiers arrested her every month, as if on some sort of schedule. Her bribes didn't always work, though. If two days passed and she hadn't returned, all five of us kids would march down to the police station and explain that our mom was the only one who could take care of us. We would threaten to lie on the ground until they released her.

"And if you kick us, we will scream until you let her go," we would shout and, believe it or not, it worked. That's how we secured her release almost every month.

People were arrested for no reason, all so the government could go in and take anything and everything of value. You had no choice but to start over. But we had already started over so many times, Mother devised a plan.

"The next time they come," she said, "one of you should jump into the toilet with all our valuables and hide. They'll never even think to look in there."

And even if they had, it was unlikely anyone would venture in sewage to chase us out. Despite it being quite possibly the most disgusting experience of my life, my oldest sister and I would sometimes take turns to lower ourselves into what felt like an abyss. We'd stand there, trying not to gag, waist-deep in sewage, the stench nauseating, the sensation on my skin even more revolting. We stayed in that hellish hole for as long as necessary, holding what few valuables we had—money, our gasoline containers, and cigarette packs stuffed into plastic bags so they wouldn't get ruined if they touched the sewage. Sometimes, as I stood there in a sludge of feces and urine, I wondered how it was possible a person's life could change so dramatically, and without warning. It didn't seem fair that I had no say in the matter at all.

* * *

I was not the only one aching to get out of there. My brother Cu began to complain to my mother, begging her to let us leave this hellhole.

"This is not the life I want to live," he would tell her any chance he got. At fourteen, he was handsome, dark skinned, charismatic, and very street smart. He could talk his way through anything. But not being able to go to school legally and living in terror and poverty every day had finally taken its toll on him.

"We cannot escape as a family," Mother explained. "They watch us too closely. But I have a connection here in Saigon— someone who can help *one* of you escape. The authorities are less likely to notice if only one of you is gone."

Days later, I awoke at 3:30 a.m. to start work, only to find my brother gone. "Where is Cu?" I panicked. "Was he arrested?

Did they take him away?" It seemed impossible that such a thing would happen and I slept right through it.

"He has escaped," Mother whispered. "I paid half of the fee when he left, and they will get the other half once I receive news that he's arrived safely in Singapore or Malaysia."

"But I didn't even get to say goodbye." And if Cu knew about this ahead of time, why didn't he say goodbye to me himself?

"He wanted to," Mother said. "And I know you wanted to say goodbye to him. But it was too risky. These things have to happen in secret. I shouldn't even be telling you this right now, but I know you'll keep asking questions until you get answers. I didn't tell you or your brother or sisters because I didn't want to risk one of you accidentally letting it slip that your brother was about to escape. That would mean big trouble for all of us."

I understood her reasoning, and though I was sad I wasn't able to say goodbye, I was thrilled my brother had escaped. I imagined him on his way to somewhere far better than where we were now. I could only hope that eventually, we would be able to follow him.

The police came to our home within days of Cu's escape, asking, "Where is your son? What happened to your son?"

"I don't know," Mother said. "He's a teenager. I don't know where he took off to. If you see him, send him home! Tell him his mother wants to know where he is. These teenagers are driving me nuts!" She shook her head and rolled her eyes as if she really had all she could take from her teenagers.

Her response seemed to satisfy the police, and they left. Mother shut the door behind them and turned to me, smiling.

"Now we just wait for the news of your brother's safe arrival," she said.

But that news would never come. Four days later, a massive storm hit the ocean in the Southeast Asia area.

We never heard from my brother again.

Tormented by the thought that Cu got swept away or captured, Mother seemed to age overnight. Her thick, luxurious hair went from black as ink to white within a year, and worry lines creased her face. I couldn't stop thinking about Cu and wondering what happened to him. Never knowing seemed an impossible pain to bear, but what could we do? We could only hope and worry and try to dilute the anguish of not knowing.

* * *

You might have thought that, after Cu's disappearance, Mother wouldn't want to try to send any more of her children to escape, but she eventually saved enough money for my older sister, Second, to try.

Sister Second had a disability, though it was not physical, rather more like a mental impairment. This was a far worse affliction than being blind or missing a limb; communist society was extremely cruel and abusive to developmentally disabled people. They went so far as to label them "dumb" and "useless." Mother believed if Second continued to live in Vietnam, she wouldn't have a life. So, she arranged for her escape.

I couldn't wrap my head around why Mother took such a risk. But I couldn't stay angry. I recognized that Sister Second had a better chance at a better life elsewhere—anywhere—even if she died on her journey.

"We are keeping our fingers crossed," Mother said. "We are going to hope for the best."

Of course I was skeptical—things hadn't worked out for Cu, so why would Mother think it would be any better for Second, who had almost none of the street smarts our older brother did?

As days turned into weeks, and we didn't hear any word, I began to fear that my sister had met the same fate. Would Mother continue to have us try to escape? I couldn't understand how she could send her children away to their deaths. But then, we received a brief letter from Second, not stating much, only that she made it safely to a refugee camp in Singapore. We shouted with joy!

"I still have some gold left," Mother said. "I can help one of you escape if you'd like."

"Hell no!" my siblings echoed. Brother Fourth and Sister Fifth knew the odds weren't in our favor. Luck followed Second. But there were no guarantees.

I didn't know what life looked like in other countries at that time because I only knew Vietnam. But in my heart, I felt the same as Cu. *There must be a better place.* I got so tired of living in an environment where I had to lie and cheat just for survival, only to have the government show up whenever they felt like it and take everything we had worked for. Life did not have to be like this.

"I'll go," I said.

* * *

Like with Cu and Second, Mother planned my escape in total secrecy.

The night I was to leave, Mother stuffed two outfits and some dried fruit in a small bag. I couldn't carry a suitcase—even if we could afford one—because people would notice a young girl traveling far away alone. She sewed pieces of gold inside the waistline of my pants to use as bribery in case of an emergency.

"You know that when you escape Vietnam, it is likely you will never see me again," she said. "But you will hopefully have a better life. Are you okay with that?"

I didn't answer right away. At the age of twelve, I'd never been separated from my mother or my siblings. Would I be able to make it completely on my own? I wasn't sure. But I had to try.

"Yes, Mom," I said.

Hours after the sun had set and my sister and brother slept soundly, I stood on the street corner with my mom, watching as she secretly handed gold to the Chinese man who would lead me out of Vietnam. My route differed from my sister's; I'd travel by way of Cambodia to Thailand, where America had an embassy.

Sadness engulfed me. I didn't know if I would live, die, or ever see my mother again. I hugged her long and hard.

"Don't look back," she said. "Just go."

As I walked away to my destiny—leaving behind my family and my childhood—I desperately wanted to glance back at my mother one last time. But instead, I did as she told me.

I never looked back. I wondered if I'd ever see her face again.

CHAPTER TWO
THE GREAT ESCAPE

Jewish history teaches us that the Hebrews escaped Egypt by wandering through the wilderness for forty days and forty nights as Moses guided them toward the Promised Land. My Chinese guide led my interminable escape from war-torn Vietnam. Although my journey to a Promised Land flowing with milk and honey didn't rival that of the Jews, like them, I would endure plenty of hardships along the way.

* * *

My Chinese guide led me onto a packed commercial bus that traveled from Saigon to a place called Chau Doc, located at the southern tip of Vietnam, bordering Cambodia. I was advised that if another traveler asked me where I was going, I'd tell him or her I was going to visit a relative.

Once we arrived at the border, I hid inside an outdoor toilet closet—think Porta Potty, but it's a permanent fixture—waiting for night to fall.

"Do not make any sound, under any circumstance," the guide admonished.

Hours passed. I waited patiently in the small space as an army of hungry mosquitoes attacked and ate me alive. They buzzed in my ears and around my face, landing on my arms, my legs, anywhere they could find exposed skin. Their bites left itchy, raised welts I desperately wanted to scratch but did not, fearful that any movement would alert the Vietnamese soldiers to where I was. So I suffered in silence.

When the sun finally reached its lowest peak, the guide came to get me. He put me in a tiny boat where we journeyed along the Mekong Delta River heading toward Phnom Penh, the capital of Cambodia. It was 1987, and everyone's movements in Vietnam were under constant surveillance. We had no choice but to stop before daybreak and take shelter. We couldn't risk public exposure, so we found refuge in a small safe house near Phnom Penh.

A woman of Chinese and Cambodian descent greeted us in her Cambodian tongue that I did not understand. My guide communicated to her in Chinese. He hadn't said a word to me since we left Ho Chi Minh City, and I wasn't allowed to speak to him unless he spoke to me.

We followed the woman into a small, barren room. Nothing adorned the walls or the concrete floor. There were several other adults already there, sitting on the floor. I was the only child.

"Now we travel as a group at nighttime," the guide struggled to say in Vietnamese with his heavy Chinese accent.

I listened to the others murmur as they peered at me, likely wondering if a child would slow them down on such a long journey. Little did they know I had as much determination and resilience as anyone and would do whatever necessary for a chance at a better life. *I'll keep up!* I wanted to tell them, but I remained silent.

"You wait here," our guide ordered, never telling us how long the wait would be. Then he left without further instructions.

I soon discovered that three of the nine people in this room were related to me. My half-brother, Thuy, was eighteen; his sister, Tuyet-Em, was twenty-two. We had never met before because they grew up in Tam Ky, about four hundred miles from where I lived in Saigon. Also, there was a bone-skinny man, Buu, who was technically my brother-in-law and old enough to be my father.

"I'm married to your oldest half-sister who lives in Germany," Buu said.

"What are you doing here, then?" I whispered back, not wanting any neighbors to overhear us.

"I was in a reeducation camp for many years. It was a prison, really. The moment I was released, I knew I had to try to escape." He shook his head. "Unspeakable experience."

"My father was at one of those places."

Buu nodded and gave me a knowing look. "Now we escape," he said. I smiled, encouraged by the fact that I had relatives with me. I wasn't alone.

I also met Dep, who was a middle-aged woman with a friendly face. She wore glasses, and she reminded me of one of the teachers I used to have. She was gentle and soft-spoken and told me as we sat there waiting that she had worked as a professor at a university. But now, like everyone else here, "the professor" was leaving that life behind in hope for a better life, somewhere else.

The first chance I had to sleep came just before dawn. Everyone slept on the floor, and the room was so small that we were pressed up against each other, whether we liked it or not. My half-brother, Thuy, made space for me next to him. Exhaustion swirled around my brain, but I was afraid to sleep, believing I'd have nightmares about the dangerous journey ahead of us. As I lay my head on the cold floor, I was thankful I could at least take comfort in having family with me. We might have only just met, but we were all in this together.

I closed my eyes, my half-brother lying next to me. I had just started to drift off to sleep when I suddenly felt a hand creeping up my chest. The shock of it paralyzed me, and I did not know how to react. I knew it was wrong and hoped he would stop. But he didn't. My shock dissipated enough I was able to swat his hand away.

But he pressed on. The more Thuy tried to violate me, the harder I pushed his hands. The harder I pushed his hands, the more forceful he got. I made noises, like coughing, hoping to wake others in the room. It worked, and Thuy rolled over, muttering something I couldn't quite make out. Too horrified and ashamed to tell anyone what had happened, I made excuses the following night when I asked Tuyet-Em if I could lie next to her. We had been waiting in that cramped room all day, and Thuy's menacing presence felt like it was going to overwhelm me, even when I tried to put as much space between us as possible. Would they ever let us out of this room? Tuyet-Em made room for me, but I couldn't sleep. My mind raced. *Why would Mother arrange my escape with someone who would molest me?* She warned me about potential rapes and death while on my journey, but I never expected it to happen at the hands of a relative.

I wanted to tell Tuyet-Em and Buu about Thuy's sickening behavior but couldn't bring myself to do it. The streets of Saigon had taught me that, to survive, I couldn't trust anyone or anything. I could only trust my instincts. I never slept in that shack another night.

Our guide returned.

"Now we go. We hike Cambodia jungle," he said.

Jungle! Fear gripped every part of me. My heart pounded so fast I thought I'd pass out, and my knees grew weak. I was not the only one to have such a reaction; others gasped and looked around wide-eyed, a few nearly collapsed. Before my escape, I often heard people talk about the Cambodian jungle where Pol Pot, the leader of Cambodia at the time, slaughtered millions of people, usually by chopping off heads in order to save bullets. But before that happened, the people were forced to dig mass graves, which became known as the Killing Fields. Even today, historians regard the Pol Pot regime as "one of the most barbaric and murderous in recent history."

"If you can't make it, we leave you behind," our guide warned.

I wasn't going to stay in that shack, so, ignoring my dread, I grabbed my small bag and headed out with the others.

The air was thick with humidity and heat. The jungle was dense as we trudged through the underbrush—always in silence for fear of being discovered. The deeper we journeyed into the bush, the more my sight and hearing sharpened. Mosquitoes and other insects buzzed around our heads; snakes slithered up trees. The jungle was alive all around us, like an enormous living, breathing monster we were trying not to disturb. I shuddered at pythons and the sounds of cobra snakes hissing as they wrapped around trees and mosquitoes that ate at my flesh. But I dared not make a noise. I wouldn't let my fear control me.

Not knowing if I'd make it to the next day or not, I began to miss home. But then I reminded myself that whatever danger lay ahead surpassed the conditions I'd left behind. So I trudged forward.

I have no real concept of how far or for how long we wandered through the bush. We didn't sleep. Nor did we stop to rest, except to use the bathroom on the side of the trail, which scared me when I saw the guide using his axes to smack down bushes and snakes to make way for us.

After one of our bathroom breaks, "the professor" Dep asked if we could stop. "I just lost my glasses."

"No stopping," the guide said. "We keep going. You want to look for your glasses, go ahead, but we keep going."

So the professor had no choice but to follow behind me, feeling her way through the foreboding jungle. I couldn't help but feel bad for her; things were challenging enough as it was, and now she could barely see.

When I began to feel weak from exhaustion and in need of rest, I knew the guide and the others wouldn't stop for me either, so like the professor, I pushed forward, refusing to be left behind.

While we marched through the jungle, I had my period for the first time. Not having anything with me, I used leaves as my pads. My stomach cramped. I bled heavily. I felt embarrassed and confused about the changes in my body and disgusted with myself for not knowing what to do. Whenever we stopped for a bathroom break, I padded myself with more leaves before catching up with the rest of the group. I'd conditioned myself to push through—no matter what—and use all my ability and strength to survive.

* * *

Just days into our journey, Cambodian soldiers spotted us.

"You come with us," the soldiers demanded. My fear of Pol Pot's carnage swept over me again. Our guide fled, leaving us to fend for ourselves. He warned us earlier, "You get caught—I leave you. Then I come back."

The soldiers marched us to a building nearby and split us up into two different groups: men and women. My inner compass spoke to me. *Something's not right!*

"They're going to rape us," one woman whispered.

I remembered Mother's words. "If you get caught, and they rape you," she said, "you might as well die. Because once they rape you, they're going to kill you."

Fight or flight! I had no choice but to bolt. I busted out of the building and ran as fast as I could. The other ladies followed. We ran in the dead of night, no clue which direction we were headed. It didn't matter—we just had to get away from that place. There were sounds behind me. I didn't know if it was the soldiers or one of the women who had escaped. All I knew was I had to go faster. I just wanted to get away. I ran for my life with so much speed and adrenalin, I'm sure I peed my pants as I made tracks. I moved so fast; my flip flops slipped off my feet, but I kept going, thorny vines and sticks and rocks slicing the soles of my feet. I continued barefoot and refused to scream at the pain. To lighten my load, I started throwing away the contents of the bag Mother packed for me: dried fruit, clothes—anything that slowed me down, I tossed as I ran.

I don't know how long I ran, but even the worst fear will give way to exhaustion. I could barely catch my breath, and my racing heart pounded in my ears. I didn't know how much longer I'd be able to go on. But then—I saw something in the distance. A bright light ahead. As I got closer, I saw it was a house. With several of the other women behind me, I ran up to the ramshackle one-story house and began pounding on the door. A Cambodian woman appeared. I pushed past her and bowed at her knees.

"Please help us," I cried.

"Help us, help us!" the other women screamed as they also fell to their knees. The Cambodian woman and her family just stared at us. They couldn't speak Vietnamese, but they could see that something had gone terribly wrong. Shouts and the sound of heavy footsteps through the underbrush got louder and louder.

The soldiers had found us.

On our hands and knees, we scurried as far from the door as we could. I cowered behind this Cambodian family, fully expecting the soldiers to burst inside and pluck us out of there, one by one.

But they didn't come inside.

Instead, the Cambodian family went outside, and I could hear the back and forth conversation, though I couldn't understand what was being said. My breathing continued to come in big gasps, and my leg muscles burned. My feet had gone numb. But if those soldiers came in and tried to take us, I would fight with everything I had left to escape.

I tensed when the door pushed open and people came inside. But I saw it wasn't the boots of the soldiers but the bare feet of the family. The soldiers were gone. I had no idea what they said to them to convince them to leave, but I did know the Cambodian woman and her family saved us from being raped and probably killed that night.

Somehow, our guide found us not long after the soldiers left, and led us back to the rest of the group where we continued our pilgrimage. I don't know how the men escaped. But, miraculously, all the men showed up with the guide to reunite with us women.

I wandered many more days in the jungle barefoot. To this day, my husband still lovingly teases me.

"You have the roughest and toughest feet I've ever seen from anyone. It doesn't matter how many expensive and fancy creams you use on your feet—it wouldn't help!" As the living proof of my escape, I've come to embrace the rough soles of my feet. My husband calls them the "Soles of a Survivor."

The constant fear running through me, the endless march through the jungle, made everything surreal. It felt as if we were stuck in an endless loop, the green of the jungle seemed as if it would never end. We put one foot in front of the other, over and over, even though the bottoms of my feet were shredded, and my bones and muscles felt like they were about to disintegrate. The thick jungle canopy provided some welcome shade, but the air felt so thick it was like you could reach out and grab handfuls of it.

Finally, we arrived at the seashore. By now, night had fallen, and there was a bit of a breeze that pushed the heavy air around. In the distance, the pale moonlight illuminated a small wooden boat bobbing on the dark surface of the water.

Relief flooded me. We had made it!

At last! We're free! I thought to myself.

"You swim to boat. Boat take you Thailand," the guide said.

My excitement evaporated. *Swim?* I shuddered. *I can't swim!!!*

Mother had insisted I take swimming lessons as a child, but I ignored her wishes and chose to hang out with other kids instead. Why would I ever need to know to swim? If I decided it was something I wanted to do later, I could learn.

Except at that moment I needed to swim. And there was no time to learn. I wished I had listened better.

I walked to the edge of the water. The waves lapped at my toes and the salt water stung the soles of my feet. "The professor" Dep and some of the others were already swimming to the boat, their heads bobbing above the water. Clearly, some were much better swimmers than others, but they all appeared to know how to do it. Thuy was out there, and so was his sister Tuyet-Em.

Standing at the edge of the water, I watched the others step in and begin their wade toward freedom. A few people hesitated, and I wondered if they too didn't know how to swim.

If only the waters would part for me so I could walk across. But that would be too easy.

My heart beat frantically. My mind raced. I had to make it to the boat, but no one—not even my relatives that I was with—seemed aware that I needed help. Or maybe they were, and they were just too eager to get to the boat.

By now, some people were quite a ways out. As the last people on the beach stepped into the water, I followed. I didn't know how to swim, but no way was I going to get left behind for the Cambodian soldiers. That beach was not where it was going to end—I had been through too much to give up. As I splashed out into the water, I knew I'd need a miracle to make it to the boat. Because if that didn't happen, my journey out of Vietnam was going to end right there, so close to the boat that was going to carry me to freedom.

CHAPTER THREE
SINK OR SWIM

Unable to swim, I waded through the salty, black water the best I could, trying to keep a tight lid on the fear, cold, and uncertainty that seemed ready to engulf me completely. The water rose. To my waist. My shoulders. My neck. My feet struggled to touch bottom. I couldn't turn back though. I kept going, hoping for a miracle. When I was so deep the water started to splash into my mouth, I instinctively grabbed the closest thing I could—a man who happened to be trying to struggle past me—and hung on for dear life. He used all his might to kick me away, but I held on like a dog with a bone—if I let go, I would drown. The man had no choice but to pull me to safety or risk drowning himself, so he struggled onward, trying to shrug me off every chance he got. But I refused to let go. My life depended on this stranger who was doing everything he could to get rid of me.

I would look back on that moment as one of those times in my life when giving up just wasn't an option. It wasn't a case of sink or swim; it was a case of sink or hold on for dear life. And that's what I did. I held on for dear life and hoped that it was enough!

I don't know how, but somehow, we made it to the small wooden boat, which was about fifteen feet long. Relief washed over me, but I wasn't able to enjoy the feeling for long, because the man who had helped me get through the water looked at me in fury.

"You evil child! You almost killed me!"

He just didn't understand. "I'm sorry." I held my hands up and gave him an apologetic look. "I don't know how to swim, I thought I was going to die—"

"Shhh!" our guide hissed. "No talking! No fighting!"

I could tell from the look on the man's face that he did not believe me, but I was glad that we had to be quiet. Even if I tried to thank him, I knew he wouldn't accept it.

"You stay below. Pirates not kill you." Our guide made a slashing motion with his hand across his throat. "If pirates see you, you die."

There was some quiet murmuring around me. Everyone wanted to avoid being seen by Cambodian soldiers or Thai pirates; they might not attack fishermen, but they would certainly attack a boat carrying refugees.

We were divided into smaller groups. There were three men, including my half-brother, and two other women, my half-sister Tuyet-Em, and Dep. Conversation was forbidden, but we were too exhausted to talk anyway. We were cramped in a tiny, dark space that was no bigger than a closet. Packed in like sardines, we were forced to sit with our knees bent and could only make the most minor adjustments in our position—there just wasn't enough room.

When you're confined like that, not allowed to speak or make any noise, your thoughts can take on a life of their own.

I tried to doze but my head would fall forward with a jerk and wake me up. The boat's rocking motion was not soothing but instead made me feel woozy; my stomach did flips and there was a sour taste in my mouth. Waves of nausea roiled through me. I was not the only one afflicted; other people in my compartment threw up, and with no way to move, we were forced to vomit on each other.

Strange what you find you can tolerate when your very existence is on the line.

Because there I was, cramped, nauseous, covered in both my vomit and other people's, the stench of it making my eyes water, but—I was alive. A fact I clung to like a safety blanket.

You might think that staring down death time after time would somehow make it easier, but it's always as terrifying as it was the first time, at least for me. I wasn't sure how long we'd been on the boat, but I could hear the waves slamming against the freeboard like an unwanted visitor trying to get in. The boat rocked and pitched this way and that like a toy boat in a child's bath. The movements were more jarring, violent, than they had been, and I was suddenly overcome with the feeling that something was horribly wrong.

This awareness crept into every cell of my being, a sensation so uncomfortable I had no choice but to sneak up onto the main deck and see what was happening. I did not want to die below deck like some trapped, helpless animal.

But the second I reached the main deck, I knew I had made a huge mistake. The sky was like nothing I had ever seen before—vast and dark, with angry clouds that dropped torrents of water. The wind howled; it felt strong enough to pick me up and fling me into the Gulf of Thailand. How had the towering waves not yet swallowed our little boat? How were we going to survive this?

That's when I started to have thoughts that you might call prayers, though I had not grown up with religion. But in that moment, when it felt as if it were just me and this giant storm, my thoughts came out in a fervent plea to whomever or whatever was out there, creating all this chaos.

Whoever you are out there, I don't want to die. I've been a bad and dishonest person, but if you let me live, I promise to change and become a good person.

I squeezed my eyes shut and repeated my prayer over and over. The storm raged, the furious wind ripping from the deck anything that wasn't bolted down. The sound was deafening, like nothing I had ever heard before. I could feel it with my whole body. Thunder cracked the air around us, and lightning flashed as the angry sea continued its relentless attack on our boat. This was the end, and I knew it. All I could do now was pray, harder and faster than I ever had before.

Sometimes not giving up means understanding your predicament and dealing with it in the best way possible. This was out of my control, so the only course of action was prayer. It wasn't that I knew all that much about prayer yet, but it seems that when things are at their most hopeless, when all has failed, and the end is measured in seconds and not days; we all cry out to something for help.

Surprisingly, the universe, or God, heard my prayer and not too long after that, the winds calmed and the ocean relaxed. The clouds broke apart and fragments of blue sky became visible. The air no longer had that charged feel to it, and then the sun appeared; hopeful beams of light sparkled along the water's calm surface. I wanted to believe that things could only get better from there, but I already knew, even at that young age, how naïve such a hope was.

* * *

The guides buzzed around, insisting we sign letters stating that we had arrived at our destinations safely, even though we had not.

"We're close," they kept saying. "We are almost there."

We were all eager to get off the boat, so we wanted to believe them. Maybe they were telling the truth. But something inside of me did not believe we were almost there, even as they had everyone sign their letter. Once our loved ones received the signed letter, the guides could secure their final payment upon returning to Vietnam. Who knew what they would do with us then? They had guns and did not care whether we lived or died—they only wanted their money. We were at their mercy, so the only course of action was to sign the letter and hope they kept their word.

As I gripped the pen, my mother's voice echoed in my mind. Not long before I left, she told me what I should do if the guide tried to force me to sign the letter before I had safely reached my destination. *If needed, sign whatever they give you, but put a star at the bottom right of the letter.*

The guide paid little attention to me, other than to glare impatiently because he thought I was taking too long. I scrawled my name and then quickly scratched a little star in the bottom right corner of the paper.

Once they had what they wanted, the guides dumped us as soon as they could, which turned out to be on a rocky, deserted island just outside Thailand. They steered the boat as close to shore as they could before ordering us off. There was whispering among some of the adults: *This might not be the right place. We are not where we are supposed to be.*

But the guides, knowing they had what they needed to get their final payment, didn't care what we did, so long as we got off the boat.

They had guns.

We did not.

It was time to go.

Because we were closer to shore, I was able to make it there myself, though it was a shore only in the most technical of definitions. There was no sandy beach, no signs of civilization at all—just a small, rocky outcropping flanked by what looked like an impenetrable jungle.

We turned to watch the boat. It got smaller and smaller until it finally disappeared.

* * *

They left us with nothing, eighteen adults and me. The jungle loomed before us, vast and tangled, dark and surely full of wild, vicious creatures. It was supposed to be a relief to finally be off the boat, yet, inconceivably, it would seem we had arrived somewhere even worse.

Night soon fell. There was nothing to eat, nothing to drink. Things got dark quickly, and a chill descended. I shivered, still damp, my lips dry and cracked, and my stomach a hard, tight knot. The waves lapped the rocky shore and the sound of the water made me even thirstier. What a cruel joke to be surrounded by so much water yet unable to drink any of it.

Sleep was hard to come by at first—what sort of terrifying animal might slink out of the jungle and drag me off before I even had a chance to wake up? But my eyelids began to feel heavier, and there seemed to be longer moments of quiet between my worry. I was afraid to go to sleep, but I also welcomed it because at least it granted me a respite from my physical discomfort, my mental unease, and my emotional exhaustion.

Because who knew what tomorrow would bring.

* * *

Tomorrow, as it turned out, would be remarkably similar to the following day, and the one after that and the one after that. I awoke to the rumbling of my stomach. No, it wasn't my stomach—it was someone else's stomach, the woman who had been sleeping a few feet from me. Some of the adults were groaning as they hoisted themselves up. I was sore, too, but only a little, certainly nothing compared to the hunger gnawing at what felt like my entire torso.

I was thirsty, too. My awareness would go back and forth between extreme thirst and the sensation that my stomach was trying to eat itself. The sun grew hotter the higher it rose in the sky. There were a few palm trees we sought shade under, though no one was brave enough to venture more than a few feet into the jungle.

We ate anything we could chew. Leaves, bark, insects. I could remember never liking to eat eel when I was younger, but I would've devoured it happily if I had a bowl of it now. Desperation thickened the air. What were we supposed to do?

The adults mostly ignored me. They mostly ignored each other, too—there would be a few conversations here and there, but they were somber and usually ended quickly. People passed the time between staring out at the ocean for any passing ships, trying to catch fish, or scouring the rocky shore and very edge of the jungle perimeter for anything edible.

Were we going to die here?

"We need to send someone out." A man's voice broke the long silence. "Someone needs to go into the jungle and see what is out there. We will die if we stay here."

There was some muttering. "Why not you?" another man asked.

Several other adults spoke up.

"There's nothing out there."

"How will we know if we don't go look?"

"If you go into that jungle, you will never come out again."

It seemed everyone was trying to talk over each other, their words blended together until it sounded like a language I couldn't understand.

But eventually, hunger would win out. Five of us—myself included—decided we would venture into the jungle to look for food. I tried to block out the image of our guide hacking at snakes with his machete, as we struggled to make our way through the Cambodian jungle. We had no machetes, no guns, no weapons or tools to speak of. It seemed unbearably cruel, and I hated to think of my mother receiving the letter I signed, seeing the little star at the bottom, and knowing I was not safely where I was supposed to be. And if I died there? She might never know. She might spend the rest of her life wondering what had happened to me. Just one more reason why I had to survive. I had to get off that island.

The fear of the wild animals lurking in the tangle of the jungle was eclipsed by the insistence of our stomachs that we locate something to eat *immediately*. And, going with a small group made it seem a little less frightening.

It was agreed the rest of the people would stay behind and continue to keep watch for any passing ships, or any plane flying low enough overhead. My mind began to entertain the daydream of finding a banquet in the jungle, only to return to the beach and see a ship had come to our rescue.

The vegetation was a thick, vibrant green as we walked, the air above us humming with insects and the distant calls of birds. The sunlight trickled through the canopy and the trees towered high above us. We walked for several minutes before someone shouted in excitement.

"Coconuts!"

Somehow, the path we'd chosen to forge through the thick undergrowth had led us to several coconut trees. I gazed up at the cluster of fruit, tantalizingly close yet completely out of my reach. We scoured the ground for any fruit that had already fallen, but there was none. The only way we were going to eat was if we could climb the tree.

But coconut palms can grow to be one hundred feet tall. I didn't think those trees were that tall, but they might as well have been. The man who had been the unofficial leader of our little group was eyeing me, like he thought because of my small stature I'd be the perfect candidate to scale the tree and get the coconuts. But my legs barely felt like they could carry me on the trek—it just didn't seem possible I would have the strength to climb the length of that tall, smooth tree.

"I'll do it," the man said. Perhaps he had heard my thoughts, or perhaps he could just tell by looking at me that there was no way I'd be able to do it. From the expressions on the adults' faces, it did not seem that they had much hope in any of them being able to do it, either. He removed his shoes and wiped his palms on his pants several times, a look of grim determination settling over his features.

My stomach gurgled and twisted.

The man walked several paces away from the tree. He stood there for a moment, took a couple deep breaths, and then burst forth, running toward the tree so fast I thought he was going to collide with it.

But no—instead of impact, ascension. He was up that tree before any of us could really register that he had done so. We stood there, mouths agape, disbelief quickly receding to allow relief to flood in.

Food.

We finally had food.

Coconuts rained down. We gathered them by the armful to carry back and share with the others. Of course, we did not have a knife. Fortunately, we had our choice of rocks to pick from on that craggy beach, so we all took turns hammering the coconuts against the rocks to get to the meat and thirst-quenching juices inside.

There were only a few mouthfuls for everyone, but oh, it might have been the best thing I ever tasted. It was a tease, though, and instead of my hunger diminishing, it felt provoked, indignant, as if it could not believe I would do such a cruel thing and only give it a few bites of coconut meat.

* * *

There were several times it rained. More likely than not, this is the reason we all survived.

The arrival of rain gave everyone a purpose and brought us together in a way that nothing else could. A few of the adults had some containers among the belongings they had managed to bring, and everyone worked together to collect rainwater to pour into these vessels.

We cupped our palms. We used large leaves. The first several palmfuls always got consumed, and I could feel my cells soaking up the water like parched earth meeting floodwaters. We focused on collecting every drop we could, and it felt good to watch as the containers slowly filled with water. That water would be rationed out for as long as possible—four medium-sized containers would not be able to sustain a group of our size for very long.

The rains provided us with a temporary solution for our thirst, but there was no quelling the ferocious hunger that we were all affected by. The longer I went without food, though, the less important it seemed. It was getting to the point where, if someone had put a plate of shrimp, my favorite food, ten feet away, I wasn't sure if I'd have the energy to get up and eat it. But whenever thoughts like this would begin to push their way into my mind, I'd think back to the man scaling the coconut tree, the way he had done so with such ease, as if he knew he had no choice but to make it.

Some people tried to meditate so they could forget their hunger. They said, "Buddha did not eat for a long time. He nearly starved himself to death before he reached enlightenment."

I tried to meditate, too, but it just heightened my awareness of my hunger. All I could see when I closed my eyes were tumbling waterfalls and valleys overflowing with foods of all types. A breeze came off the ocean, bringing with it a damp coolness, the smell and feel of the ocean making us even thirstier.

I began to imagine what would happen if we were never rescued. People would begin turning on each other—at that point, I was no stranger to the limitless depths of human desperation.

They would try to eat me first.

And maybe I deserved that—after all, hadn't I almost killed a man just to get to the boat that would ultimately get me here? Could I even blame them for doing something like that, when I myself had nearly cost someone else his life?

I kept praying. I didn't know who exactly I was praying to, but I prayed fervently, for rescue. Yet even that prayer was interlaced with fear—what if we *were* discovered, but it was by Thai pirates? Or people who would do us more harm than being left to die on that island?

The unknowing was as unbearable as my hunger.

The adults around me also grew listless. People continued to watch the horizon for any glimpse of a passing boat. I sat on a rock in the shade, my head resting against another rock, thoughts of my mother, my other siblings, my brother Cu who had disappeared at some point during his escape, streaming through my mind.

The sun reflected off the water, an expanse of blue that seemed to go on forever. It would be easy to lose hope completely, to just give up. As I looked out at the ocean, no sign of help in sight, it was as if I could feel the pull of despair, a whisper in my ear, beckoning me to follow that trail. It would be so easy. The hunger, the thirst, the pain of being out in the elements this whole time, it was as if they were circling my psyche like a pack of wild dogs, just looking for their way in, that point of weakness.

And then it happened.

A ship in the distance.

People began to shout and wave their arms.

I blinked, wanting to believe what I saw on the horizon, but wondering if it was a hallucination, if we were all hallucinating the same thing.

Two men took off their ragged shirts and waved them over their heads like flags.

The ship got closer. Yes, it was real—but now that we'd gotten its attention, another question muscled its way into my thoughts:

What if the ship wasn't the Thai military? What if it was pirates?

CHAPTER FOUR
REFUGEE CAMP

Somehow, some way, every single one of us scraped together the last bit of our energy. We stood on the tallest rocks we could find. We jumped up and down. We shouted, and then we screamed. The men with their shirts off continued to wave them frantically. We had no way of knowing if they would be rescuing us or capturing us, but at that desperate point in time, it was a chance we were all willing to take.

It was a Thai military ship.

They rescued us.

Much of what happened after we were rescued is a blur, like trying to recall a dream. Bits and pieces I still recall vividly, though large swatches during that time are hazy. The reality is that I probably would not have survived much longer if the Thai military had not happened upon us.

But our time on the island had taken its toll, and I had used every ounce of my strength and adrenaline to survive. My body was giving out. As I lay on a cot aboard a ship taking me to safety, I realized how close I was to death.

The irony that slammed into me like a ton of bricks—I had, somehow, managed to survive dozens of harrowing situations only to meet my end because I tried to eat. And I had been so hungry on the island, dreaming of foods of all types, and now that I was finally able to eat, my stomach simply couldn't handle it. The rice, which was plain but tasted better than anything I'd ever had, left my stomach cramped and bloated. The pain was dizzying and left me writhing, miserable, and confused.

I became very ill. I lay on a mat, writhing in pain, wondering if I had survived all of this only to die after being rescued. Bits and pieces of people's conversations would drift over—I could recall hearing several people exclaiming about seeing dolphins playfully leaping through the waves as they followed the ship. Another time, it was sharks circling, and someone said, "We're lucky we're on this ship and not in the water."

Somehow, the team that rescued us kept me alive until we reached land. I spent the next several days in the hospital, regaining my strength and trying to get well. But it's hard to focus on healing when you feel as alone and isolated as I did. The familiar faces of the people I had escaped with were gone, replaced by strangers who spoke a language I could not understand. The people in the hospital were kind and only trying to help me, but there were no interpreters, which meant communicating with anyone was extremely difficult.

But even as I began to regain my strength slowly, my worry about what was going to happen continued to grow. Where would I go after I left the hospital? Perhaps I should've been used to not knowing what was in store for me, but the uncertainty and loneliness seemed to have a mind of its own. It was a cancer within me, growing, multiplying unchecked, until I felt as if I was going to be consumed. I missed my mother. I missed familiarity—I even missed that hole in the ground that we used for a toilet. It was disgusting, but familiar. It was strange to continually be somewhere you'd never been before, everything new.

For the next several days, I remained at the hospital, one of dozens of people in a large room, all of us in varying stages of recovery. I was still very weak and spent most of my time in bed. I had so many questions yet no way to ask or get any answers— where was I? What happened to the rest of the people who had been on the boat? Would I ever see them again? Where would I be sent once I was well enough to leave the hospital?

The nurses would come through a few times a day with trays of food. I found Thai food to be extremely hot and spicy compared to the milder cuisine I had grown up with. The first time I tried Thai curry, it felt as if my entire mouth and throat had caught on fire. I stuck to the rice after that.

When I was well enough to leave the hospital, the authorities decided to send me to Panat Nikhom, a refugee camp in Thailand. The year was 1987, and I was with hundreds of thousands of other refugees. There simply weren't enough resources to handle such a vast number of displaced people.

And oh, there were a lot of us. There were Vietnamese, Hmongs, Laotians, and Cambodians all confined within a half-mile radius. I was reunited with the people I had escaped Vietnam with, and felt relief at seeing their familiar faces again. We were considered fortunate, though, to be moving into a small building with a dozen others who had been there quite a while. The living space was about one thousand square feet and covered with a tin roof to protect us from the blazing sun and torrents of rain. Escape was not an option, as there was fencing and, for good measure, an eight-foot tall metal wall, guarded by Thai soldiers, twenty-four hours a day.

Perhaps it might seem strange to want to escape—surely the camp was far better than the deserted island we had just been rescued from. But at the camp, people were crammed in like cattle in a feedlot. At night, we slept on cold concrete, everyone pressed up against each other because there was so little room. The stench of body odor permeated the area, and my nose refused to get used to the disgustingly pungent smell. Simply breathing made me feel sick to my stomach.

But what was even worse than even the most foul-smelling body odor was my half-brother, Thuy. While some little sisters might have welcomed the presence of an older brother in a situation like that, my half-brother instead chose to continue to try to molest me every single night. He'd be certain to position himself next to me and then slide his hand down where it shouldn't be.

Around 9 p.m. each night, the Thai guards demanded that everyone blow out their candles because it was bed-time. If anyone disobeyed, they'd be beaten. But when the lights went out, the molestations would begin. Many people at the camp looked forward to sleep, for the chance to be somewhere else, even if it was only in their dreams. For me, though, nightfall brought with it dread, pain, and fear. *How would I ever survive this place?*

The first night Thuy did this, I swatted his hand away. There was enough of a pause that for a moment, I thought I had succeeded; there was no time for relief though, because his snaking fingers slithered their way back, and I felt his hot breath against my ear.

"If you ever tell anyone what really happens, I will KILL you." I had no reason not to believe him. The first night it happened, all I could do was lie there as my half-brother violated me, thousands of adults all around us.

There was always a shard of relief when Thuy fell asleep, after he was done doing what he did. His breathing would slow and he might even turn away from me, which I always hoped for. I knew what he was doing was wrong, but all the adults seemed too caught up in their own problems to notice anything was amiss.

Thuy's abuse continued. Each and every night. Sometimes, I'd lay there and wonder how much more I was supposed to endure—each experience I went through I hoped would be the worst, yet I would somehow always find myself in an even more wretched situation. Sometimes I thought about my mother, and the way her hair had turned completely white within a year of my older brother's disappearance. I would think about dying because that seemed a far better alternative than nightly molestations in this dingy refugee camp. But if my mother ever found out, I knew how upset and guilty she would feel. I could not do that to her.

I did what little I could to thwart his nightly advances. Mostly, that came in the form of trying to place some sort of barrier between us—a few balled up shirts, a book, anything I could get my hands on that might create some space. It was foolish to think that such a thing would stop him—all it did was make him angrier.

Unless I was anything but cooperative with him, the following morning, he would beat me. He did this openly, often dragging me across the complex by my hair. Once he'd made a show of this and gotten people's attention, he'd proceed to kick, hit, and punch me. When he got tired of using his fists, sometimes he'd use a big stick. He would make sure it was in front of everybody so that there was no question about who was in charge.

"You're a bad girl who deserves to be beaten," he'd announce. The stick was painful, yes, but it was better than feeling his hands on me.

"What did she do?" a man asked.

"She's done many bad things," Thuy said. "Too many to name. And she deserves to be punished." People would watch, though no one intervened. The closest I came to getting help from any of the adults was from Thuy's sister, Tuyet-Em.

"Enough beating!" she screamed. "Stop it!" Thuy stood above me as I curled on the ground, trying to protect myself as if I were a turtle who could draw up into its shell. For a moment, at the sound of her voice, I had a burst of hope that he might listen. No one else had spoken up before.

I dared to move my arm back enough that I could look up and see Thuy. He glared at his sister.

"Shut up," he said. He looked down at me, and our eyes met. It only lasted a split second, but it was as if I could see the fear in his soul, the knowledge that what he was doing was wrong. Yet for some reason, he couldn't stop himself. He was sick, and maybe he did feel guilty, though his guilt was never so great that he stopped either the beatings or the molestation.

It may be difficult to understand why no one, out of the thousands of adults I was surrounded by, stepped in to help out a young girl who was clearly in an abusive situation. But when you are tired and wounded from your own journey, and still overwhelmed with hopelessness and despair that lingers in the air like poison gas, it can feel insurmountable to take care of yourself, never mind anyone else.

Everyone here was drained mentally, physically, and emotionally, and we were all just trying to survive. Thuy could have taken on the role of a protective older brother instead of abuser, but he did not. Outwardly, I trembled at the sight of him and kept my head down to avoid eye contact whenever he was near. I had no idea how long I'd be at this camp, and no clue how much longer I would be able to endure Thuy's abuse.

Though it seemed naïve, foolish, I prayed for someone, for anything, to help me, to intervene when no one else would and just take all this pain and fear away.

* * *

A daily routine was essential to my survival. Goals and even the slightest semblance of order allowed me to hold onto my hope, as tenuous as it sometimes seemed.

I would try to start each morning early, before Thuy woke up. I would head to a designated center to collect the food rations that the United Nations distributed, lugging with me a five-gallon plastic container of allocated water to use for bathing, cooking, cleaning, and drinking.

I began to notice that some of the long-time refugees were able to communicate with their families back in Vietnam at the communication center. The center was really just a large booth, maybe ten feet by twelve feet, located on the opposite side of the camp. To get there you had to take a narrow dirt path. The center was stationed by a UN volunteer and a Thai employee who would distribute incoming mail and send outgoing mail where it needed to go. As you can imagine, the communications center was one popular place; lines would sometimes form before the two workers got there. We were all eager to hear from our families. Some people even got care packages with food or books. My heart leapt at the possibility of being in touch with my mother.

I cashed in the gold that my mother had sewed into my pants so I could pay for postage, opening a channel in which, I hoped, would allow me to be in touch with my family. I made sure to never tell Mother about the horrors I was experiencing because it would have devastated her. So instead, I led her to believe that things were hard, but okay.

I am in a refugee camp in Thailand. There are many of us here and things are not easy, but we have food, water, and shelter. I am here with my half-siblings, but I think I might need to find a way to live separately, if possible. I am not sure how long I will be here.

I kept my letters vague, hoping my mother would not be able to glean the magnitude of my desperation through my handwriting. She probably would though—Mother was smart and perceptive.

Sometimes, I'd even try to add a dash of hope—*When I finally make it to America and am making my own money, I am going to send you some to build a decent toilet.*

It took about a month for my letters to reach my family, and then about another month for their correspondence to find its way back to me. It was a long wait, but it gave me renewed hope, to wake up each morning and think that maybe today would be the day I'd receive a letter back.

The day I finally received a letter was perhaps the most uplifting day I'd had since I left Vietnam.

Though it was only a piece of paper, seeing her hand-writing and reading her words almost felt as good as seeing her in person. I felt connected to my family again and that reenergized me and gave me new hope. Mother's letters were worth more than gold—I read them count-less times, savoring each word, imaging her writing them. Mother kept me updated with things that were happening in Vietnam, mostly mundane, everyday sorts of things, but it made me feel as if I were more informed than many others, as there were no newspapers, radio, or TV at the camp. Like me, though, I felt that Mother might be hold-ing back—she did not mention whether or not she was still getting arrested, or what illegal items she was selling to make ends meet. In this way, I think, we both wanted to protect each other from the more painful realities of our living situations.

Getting letters from my family bolstered my spirits so much I couldn't help but wonder how it was for many of the refugees who were not able to get in touch with their loved ones, to feel like they had love and a lifeline to the outside world.

* * *

There was at least one thing about being at the refugee camp that would make my mother happy: I finally learned to cook.

At twelve years old, I didn't have much culinary talent. Sure, I had plenty of street smarts, but when it came to preparing food, I was clueless.

Our original group of nineteen had been split into smaller groups, so now I lived with a very tall Chinese-Vietnamese woman named Van Le, along with Thuy, Tuyet-Em, and Buu. Our group was housed with several other people, refugees who had been at the camp for far longer than we had. This regrouping and shuffling and moving around happened quite a bit, as some people left the camp and new people arrived.

I helped Buu and Tuyet-Em using old rocks and rubble that other refugees left behind to construct a fire pit so we could cook. We had one pot and one pan, a donation from the previous person who had lived in our building but had finally been able to leave the camp. Not everyone had cookware, so to protect our new possessions when they were not being used, we used a blue tarp to cover our cooking space. As I helped arrange the rocks, I could hear my mother's voice as if she were right there next to me.

"You need to learn how to cook from our family chef," she used to preach, back when we still lived in my childhood home by the lake.

Being the stubborn, inquisitive child I was, my reply was always the same: "Why?" The few times I had ventured into the kitchen when the family chef was cooking, I found myself bored and eager for something more interesting to do.

"Why do I need to know how to cook?" I'd ask my mother.

"Because if you don't know how to cook, nobody is going to marry you."

A response which would usually elicit a hand on my hip and a defiant tone: "I will NOT learn how to cook! I don't need to know how to cook because when I get older, I'll make a lot of money—maybe even become a doctor like Dad—then I will hire someone to cook for me. I'll have my own nanny. And I don't need to cook for a man."

Those conversations seemed like a lifetime ago, or someone else's life. My flippant attitude toward learning how to cook always shocked Mother, and I knew she hoped I would eventually change my mind. Now, I was living among strangers with no family support, and I barely knew how to cook rice.

I began to watch people and observe all the things they did to cook and prepare food. The menu mainly consisted of rice and ramen noodles, with plenty of soy sauce. Occasionally we were given some salted fish which we would mix in with the rice or noodles, trying to stretch the meal further. This useless talent I once considered a waste of my time became vitally important for my survival.

Being able to cook food for myself filled me with a sense of accomplishment I would not have thought possible in a place like this. This all went on for days and days and little did I know that soon, very soon, my plight would improve thanks to an American volunteer who would see my pain and try to help.

* * *

Her name was Bridget and she was an American worker at the orphanage center inside the refugee camp. To me, she was like Mother Teresa, an angel, the answer to my prayers.

I assume that, after seeing the sad, defeated expression on my face, Bridget knew right away what was happening because she probably had seen it many times before. She asked me about it in English, but she also used her body language to communicate with me. I can recall her first words to me like it happened yesterday.

"Hi there. Are you with your family?" she asked slowly, her tone warm and loving.

I shook my head. "No."

"Where are you staying?" she asked.

I tried to recall the private English lessons Mother forced me to take before my escape. I had only gone to a few, though I had also flipped through the pages of a few English-language books that I'd come across here at the camp. Would I be able to piece together enough of a sentence to communicate with Bridget? I was certainly going to try. I used my hands and spoke in broken English.

"I with people escaped Vietnam with." Like Bridget, I spoke slowly and tried to pronounce the foreign words the best I could. I was afraid to make direct eye contact with her—could she be trusted? I wanted to believe so.

She gave me an encouraging smile and nodded, though her eyes seemed sad. When I look back on it now, I realize how frightening I must have looked—rail-thin and dirty, with the latest bruises blooming across my face.

"Would you like to go somewhere with other children?" she asked. "There is an area that's reserved for children sixteen and under who don't have any family with them. I think you'd be much more comfortable there."

I nodded and Bridget said, "Why don't we go get your things and I'll bring you over there."

I had no idea this place existed, but finding out that it did was the best news I'd received in a long time.

Bridget walked with me to my sleeping quarters and waited outside the building on the dirt path. Like me, she was not tall, but I felt safe with her. She exuded a kindness I felt I could soak up simply by being in her vicinity.

Thuy was there when I returned. I made sure not to make eye contact with him, but that didn't stop my knees from shaking, my hands trembling as I reached for my things.

"Where do you think you're going?" he demanded.

"There is an American lady standing nearby," I said, keeping my gaze fixed on the ground. "She's going to take me to an orphanage."

Rage filled his eyes, but with Bridget standing outside the building, I knew he wouldn't try anything. He leaned toward me. "You can never escape me," he whispered, his tone menacing. "I'll kill you when I have a chance and you'll never have peace." I continued to gather my things, my insides quaking. All I wanted in that moment was to get as far away from him as possible. I had no idea what the orphanage would be like, but surely it could not be any worse than what I had gone through with Thuy.

"Just remember, I will find you," Thuy shouted as I walked away with Bridget. But already, his words were losing their power. My fear lessened with each step I took. It would seem my prayers had finally been answered—I hoped I was walking toward a new future free from pain, suffering, and fear. Yet this hope was tinged with the apprehension that, despite Bridget's arrival in my life like an angel, there were still plenty of things that could go catastrophically wrong.

CHAPTER FIVE
MINORS CENTER

The Minors Center, the only one of its kind in Southeast Asia during that time, was located in the center of the refugee camp. It was a sanctuary, full of other kids and free of molestation and physical abuse. It was the only area in the whole camp that had a big open space kids could run around and play in. At night, boys slept on one side of the building and girls on the other, our sleeping area separated by a collapsible wall. We were still sleeping on the floor, but I had a quarter-inch thick pad to sleep on that felt like the most luxurious bed imaginable. Two Vietnamese men watched over the boys and a woman from Vietnam watched over us girls at night. Foreign workers like Bridget always went back to the boarding house they stayed at outside the refugee camp at six each evening. I was always curious to know what her living space was like outside the camp, or back in the United States where I imagined she had a nice home. But due to my language barrier, I could not communicate with her much.

There were so many things that struck me about the Minors Center—one of the first things I noticed was the number of young children, years younger than myself. Why would their parents send them away when they were still so little? They were all but assured to never see them again, as some of the children were so young they couldn't write to communicate with their families back home. I would learn later that those parents believed sending their kids before they reached puberty would lessen the likelihood of rape and sexual assault. What a choice for any parent to have to make. How heartbreaking it must have been for those parents, willing to lose their kids permanently in the hope that someone would take better care of their babies.

I was also amazed to see water flowing freely from a hose. And not a little dribble like the hose we used to have to shower with in the Ho Chi Minh slum. Water bubbled out of this hose with force. What a welcome sight! Though we were still restricted to an allocated amount of water for washing, I no longer had to carry that five-gallon container through the dry, dusty heat, my shoulders and arms aching at the weight of it. Things certainly seemed like they would be easier there, and for that, I was immensely grateful.

At the Minors Center, our meals were cooked for us. Our dining area also doubled as a classroom when food was not being served. We'd sit at the long wooden tables with benches on either side, sometimes with metal trays of food in front of us, sometimes workbooks. If it was food, everyone scarfed down their meal as quickly as possible. Everyone got his or her own portion, but it was like we were all ingrained with the fear that someone was going to come along and steal what we had. I never saw another child take someone else's food, but we also had two supervisors there, a man and a woman, who walked around and made sure that everyone was behaving. One day, I told myself, when I have enough food to eat, I'll take my time to enjoy and be thankful for what I put into my mouth.

* * *

Life in the Minors Center was a drastic improvement. Once in a while, the center had a treat for us and brought in a TV. We were so excited to watch a movie even though we had no clue what it was about and couldn't really understand what the actors were saying. We just enjoyed staring at the lives of some white kids living these fantastic lives in big homes, fridges full of food, bikes to ride, and happy songs to sing as they frolicked through verdant green hills. We couldn't relate at all to any of it, but it was still such a thrill to watch. Later, I would find out that the two movies we watched were *E.T.* and *The Sound of Music.*

Despite these occasional special treats and the fact that I did not have to worry about nightly molestations at the hands of my older half-brother, we could not come and go as we pleased. My memories of the outside world were starting to seem like they belonged to someone else. Waiting for a letter or care package from my mother was the only real thing that brought me any joy; sometimes I would let my thoughts drift to what the future held in store for me, but that was also a scary prospect, as who knew where I might end up next.

I knew most days would end in disappointment that no letters from my family had arrived. Yet the disappointment would quickly give way to the hope of tomorrow. Yes, tomorrow was another day, another chance for a letter to arrive.

Many of the children I lived with in that camp did not have anyone to write to and never received a single letter or a care package. For this reason, I did not try to make a huge deal when something finally arrived for me, though inside I felt like spreading my arms wide and spinning around while I sang a song, just like that lady in *The Sound of Music*. I devoured my mother's letters as it was my only connection to the outside world, even though I knew the government monitored our correspondence and usually opened our letters to read before delivery.

Mother often included educational books in her care packages, along with food. We might not have been living in the same country, and it was debatable whether we'd ever see each other again or not, but Mother continued to persist in her efforts to instill the importance of education, no matter the situation. I was malnourished, isolated, and essentially being held captive, but that did not mean the pursuit of knowledge needed to stop.

And indeed, it did not. Education, as it turned out, was a great distraction to my current situation. I pored over each and every book, and when I was done, I'd share them with any of the other children who were interested. Some were, and some were not. But for me, education became a lifeline.

There was also a center where refugees could learn how to sew and knit. Like cooking, such skills were never something I was interested in doing, and most of the time, I was bored out of my mind. To keep busy, I learned these skills even though it was not something I'd ever be interested in doing in the real world.

I found far more enjoyment in my academic studies. One of the first classes I took was a cultural orientation class that Bridget taught. At first, the class focused on teaching us about things like seasons and geography, how to use a fork and a spoon, and dressing appropriately depending on the weather. Snow? Hats and mittens? In Vietnam, we didn't need such things, but there was a good chance many of us would need to know about these things when we finally headed to our next destination.

But Bridget also taught an advanced English class, for kids who had at least a rudimentary understanding of the language. I made sure to stick around for that class. She did not speak Vietnamese or any other language to us during the class—only English. But she would speak slowly and enunciate each word. She would write words on the blackboard and sometimes use pictures or body language to help us understand just what the word meant.

She fascinated me, not just because she had saved me from my half-brother but because I couldn't quite wrap my head around the fact that this American woman was dedicating all of her time here, with us. I wanted to have long, full-throated conversations with her, yet I couldn't since we didn't speak the same language. Some of the kids would whisper that she was a nun, she had to be, what other explanation was there for such selfless kindness? Even though we were just kids, we knew how admirable it was, how it must take a special person, to be so willing to spend so much time with children starved for adult attention.

It was in Bridget's English class that I found myself sitting near a handsome and quiet boy named Cau-Thien. He was around fifteen, or sixteen; I had recently turned thirteen and found myself experiencing the first pangs of a crush. These new feelings intrigued me—where were they coming from? What was I supposed to do about them? Not having anyone else to talk to about it, I kept the feelings to myself.

It was obvious, though, that I was not the only girl who had feelings for Cau-Thien. Many girls would talk about him at night, and sometimes felt comfortable approaching him after class. I would observe them from a distance, marveling at the ease of their conversation, wishing that I, too, could carry on that sort of light, happy talk with him. I never once saw Cau-Thien be anything but kind to the girls clamoring for his attention, and this made me like him even more.

Along with Bridget's English class, I also discovered that the two male supervisors who watched over the boys at night had academic backgrounds; one was a high school teacher and the other had been a college professor, prior to their escape.

I approached them one day and showed them two of the books my mother had sent that I was having difficulty with. "When I read these math and science books and don't understand the concepts, may I come to you for help?"

Seeing my inquisitive mind and my desire to learn, these two men were willing to tutor me in math and science. It worked out on both ends—I was thrilled to receive free tutoring and they felt good helping me and also, being needed. I suggested that they might extend their teaching services to some of the other kids, too, and they attempted to do this by hosting a group math session, which was attended mainly by younger kids.

"Most of the kids here aren't interested in learning," one of them told me after. "It's frustrating trying to teach kids who aren't interested."

And it wasn't just the younger kids who weren't interested—a lot of the older kids, too, couldn't seem to wrap their heads around why I wanted to learn so much when we were stuck in such a hopeless environment.

"What's the point?" they asked. "Why are you spending so much time reading and studying?"

Sometimes I would just ignore them, but other times, I would try to explain myself.

"One day, I'll get out of here and will need to catch up with other kids in other parts of the world. My mother said education is important, especially math and science because it's the same around the world. So I'm doing it even if I don't know what the future is like."

Such a reply would usually be met with blank stares, or sometimes laughter, though it was never cruel or malicious—they really just got a kick out of it.

"You are such a geek!" was the common exclamation. One day, Cau-Thien happened to be walking by, English book tucked under his arm, when he heard a group of younger kids joking around about my geekiness.

"If learning and expanding your mind makes you a geek, you should be proud to be one since it's better than sitting around doing nothing," he said as he ambled by. He didn't stop and didn't say anything else, but he caught my eye and smiled before he had passed us by.

I blinked, almost unable to believe what had just happened. The other kids barely even noticed; they had gone back to their laughing and joking, talking about whatever it was they'd been talking about before they decided to direct their attention at me and my armful of books.

One of the things that was so wonderful about the Minors Center—there was no bullying, no fights, no drug or alcohol use. There was no violence because we didn't have access to guns or drugs, and besides—we all knew the harsh reality: any misbehavior would likely result in our being kicked out of the Minors Center. We had next to nothing, but when that is the case, there is no competition, no trying to one-up each other.

I would later, as an adult, be reminded of this when watching my own children navigate adolescence; as I write this chapter, my kids are the same age that I was when living in the camp, and I see the pressure that so many American kids are faced with, to have all the right "things": clothes, shoes, phones, cars. At the Minors Center, we had so little that we truly appreciated anything that made its way into our possession.

Once, Mother surprised me by mailing my favorite snack— dried squid. What a welcome surprise! I had some right away, and closed my eyes so I could fully focus on the briny flavor and chewy texture of the most cherished treat. When I opened my eyes, I saw that something of a crowd had gathered, and several of the other kids stared, wide-eyed, at the remaining dried squid. Of course there was a part of me that wanted to cram the rest of it in my mouth, or hide it somewhere so I could enjoy it all to myself later, but I recognized the expressions on those children's faces; I knew exactly what they were feeling.

"Would you like some?" I asked, and the crowd encircled me, palms outstretched. I passed some to Nhieu, a girl two years older than me who had also fled Vietnam. Her eyes lit up and a smile stretched across her face. In the end, we all probably only got a small morsel, but for those several moments, the air felt lighter, and the mood seemed uplifted. It felt good to share a positive experience, to have something we could enjoy together, as a group.

* * *

But it still felt like being in prison.

We were eager for any experience that was different, that might help us forget that we were trapped within the confines of fences. One day, a volunteer and missionary named Julie, from New Zealand, invited some of us to church. I had never been to church before and was a little curious, though when Julie announced that there would also be free food, well . . . that attracted a whole lot of us.

The church turned out to be a tiny single-story building with a tin roof and a dusty concrete floor. Julie and a few other adults were there, and they talked about God and Jesus and the Holy Spirit. I wasn't familiar with anything that they were talking about, but, when I was there, I prayed to God because I was thankful for Julie's kindness . . . and for the free food.

Sometimes, I would think about God, not necessarily the Christian God they talked about in that little church but some sort of higher power when I would often find myself standing by the fence, gazing out through the gaps, beyond the guards. Freedom was right on the other side of this barrier, yet it might as well have been on the other side of the world. I missed the ability to go out, not even anywhere specific, just knowing I had the freedom to come and go. I missed my family, too. It was hard, being surrounded by so many other children, all of us—whether we were aware of it or not—longing for the love and support that comes with having a family.

At least I had such memories. Some of the children in the camp were so young, there is no way they would have any recollection of a family life. They didn't know that the absence of love and someone to look after you—to *really* look after you—was not normal, was not the reality for many children.

Or were they, perhaps, better off? Would it be easier not to have such memories, not to have experienced such feelings? Because of course, as I stood there against the fence, I wondered if I would ever be part of a family again, if I would ever get to experience that kind of love. If there was a higher power, some force that was bigger than me, bigger than anything, might that force be listening? I had overheard whispered prayers and exclamations, and I thought of my own experience on the boat in the middle of the storm. It had seemed the sky was responsible then—and in Vietnam, many people considered the sky an omnipresent force—*Dear sky* was the Vietnamese equivalent to the English phrase *Oh my god.*

But I was beginning to think there must be something less impersonal than just the sky, something or someone who was watching over us. I had no way of knowing for sure, but the thought gave me comfort.

God, Universe, whoever you might be, if you really DO exist, please give me a family to love, who also loves me in return. I'm not asking for material things, just the care and love of a family. I made this silent prayer daily, and hoped, if someone was out there, they could hear me.

* * *

One day, Cau-Thien was not in English class. I was disappointed that he wasn't there, though it wasn't like I was going to say anything to him anyway—I still hadn't worked up the courage to do so. But he wasn't there at our next class, and I found out from one of the boys that talked to Cau-Thien all the time that he had gotten very sick two nights ago and had been taken to the hospital outside the refugee camp.

I had so many questions, but I was so shocked I didn't ask. But the questions, the worry, streamed through my mind—*Was he okay? When would he come back? Was he being taken care of?*

Those answers would never come.

A week went by and still no Cau-Thien. No one seemed to want to give us any answers; in some cases, like Bridget's, because she didn't know. But finally, several of the other kids and I were able to ask the supervisor who oversaw the Minors Center.

"He died," he told us. "We don't know what happened. He was sick and died suddenly and the hospital didn't tell us the cause of his death."

I was heartbroken.

There was no funeral or memorial service for Cau-Thien. It was like he never existed, except for those of us who were missing him. I started to talk with one of his roommates, a sixteen-year-old boy named Hai-Ho. Initially, it was because I wanted to find out more information about Cau-Thien, anything really, not just about his death. But Hai-Ho didn't know much about Cau-Thien's death, or his history. Hai-Ho and other people did go through the few possessions Cau-Thien left behind, hoping to find some clue as to how we could inform his family back home. We were about to give up when Hai-Ho found a crumpled envelope containing a letter from Cau-Thien's family. The letter, like many of my own, had been read so many times the corners and creases were soft, the paper nearly transparent.

"I'll write his family," Hai-Ho said.

I nodded, relieved that Cau-Thien's family would at least know. It was an awful truth, but it was better than not knowing. I couldn't help but think of my brother, Cu, who had gone missing. Perhaps my brother had reached safety, but more likely he, too, was dead. So I knew the sort of painful grief Cau-Thien's family had ahead of them, the not-knowing, the wondering. I was grieving not only for Cau-Thien but also for my brother.

At night, as I lay on my thin pad atop the concrete floors in the Minors Center, I tried to keep my sobs quiet. I didn't want to scare the other children or add to anyone else's grief, but there was no way I could've kept all of it in. My silent tears were the only outlet I had, the only way to process the grief I felt in losing Cau-Thien, in not knowing my brother Cu's fate.

The magnitude of my crush on Cau-Thien now made me feel as if I were about to literally be crushed. The mental anguish felt as if it were going to consume me. I had been through so much, yet this inner, emotional and mental pain was staggering—it was like nothing I had ever experienced. It felt permanent, etched into my soul, something I would carry with me forever.

But that did not mean I had to wear it on my sleeve. No, instead, I took Cau-Thien's memory, all the pain associated with his death, and I locked it away within myself. It was the only way to numb the pain. It was the only way to be able to get up each morning and try to carry on with my day.

The message was clear though: Anyone I loved had been taken away, leaving me eviscerated, empty, raw. As such, the remedy seemed equally clear: Do not open your heart to anyone. Numbing my emotions would be the best way to move forward.

And this was exactly what I did, for a long time.

* * *

After two years in the refugee camp, the US Embassy finally granted me an interview. In order to be approved for refugee status, I needed to provide documentation showing that my father had been a physician working for the American military during the war, and that my family was politically persecuted. My mother included the needed paperwork in one of the letters she sent. I was quite fortunate in this regard—many of the kids at camp did not have paperwork and had no way of getting it, which meant they would have a much longer wait to be granted an interview. The letter also had more good news: my eldest sister, Second, had made it to Kentucky, and it included her address. Along with the documents Mother had sent, I shared my sister's information with the interviewers. I was thrilled to finally have an interview, but also nervous, knowing that if I messed up and was rejected, it could take a very long time before another country would decide to accept me as a refugee. But I answered all of their questions, and they processed the paperwork and approved me for refugee status.

One thing that the interviewers did not know, and that I did not disclose, is that Sister Second has a learning disability and some developmental delays. Such a thing is rarely spoken about outside of immediate family; in Vietnam—and most East Asian cultures—mental disabilities were looked down upon, harshly. You are either smart or you are stupid—there is no in-between. Sister Second was often teased and sometimes beaten up by kids in the neighborhood, who used to laugh at her and tell her she was dumb as a cow. Even Mother would get physical with her sometimes, or deride her by saying things like, "How can all of my children be so smart, except for you? You are so dumb."

It was true that Sister Second had difficulty grasping new concepts; she was also brutally honest, which, in certain situations, made her appear dumb. While my other siblings and I were out hustling on the streets of Saigon, Sister Second was never allowed to, because she wouldn't hesitate to tell a potential customer just how much she had paid for something and how much she was planning to sell it to him for. But my older sister also has an incredible long-term memory, and is able to recall things in vivid detail from long ago that most people would be unable to.

Still, people were cruel to my sister because she didn't act normal. Special needs do not exist in Vietnam, because people refuse to acknowledge it as a legitimate state of being. There are no special classes, no one-on-one attention. Those who have mental health issues or developmental delays could expect to be bullied and looked down upon for their whole lives, which was in stark contrast to, say, if you were missing a limb. Vietnamese people are far more understanding in that case; they assume it was a result of the war.

But I kept this information about my sister to myself. There was no way she could actually take care of me, but the Red Cross and the Catholic charity who were my sponsors didn't know that. She was family, and they were going to send me to live with her in Kentucky.

* * *

For two years I had stood near the fence, gazing out, yearning for my freedom, saying prayers I wasn't sure if anyone was really hearing. Yet the day had finally arrived—I was going to leave the Minors Center and start my new life. The excitement coursed through me—I was going to fly on a plane for the first time! I was getting out of the camp! I was going to America!

It was almost too much to process.

But I did try to keep my excitement in check; I did not want those I was leaving behind to feel bad. There was Nhieu and Hai-Ho and many of the other kids I had spent the past two years with. I received a special gift from them—they had pooled together the little money they had and bought me a brand-new skirt and blouse. The majority of clothing that came through the camp was donated, but occasionally, some of the Thai workers would bring in new clothing to sell to the refugees who had money.

"We wanted you to have a nice outfit for the plane ride," Nhieu said, and my eyes filled with tears. They could have spent their money on food, or something for themselves. But they had not, and now I was going to have to leave them all behind.

I was excited to go, but I felt sad to be leaving, which I realize might sound strange, considering how badly I wanted to get out of there. But the camp had been my home for the past two years, and the other children, my family. I would never see any of them again, and, much like when I had said goodbye to my mother on a street corner in Saigon, when I passed through the camp's gates, I didn't want to look back. I boarded the bus that morning, filled with both excitement and trepidation because, once again, I had no idea what my future would bring. My mother's wishes—that I make it safely to America—were coming true. Yet I couldn't help but wonder: Would my twenty-year-old sister be able to take care of me when she was barely able to take care of herself?

PART TWO
MY NEW LIFE IN AMERICA

CHAPTER SIX
COMING TO AMERICA

I'd never seen such beautiful clouds.

They were all different shapes, all different sizes, and from my vantage point at the airplane's window, I was seeing these clouds from a whole new perspective. It was September 1989, and I was on an airplane for the very first time. I was up in the sky, flying through the clouds! I couldn't believe how beautiful it was. It had been cloudy when we'd taken off, but once the plane had broken through the clouds, it was a beautiful sunny day, and I realized then, no matter how stormy or turbulent things were on the ground, somewhere, the sun was always shining. I gazed out that tiny window at the azure blue sky that seemed to stretch forever. I thought of my friends and the other children I had left behind, thought of how exhilarating they would have found this, too.

Though the views were exquisite, I was uncomfortable for a good portion of the thirty hours I spent traveling. My stomach rumbled, but I didn't have any money for food, so I could only look hungrily at the flight attendant and her cart stocked full of all sorts of delicious things I had never tried before.

"What would you like to eat?" she asked, her smile bright.

I didn't realize the food was complimentary, and I didn't want to admit to the fact that I had no money. So I tried my best to return her big smile when I shook my head and said, "No, thank you!"

The woman who was seated next to me had a coffee she emptied sugar and milk into, and the flight attendant had given her a tray full of food, the delicious smell wafting over, taunting me, making my stomach rumble even louder.

Of course, this was nothing at all like the hunger I'd experienced when we'd been on the deserted island. But I had also not been seated next to someone who was enjoying what looked to me like a gourmet meal. All around me, I heard sounds of soda cans opening, wrappers crinkling, someone chewing something crunchy.

My best hope, then, was that I could sleep. At least then I wouldn't be conscious of my hunger, and perhaps when I woke up, we'd be close to landing. Sleep was difficult to come by, though. The lovely outfit my friends from the Minors Camp had given me was perfect for the hot climate I was coming from, but not enough to keep me warm in the cool, conditioned air that circulated throughout the main cabin. Even the blanket provided by the airline wasn't enough; it was thin and small, so my body was cold and covered in goosebumps for the duration of the flight.

It took me a while to fall asleep, and when I finally woke up, I did not feel refreshed. My hunger had not abated and a dizzying wave of anxiety was there to greet me when I opened my eyes, shivering. The pilot's voice came over the intercom, informing us passengers that we were close to landing at Los Angeles International Airport.

I gripped the armrests as the plane made its descent, my stomach flip-flopping. The landing was rougher than takeoff, and momentary relief flooded me when the wheels finally made contact with the tarmac. As the plane slowed, my anxiety roared back in, usurping my hunger and any relief I had just been feeling.

What was going to happen now? Where was I supposed to go? Why isn't there anyone here to help me?

The thoughts spun through my mind as I exited the plane, clutching the folder of paperwork the immigration representative had given to me before I'd left, my heavy backpack straps digging into my shoulders. My backpack contained two outfits, my journal, some photos, and every book that I had read at the camp and enjoyed—some sent by Mother, others that had been donated. Having not yet heard about the libraries in America, I didn't know when or if I'd be able to get more books.

I let myself be carried along with the flow of people until we got to the gate where a man directed people to go through customs. Thanks to Bridget's English class, I could read some of the signs. I knew I needed to find someone who might be able to point me in the right direction; otherwise, I feared I'd be lost in the airport forever.

I stopped and took my backpack off, tried to stretch the soreness from my shoulders. When I saw the flight attendant who had been serving food on our plane, a woman with wavy, dark blond hair and pretty earrings, I showed her my folder of paperwork, which she looked at in confusion at first.

"I need help," I said. "Not speak English well."

"Ah!" she said, her face brightening. "I'd be happy to show you just where you need to go. Follow me! Let me walk you to customs and to your next gate." She saw me struggle to lift my backpack and held out her hand. "Here, I'll take that for you."

There were so many things that my eyes couldn't quite believe as I followed her. The airport was immaculate. The floor seemed to gleam, and there was no hint of dirt or grime even though there were people coming and going in all directions.

And the people—I saw white people, black people, Hispanic, Asian . . . the variety was astounding, all of them there, in one place. I had not seen many people of a different nationality when I'd been in Vietnam—in fact, I suddenly recalled seeing a Russian man once, many years previous, and wanting to chase after him to see if he was a real person. That was how rare it was to see someone of a different nationality. Yet suddenly there I was in LA, seeing all that diversity for the first time, at the tender age of fourteen. Everyone looked different, yet it didn't seem to be a big deal at all. Everyone went about his or her business, as if all the diversity was simply a normal part of life.

I went through customs and then to my next gate, where I was shown how to get on a different plane, heading to Kentucky. My whole body buzzed with a blend of excitement, hunger, and anxiety. I could barely understand a word of what was being spoken around me, and it was very difficult for those I encountered to understand what I was saying. I longingly thought of Bridget, who had spoken English to us so slowly and so clearly. Though I had both the powers of hearing and speech, I felt as though I deeply understood the challenges those who cannot hear or speak encountered on a regular basis. Not being able to communicate left me confused, vulnerable, and exposed, and though I could not know at the time, that experience would be the catalyst for me to become an interpreter many years later.

* * *

I arrived in Louisville, Kentucky, in the evening. I peered out the window as the plane descended, mesmerized by the twinkling glow of the city lights. At first, I wasn't even sure what I was looking at, having never seen anything like that before. In both Vietnam and the refugee camp, it was always dark, even in the city. Families were lucky to have electricity just a few hours per day, so seeing an entire city lit up was stunning. Despite how beautiful I thought it looked, I couldn't help but think how wasteful it was, too.

The pilot announced the local time after we landed, and I realized that, despite traveling for the past twenty-four hours, I had arrived at my destination on the same day I had departed Thailand. That was really something to try to wrap my mind around.

Sister Second and her husband, Kinh, were there to meet me at Louisville International Airport. They were with my nephew and nieces, whom I had never met before. Though it was a relief to know my long journey was winding down, now that my family had come to pick me up, it was also strange to reunite with my sister.

Much like the airport in Los Angeles, the airport in Kentucky was pristine. Was everywhere in America always super clean? But perhaps more shocking than that was the way people drove. My sister's husband drove us to their home, and I was amazed at the orderly way in which all drivers obeyed the rules of the road. There were so many sleek cars, all with working headlights and glowing red taillights. Drivers used their blinkers to signal when they were going to turn. People obeyed all

stop signs and traffic lights and stayed within the confines of
the lines painted on the smooth black pavement. It really was
something to witness, compared to the chaotic nature of traffic
in Vietnam.

* * *

I was in for a surprise when we arrived at my new home. Not
only did my sister, her husband, and their children live there—
so did five other people. Kinh's three brothers, one sister, and
his father all lived there too.

The house itself was not large, with three small bedrooms
and one bathroom for eleven people. But the size of the home
didn't bother me as much as living with several strange men.
They were Chinese, but had lived in Vietnam, so knew the
language. They frightened me because of everything I'd been
through in the refugee camp. When my sister told me I'd be
sharing not just a room but also a bed with Kinh's eighteen-
year-old sister My-Le, I was relieved. She was not much older
than I was, and I hoped we could be friends.

It was late when we arrived, and I was tired, but I still hadn't
eaten anything. Sister Second asked if I was hungry and when
I told her I was, I watched in amazement as she crossed the
small kitchen to the refrigerator. My jaw dropped when she
opened it. Not only did a little light come on, illuminating
everything inside, but the shelves were also full of food and
cartons of beverages. I watched as Sister Second took a few
jars out of the fridge and one of the cartons. She rummaged
through a cupboard, then another, pulled open a drawer. She
offered me some rice with pork and shrimp, scooping the rice

out of something that looked like a bucket with a lid—the first rice cooker I had ever seen. She gave me a glass of cold milk. I probably could've eaten anything at that point and it would've tasted heavenly, but I can still recall my delight at tasting fresh milk for the first time.

After my meal, it was time for everyone to go to bed. The full-size bed I shared with My-Le was not spacious, but it was comfortable. I had my own pillow, and we were on a thick mattress with both sheets and a blanket. Despite being in new surroundings, I fell asleep quickly.

I awoke many hours later, the feeling of something warm and wet spreading against my legs. It was disorienting, the warm, wet sensation, coupled with waking up somewhere unfamiliar. It took me a moment to realize where I was, who I was lying next to, and finally—what was happening. My-Le must have wet the bed. I tried to move over, away from her and the wet sheets; my movements must have woken her.

She sat up. "You peed," she said, her voice accusatory.

Even though I had been asleep, I knew I hadn't. Though it also seemed just as unlikely to me that *she* had, but what other explanation was there? I was certain it hadn't been me. My-Le threw back the damp covers. "Let's change the bed sheets!"

My-Le's bed-wetting would continue, though it wasn't every night. "You better not tell anyone," she told me one night. "You'll be sorry if you do."

I wasn't sure exactly what she meant, but I knew she could make my life miserable if she wanted. I wasn't trying to embarrass her, either; I just didn't want to continue to share a bed with someone who kept having accidents. I tried to talk to Sister Second about it.

"I just want you to know that it's not me who's wetting the bed," I told her one evening as she prepared dinner. I kept my voice low, not wanting My-Le to walk in and overhear me. "It's My-Le."

Sister Second looked up from the pot she had been stirring. "That makes sense," she said. "I didn't think it was you anyway; My-Le's room has smelled like urine long before you got here."

I felt relieved that my sister believed me, though she went back to her cooking and didn't say anything else about it. And it wasn't as if there was an extra bedroom or even a spare sleeping space—I was stuck sharing a bed with My-Le, and I continued to keep quiet about who was responsible for wetting the sheets on a regular basis.

* * *

My first week in America, I accompanied my sister and my brother-in-law to the grocery store. More amazing than the sight of a fully stocked fridge was the supermarket, where the floors were as clean as the airport, where there was aisle after aisle, and in each aisle, shelves atop shelves, flush with food.

But first—we had to get into the store. As we walked across the massive parking lot, Second suddenly clapped her hand to her forehead. "I forgot my purse in the car," she said. "I'll be right back. You can go in and I'll meet you. Just wait by the shopping carts." Kinh followed Second back to the car, and I enjoyed the freedom of walking across the parking lot toward the huge store on my own.

I stepped up onto the curb and saw the way the door just opened for the woman ahead of me. The door closed before I could slip through, so I waited, thinking it would open for me the way it just had, but it didn't. Was I too short? I tried jumping up and down. The door didn't budge.

Finally, Kinh and Sister Second returned, her purse swinging over her shoulder. She walked right up to the door, like she was just going to walk through it even if it didn't open, but at the last second, it did.

"You just weren't getting close enough; you have to be in the right angle of the laser," she said.

Kinh selected a shopping cart and he followed Second as she led us up and down aisles, filling the cart with unfamiliar things. I was used to the Vietnamese market, where chickens were still covered in feathers and pig heads gazed out with unseeing eyes. Here, meat was sold already cut, in neat plastic-wrapped packages. There was beef, chicken, and pork, as well as many different types of fish. In the produce section, the vegetables were orderly and, as I stood there looking at the bunches of broccoli, a mister came on, gently covering the vegetables with a fine sheen of droplets.

In the cereal aisle, I was confronted with a dizzying array of brightly colored rectangular boxes. There were so many choices! The other shoppers pushed their carts along, looking bored as they selected their items. How did they know what to get? Did they not realize what an incredible thing it was, all that food, right there, just waiting to be selected?

"I am going to get you a treat," Second said. We were already standing in the checkout line, and I was watching in amazement as my brother-in-law placed the items from the shopping cart onto the conveyor belt. Second gestured to the rack of candy and gum. "Pick something."

I chose a chocolate bar. I waited until we were driving back home to unwrap it and take a bite.

Now, I had never had chocolate before, so when that first, delicious morsel touched my tongue for the first time, I really thought I was in heaven. The flavor was sweet and rich and a little earthy, like nothing I had ever experienced. I swallowed that first bite and took another, this time letting it melt on my tongue. I closed my eyes so I could better focus on the flavor.

And so would begin my love affair with chocolate. Though I was living in the land of abundance, with all types of food available, the only thing I wanted to eat was chocolate. I would've eaten it for breakfast, lunch, and dinner, and I often did, which surely was the main reason I went from being bone skinny to a plump teenager with plenty of acne!

Though the sheer abundance and availability of all types of food was what amazed me the most, there were so many things in America that I was seeing and experiencing for the first time.

* * *

Fall arrived in Kentucky two months after my arrival. The leaves changed from green to gorgeous hues of scarlet, cinnamon, orange, and gold. In Vietnam, the leaves were always green, and so to witness that glorious change seemed like magic. I noticed the changes every morning on the school bus as we headed toward Iroquois High School. It was not in the best part of town, but it was one of the few schools around that had an English-as-a-second-language program. As the weather got cooler, the air had a crispness to it that I had never felt before, and I could smell the aroma of wood smoke on the cool breezes. The sun set earlier and earlier.

As the days grew shorter and the air colder, my classmates began to talk about Halloween. Apparently, on the last day of October, you would dress up as something else and go door-to-door and be given candy. For free! I wasn't sure what it was celebrating, exactly, but it was an activity I was happy to participate in.

One thing I was not well prepared for, though, was winter. Mornings would dawn clear and cold, and the sun would set not long after I got out of school, when it was still the afternoon, really. I was always shivering, as the secondhand clothes I had were unable to keep me warm enough.

But snow—I had never seen snow before, until one morning in late December. I looked out the window and there was stuff falling from the sky.

"It's snow, stupid," My-Le said, from where she sat at the kitchen table. "Who doesn't know what snow is?"

If you had lived in Vietnam your whole life, you wouldn't, and I hurried outside to experience it myself. The cold didn't even bother me because I was so enraptured by the way the snow had transformed everything. There was maybe an inch or two already on the ground, and it was falling steadily. I held out my hand, palm up, and watched as the snowflakes landed, then began to melt. The sky was covered in thick, gray clouds, solid looking as a tabletop. By that point, I was freezing, but so transfixed by the beautiful snow that I stayed out there for quite a while, until I couldn't feel my toes anymore. What a thing to experience such differences in the seasons!

* * *

By American standards, my sister and her family were low-income. They did not have a lot of money, but there was always food in the fridge and a bed to sleep in at night. I was eligible for welfare, and received 120 dollars a month. Not a lot, but it allowed me to contribute toward food, which I was glad to do because I could see how hard my sister and her husband worked.

Because I did not have much money, I only sent Mother money once. I wired her money with a note:

Please use this money to bury that hole from hell and build yourself a better toilet—hopefully no one will ever have to use it as a hiding spot again!

But this was before the US embargo against Vietnam was lifted, which meant we couldn't send money directly to Vietnam. In order to get my mother the money, it had to be sent to Canada, and then could make its way to Vietnam. Regardless of the journey the money had to get to her, I knew Mother would appreciate it.

* * *

Because I had Medicaid, I was able to see a doctor and get a physical. I also had an eye exam, and it was determined that I needed glasses. Medicaid would only cover a very basic, inexpensive pair of frames that did not fit my face correctly. The glasses were huge and felt as if they covered half my face; they also slid down my nose, so I constantly had to push them back up. I knew I looked like a serious geek, but really, I was just grateful to have received the care in the first place.

As the days passed, it was harder to feel gratitude for my living situation. It had turned hellish because of My-Le's refusal to ease up on me. In fact, her bullying had intensified, and she continued to wet the bed and blame it on me in front of her family. To make matters worse, My-Le and I went to the same school, and she was not as good of a student and had trouble picking up new concepts. I did my best to avoid her, but that still didn't change our sleeping arrangements and riding the school bus together. Even on the rare day I would manage to not see My-Le all day, I knew we'd be sharing the same bed come nightfall.

One evening, after brushing my teeth, I went into our bedroom. I caught a flutter of movement out the corner of my eye and turned in time to see My-Le try to hide something under the bed.

She wasn't fast enough, though—I saw what she had. It was a journal that I had started keeping, a private place where I was able to write about all the experiences I'd been through. I never thought someone would read it.

"Please give it back," I said. "My journal. It's not yours."

For a split second, I thought she was going to hand it over. But then the apprehension I thought I had seen on her face vanished, and she smirked.

"This garbage?" she asked, pulling the journal out from underneath the bed. She opened it, fanning the pages. "*Cau-Thien's family will never know what truly happened to him.* Who is Cau-Thien? One of your dumb friends? What happened to him?"

I hated the sound of his name coming out of her mouth. "Shut up," I said. It was barely more than a whisper; I didn't want to make things worse, but I couldn't just stand there and say nothing.

Her eyes narrowed. "*What* did you just say? How dare you say that to me. We welcomed you into our home. It's not like we have all this extra space for people that can't even pull their own weight. And who *wet the bed*."

She held my journal up, and for a moment, I thought she was going to give it back. I even extended my arm to take it, but instead, she began tearing out the pages. "Nobody cares about you or will protect you, except your sister," she sneered. "But your sister cannot do a thing because she's 'off' and my family can control her—and you."

I hated that she was right, and she knew it. And she knew that *I* knew it. Who knew what sort of lies she would tell the rest of the family? If I told her family she stole my journal, she would probably blame it on me, say that I was trying to get her in trouble, and seeing as they all seemed to believe her when she blamed me for wetting the bed, why wouldn't they continue to believe her lies? What if they threw me out? I had nowhere else to go, so even though I didn't have any personal space to speak of and was subject to constant bullying by My-Le, the idea of being kicked out was terrifying.

"What is going on in here?" Sister Second appeared in the doorway, a frown on her face. "What is all this shouting?"

"She's destroying my journal!" I screamed.

Sister Second came all the way into the room and turned toward My-Le. "You give that back to her right now, and stop being a bully! I'm going to talk to Kinh about this—he is not going to be happy to hear about your behavior!"

For all her talk about her family controlling my sister, My-Le shrank back from my sister and held my journal out to me. I snatched it out of her hands, ripped pages and all.

"Now just stop it," Second said before she left the room.

I had managed to escape Vietnam, I had survived a deserted island, and I had endured years in a refugee camp. And finally I was there, in America, the land of opportunity, a country made up of people of all nationalities, where anyone could achieve anything if he or she was willing to put in the effort. The American Dream. But for me, the nightmare had not yet ended because my living situation was so deplorable. I burned my journal because I was afraid My-Le would try to take it again. There was no one to talk to about it, no one who could help.

Or so I thought.

CHAPTER SEVEN
MARY LOU

Mary Lou Hearn was a teacher at Iroquois High School, and she would transform my life. She was petite, like I was, and she saw something special in me. One day, as I was walking down the hallway to my next class, she fell in step next to me.

"Nhi," she said. "I can't help but notice what a diligent student you are."

"Thank you," I said, smiling. I liked Mary Lou immensely—most everyone did. She was just one of those people who radiated this kind, caring energy—in many ways, her demeanor reminded me of Bridget, and she spoke English to me slowly, so I was able to understand each and every word. Being new, in such a large school, it was nice to receive some encouragement.

"I see how hard you work," she continued. "You've got an intense drive to succeed. I just wanted to extend the offer to you—if you're ever interested, I'd be happy to tutor you before school."

"I'd love to get more help!"

For all the time I spent studying, I really was thrilled for the opportunity for some one-on-one assistance. I rose an hour earlier so I could leave the house with enough time to walk to school, as the buses wouldn't start running for another forty-five minutes.

I flourished under Mary Lou's attention. At the end of each of our sessions, I would regret the time passing so quickly, and also already be looking forward to tomorrow morning. During our science tutoring sessions, Mary Lou would help me with my English, which was the area I really needed help in, especially if I wanted to keep up with my peers.

As part of improving my English skills, Mary Lou and I would sometimes just have a conversation. Though I sometimes struggled to find the right words, or utilize the correct pronunciation, these talks were more than just science and language practice; we were two friends getting to know each other better. I learned that Mary Lou was married to a man named Lewis, and they had three sons: Tom, Alan, and Bryan. Tom, their oldest, was two years younger than I was. *What a happy family they must be*, I thought.

I didn't give Mary Lou too many details about my own home life; I told her I was living with my older sister and her husband and his family—eleven of us in a home.

"That's a lot of people," Mary Lou said.

I nodded, not wanting to speak further about it because I was afraid if she asked, I'd tell her the truth about just how awful it was. My-Le's torment had not let up; if anything, it was getting worse because she could see that I was doing far better than she was at school, despite being younger, and not in the country for as long.

We started to meet after school for an hour or two a few days a week. Instead of walking home, Mary Lou offered to give me a ride home.

"Do you or does anyone in your family need anything?" she asked me one day as we pulled out of the school parking lot. "Clothes or anything? There are a lot of people in our community who are more than happy to help with clothes or other items you might be in need of. You can think about it and let me know, okay?"

That was how Mary Lou was—she radiated goodness, and she was always willing to help anyone who was in need. "Thank you," I said.

As she pulled up to the house, My-Le was just getting home. She stood there, as if she was waiting for me. If you didn't know any better, you might think she was happy to see me.

"Why are you always with that teacher?" she asked as I approached the house. I wanted nothing more than to turn and get right back into Mary Lou's car, but she was pulling away from the curb and driving away. I returned her wave and then turned to face My-Le.

"She's tutoring me. That's all."

My-Le smirked. "Why bother? It's not like you're going to do anything with your life. That teacher will realize what a loser you are, just like the rest of us know." She shook her head in disgust and then turned and went inside, shutting the door in my face.

I stood there for a moment, unsure if My-Le was waiting right there behind the door, just so she could lean all her weight against it if I tried to let myself in—it wouldn't be the first time.

"Nhi?"

I turned. It was Mary Lou, her car parked right where she had been when she dropped me off. She had gotten out and was walking toward me, my science textbook in her hand. "You left this in the car," she said. "I circled back when I realized it; I figured you might need it tonight."

"Thank you," I said, taking the book from her. She was right—I planned to find a quiet corner and spend the rest of the day studying, until it was time for bed.

Mary Lou's eyes went past me, to the house, the front door still closed tightly. I wondered if My-Le was now peeking out one of the front windows, if she'd use the fact that Mary Lou had returned as more ammunition against me.

"Everything okay?" she asked.

I swallowed away the ache in my throat—all I wanted was to tell her the truth, but what would happen then? She had already done so much for me, spending all the time she did, both before and after school, helping me. So I forced a smile and nodded emphatically.

"Everything is okay," I said. "Thank you again. I'll see you tomorrow."

I waited on the front step and waved to Mary Lou as she drove off. I imagined her going to her home, with her husband and her three sons. They probably ate dinner all together and talked about their day. After dinner, maybe they played games or watched television. I took a deep breath and went into the cramped house that I lived in but simply could not think of as *home*.

* * *

Not long after that day, Mary Lou asked if I would be interested in getting tutored over the weekend, too.

"But isn't school closed?" I asked.

"It is, but we could come back to my house. Or we could go to the library." She smiled. "There are lots of options."

Of course I was more than happy to go to her house. And the rest of her family welcomed me with open arms, too. Her husband, Lewis, was tall and handsome, and the three boys were happy, energetic, and friendly. Alan, the middle son, with beautiful platinum blond hair and hazel green eyes, was four years younger than me, and immediately asked if I wanted to play.

"Nhi came over to do some studying," Mary Lou said. "Would you like to do some studying with us?"

All three boys took off to play sports, and I didn't see them again until I was getting ready to leave.

I didn't realize it that first day, but we were starting a weekly tradition, and for the next year, I would go over to Mary Lou's every Saturday. My visits would stretch longer and longer, and did not just include study time. The family began to include me on various outings and I was thrilled when I was invited to stay for dinner. I felt safe, and I felt like I was surrounded by people who really were interested in seeing me succeed.

I was not familiar with using a fork and spoon, so Mary Lou's sons all took turns showing me how to do it.

"You hold it like this," Alan said, demonstrating. "If you can use chopsticks, you'll figure this out in no time. I've tried to use chopsticks but it's really hard!"

"You hold it kind of the same way you hold a pencil," Tom said.

The utensils felt foreign and clumsy in my hand, but that didn't matter because the Hearns were so encouraging. The boys taught me other things, too. They encouraged me to play more when I sat in their home reading textbooks.

"I can't," I would say. "I've got so much catching up to do. Study now, play later."

They laughed when I said this, though not unkindly. Alan was always at the ready to help decipher any word I was too tired to look up in the dictionary—one day, it was "jump" and he climbed onto his twin-size bed and leaped off. He did it several more times.

"See?" he said. "Jump. That's what I'm doing. I'm jumping from the bed—" here he was airborne, before landing on the floor softly, like a cat—"to the floor."

Although all the boys were into sports, I was surprised they were not jealous of the attention their mother gave me. They didn't seem to mind or think it was at all strange when they'd come in from playing soccer to find me sitting at the table with Mary Lou, textbooks open in front of us. Over time, the boys and I would grow closer and I would begin to think of them as brothers. In a way, it seemed inevitable; I was spending so much of my free time over there, and Mary Lou's family had been just as kind and welcoming as she had been. I hated having to leave and go back to my sister's house, to sharing a bed with My-Le, to being surrounded by people who really did not care either way if I succeeded or failed. Though I knew Sister Second did not wish me ill, the way My-Le did, my sister simply had too much going on to be able to provide me with a solid foundation, a home base where I felt like I could flourish. I didn't blame my sister; I knew, even without the developmental delay and mental challenges she had, it would be difficult, but that didn't stop the longing that things could be different for me. I kept telling myself that this was not the America my mother envisioned for me—she wanted me to succeed, which

I knew meant I would have to assimilate in ways that my sister and her family were not going to.

About a year after I began spending more time with Mary Lou's family, it seemed things finally were going to change, for the better. One afternoon, after working on an English lesson, Mary Lou closed the textbook and looked at me.

"My family and I had a discussion and we want to know whether you would be interested in having me as your legal guardian."

I was speechless, certain I had heard her wrong.

"I realize that you are pretty much on your own," Mary Lou continued, "because your sister simply cannot take care of you."

Tears blurred my vision, but I blinked them back before they could start sliding down my cheeks. Crying was something I hadn't been able to do since I had left Vietnam. "Yes, I'd love to have you as my guardian."

In order to become my legal guardians, Mary Lou and Lewis had to file a petition with the court. During this process, it was discovered that, because of a loophole in the filing, my sister wasn't even considered my legal guardian. And because I was over the age of fourteen, I was able to nominate my guardian of choice. It did not take long for the Hearns to become my legal guardians, and shortly after that, I moved into the home I had, up until that point, only imagined in my wildest dreams would ever be *my* home, too. But now it was.

* * *

In 1990, as I headed for the Hearns' residence, I made a commitment to myself to always treat people with kindness, the way

Mary Lou had treated me. It was important to pay it forward whenever I could, and I knew that no matter what, kindness would always be a universal language. I welcomed my adoption into the Hearn family.

With my childhood lost, the Hearns saw to it that my teen years would be some of the best years of my life. Christmas that year I received my very first stuffed animal, at fifteen years old. It was a plush bear with round dark eyes and a velvet nose and it was the softest thing I had ever felt. Yet there were also some things that took getting used to, and that my mind had trouble grasping, particularly overwhelming abundance—food, clothes, and freedom. It seemed everyone took it for granted. Although I love my American brothers, they appeared clueless at so many opportunities in front of them, and thought it was normal. Their closets were not just full of clothes but also an array of different sports uniforms and special shoes—you wouldn't wear the same shoes you played soccer in to play basketball. I could recall kicking the soccer ball around the big play area at the Minors Center, all of us barefoot in the same clothes we wore day and night.

The refrigerator and cupboards were well stocked, and they kept plenty busy because of all the extracurricular activities they did. They were so busy, in fact, that Mary Lou paid a woman to come in once a week and clean the house—to wipe down counters, vacuum the floors, and dust.

"I could clean the house for you," I told Mary Lou one afternoon, after the cleaning lady had left. I had seen the cash she left in an envelope each week for the woman, and I would've been more than happy to do the work for half of what Mary Lou was paying.

"Nhi, you are part of this family, not the maid," Mary Lou said. I understood why she would say that, yet it was also hard for me to believe how much money she was paying this woman. It wasn't just Mary Lou and her cleaning lady, either; I was shocked at the amount of money Americans spend on their pets. Expensive food, lots of toys, annual trips to the veterinarian—all that money could have easily fed and housed a number of families for quite some time back where I came from. I didn't feel angry or judgmental over such things, just felt surprised and impressed by the tremendous wealth that simple, ordinary Americans were blessed with. I often wondered if they knew just how blessed they really were.

I wondered though: Would Mary Lou come to think she made a mistake? She already had three children of her own, after all, just like my sister did. I didn't want to be a burden, and I knew that, as a teacher, Mary Lou's salary was modest.

Once, she bought me two sweat suits. This was one of the styles of the time, these nylon sweat suits, often in bright, sometimes clashing, colors. The two Mary Lou brought home for me were pink and purple—one was made of purple fleece, the other was pink. To say they were a little hard on the eyes was putting it kindly. Still, I loved those two outfits, and would become so attached to them that even years later, when I was grown and married, I would still wear them around the house.

One morning, my husband just couldn't hold back the truth any longer.

"I'm sorry, honey, but you look ridiculous in that outfit. It's not the nineties anymore. Why do you keep wearing these things around?"

"Mary Lou bought these for me way back when I had nothing. These were the first gifts I ever got," I said.

"I see," he said, smiling. "Well, maybe instead of wearing them, you could give them an honorary place in the closet. Or, you know, you could just move on, divorce those outfits, give them to someone who's nostalgic for the nineties."

My husband was right; the outfits were outdated, and by that point, getting worn out. But they were as comfortable as a second skin, and, more importantly, had been a gift from Mary Lou. Though I did eventually find the strength to donate them to Goodwill, the kindness of the gesture will always stay with me.

* * *

Within two years of living with Mary Lou and her family, I blossomed from a geeky girl who had little support into a confident, academically successful young woman (still nerdy looking though!). During my junior year, at Mary Lou's encouragement, I applied to the Governor's Scholar Program. The program, which began in 1983, was intended to assist the "best and brightest" high school juniors to further their education and start a career in Kentucky, as opposed to looking at out-of-state options. Though Mary Lou seemed to think I could get in, I wasn't so sure.

"How could I be considered one of the best and the brightest?" I asked her one evening as I helped her clean up from dinner. "My English is still not as good as it could be."

Mary Lou stood at the sink, washing dishes. With my application submitted, we were now just waiting to hear back. She set a plate in the drying rack and turned to me. "Nhi," she said. "Your English is quite good, and every day, it is getting better. You are one of the hardest working, most dedicated students I have met, in all my years of teaching. The Governor's Scholars Program is meant for students like you, and you have to remember—they consider multiple factors when deciding who they accept, not just academic achievement, but also your extracurricular activities, who you are as a person, the ways in which you give back. There's a lot more they look at than whether or not your English is perfect."

Mary Lou had reviewed and edited my essays, and I knew she and a few other teachers at school had written recommendation letters on my behalf. When I received the letter in the mail a few weeks later that said I'd been accepted into the five-week summer program, I was thrilled. But I knew that it hadn't happened on my own—Mary Lou had played a big role. I probably would not have applied to the program in the first place if it hadn't been for her encouragement, and her unshaken belief that I would get in.

I didn't have many friends in high school, but I did make a few friends through the Governor's Scholars Program. I think that's because they were all high achievers like myself. After I completed the program, Mary Lou encouraged me to reach out to them, so I did. Some of them would come over to the house from time to time and we hung out together. One of them, Rebecca, and I became good friends. Yes, we geeky girls bonded together. We weren't interested in going on dates or trying to find boyfriends—we were going steady with our studying, and that kept us plenty busy.

My goal at the time was to do exceptionally well in school so that I could get a scholarship. I studied day and night and had "no life" compared to your typical American teen-ager, my brothers included. Sometimes I was up until two or three in the morning, studying to catch up with other native English-speaking students. I got dumped into a class where I had to read *Romeo and Juliet*, *The Scarlet Letter*, and all the other classic pieces of American literature. Extra study time was needed!

* * *

The Hearns always seemed to know just what to do to make me feel like part of the family. One day, I was helping Mary Lou put away groceries.

"I got some of that yogurt you like," she said. "Make sure you have some before one of the boys eats it all."

"Thank you, Mrs. Hearn," I said, as I put boxes of cereal away in the pantry.

She closed the refrigerator and turned to me. "Nhi," she said. "You know, I've been thinking about it. If you'd like—and only if you feel comfortable with it—you can call me Mom."

Because she had been my teacher, I still called her "Mrs. Hearn." But now she was saying I could call her Mom?

"I know you have a mom," Mary Lou continued. "And I am not trying to take the role away from her. She'll always be your mom. But I consider myself your mom too, and if you want to call me that, you can. You're a young lady going through her teen years—you can't ever have too many moms." Mary Lou smiled—she has a great smile that reaches all the way up to her beautiful blue eyes and lights up her whole face. The sort of smile you can't help return.

"Thank you for always making me feel like I'm a part of the family," I said. Whether or not I called her Mom, just knowing she wouldn't mind made me feel so special and loved.

"Not *like*," Mary Lou said. "You *are* a part of this family."

* * *

Despite my close bond with Mary Lou, I didn't feel comfortable sharing the details of my past with her. I just didn't feel comfortable talking about my past with *anyone*. Maybe out of shame, or fear of judgment, or being rejected if people knew about the horrible things that had happened in my past. Maybe all three of those things. If I talked about it, I'd be reliving it, and I wanted to put all that behind me. But one day we were in the car on our way to school and a talk radio program was on. One of the guests was talking about how she was abused as a child. She was really going on about it in a way I could never imagine, especially on the radio with who knows how many people listening in!

"There was probably a reason for it," I said. "She might have done something bad to deserve it."

It was, perhaps, a harsh comment from someone who herself had been beaten countless times, never having done anything to deserve it.

Mary Lou glanced at me. "That is a sick comment! No one ever deserves to be beaten. People sometimes do the wrong thing, yes, but that does not give anyone the right to violate your safety." She paused. "Were you abused in the camp?" She slowed the car and pulled over to the side of the road. I stared straight ahead.

My childhood home once it had been converted to a police station.

My mother with five young kids after we moved to Ho Chi Minh City.

My missing brother who attempted escape before I did.

My mother wanted a photo of me before my escape.

All the kids staying at the Minors Center.

English class at the Minors Center.

Outside the sleeping area at the refugee camp.

With the other kids at the Minors Center.

Goodbye refugee camp!

My adoptive parents, Mary and Lewis Hearn.

My two mothers meet for the first time.

With my two moms, Lewis, and Jeff on our wedding day.

The Hearn family and my Vietnamese mother.

Jeff's first trip to Vietnam—meeting my relatives—at the lake in front of my childhood home.

My family challenged Jeff to eat a scorpion!

The B'Nai Mitzvah ceremony at the ancient synagogue on top of Masada in Israel.

"We've never talked about it," she continued. "And I don't want to push you to talk about anything you don't feel comfortable speaking about. But . . . if there is ever anything you want to talk about, I want you to know I am here to listen. And I don't just mean school-related things. I can't even begin to imagine the experiences you must've gone through when you were escaping Vietnam, and I know people will often try to forget or push down negative experiences and never bring them up again. But sometimes it can really help to talk about it."

An ache started to build in my throat and my vision blurred as tears gathered at the corners of my eyes. No one had ever told me he or she was willing to listen if I needed to talk.

"Some bad things did happen," I barely managed to whisper before the tears started flowing. Mary Lou leaned over and pulled me toward her. She held me close for a few minutes, until my crying began to subside.

"Do you want to talk about it?"

I wiped at my eyes and shook my head vehemently. "No!" While I believed what she said about being there to listen, I couldn't help but worry that if Mary Lou and the Hearns knew the whole story about my past, they would surely stop loving me; they might even send me back to my sister's home. That was something I wasn't willing to risk yet.

* * *

It was my senior year of high school when Mary Lou came to me with great news. "Since Iroquois has mostly underprivileged students, the University of Louisville offers a full scholarship to one student to attend the university while this person is still in high school. Among all the students at this school, the other teachers and I can only think of you for that academic scholarship!" she exclaimed. "How would you like to attend the University of Louisville while you're still in high school?"

College classes? While still in high school? It sounded a little intimidating, to be honest. But I could tell just by the look on her face that Mary Lou was excited for me and thought this was a great opportunity.

"I don't know how well I'll do taking classes with other college students," I said. "But . . . if you think it's good for me, then I'll take a chance."

Mary Lou beamed. "Nhi, you're going to shine."

In order to get to the University of Louisville, I had to take a public bus from my high school to the campus. U of L was huge, with over twenty thousand students. Learning to get around the school and finding the right classroom was an experience in and of itself. I did not go through the school orientation and had no clue where I was going. But I used the campus map and also asked for help along the way, a much easier process because by that point, I could speak English pretty well.

Once I got used to my new schedule, I did quite well with my classes at the university. Quite a few adult students were surprised to learn that I was only a high school kid. Mary Lou was right—I did shine at U of L, so much that they offered me a full-ride scholarship to attend their four-year program.

U of L was not the only school I received an offer from, though. I had also applied to the University of Kentucky and a private liberal arts school called Centre College. It was ranked the second-best liberal arts school in the South, and when I found out they were also offering a scholarship and a financial aid package—enough to cover my tuition, room, and board—I knew that was the school I was going to attend.

But before looking forward to college, there was still high school. I graduated from Iroquois High School in three years, as valedictorian. As such, I had to give a speech—me, knowing nothing about public speaking, who still spoke English with an accent. I was supposed to stand up there in front of the entire school and give a motivating speech.

Delivering that speech was one of the most intimidating experiences for me—standing in front of about two thousand people giving my speech with a heavy accent. I was so concerned whether people could understand me. People came to me after and told me I did great, but I personally think my delivery was terrible and that I would have done a much better job if I had some personal coaching for my public speaking skills. But I overcame my fear and I did it.

The nervousness I had felt about giving the valedictorian speech paled in comparison to my anxiety about college life. Again—it was the unknown, and perhaps you'd think I'd be used to that by now. But it was still scary. I would be leaving the Hearns, the one place I had truly felt safe and like I could call home. Now, I was about to go off on my own, and though I knew the Hearns would always be there for me, I was determined not to ask them for any financial support, as they had already done so much. I wanted to show them that, thanks to their kindness and generosity, I could stand on my own two feet and make my way in the world. Yet inside, I was fearful I would not succeed in the competitive academic environment, and I imagined my future classmates to be privileged and well-off. How would I ever be able to measure up against that?

CHAPTER EIGHT
COLLEGE

Mary Lou drove the two hours to Centre College to drop me off. I had a suitcase with my clothes and some toiletry items, my backpack and a few school supplies, and a new set of sheets and a comforter. Over the summer, I found out that my roommate's name was Zita. Though I hoped we would get along, I had been through enough horrible living situations that I wasn't too worried about that aspect of college life.

The school itself was beautiful, with its stately brick-and-column buildings and lush, manicured lawns, bisected by neat concrete pathways. It was built in 1819, and you could just feel the history of the place as you walked around campus. For the next four years, it would be my home.

* * *

I had arrived at Centre as the high school valedictorian, but I quickly began to feel extremely inadequate academically, compared to my college peers, many of whom were also valedictorians or highly ranked in their graduating classes. Not only did they all speak impeccable English, but it appeared that quite a few students came from privileged families. They were easy to spot—they had nice clothes, fancy cars, and a seemingly endless supply of money to go shopping or out to eat. Yet despite our vast socioeconomic differences, everyone was very welcoming and nice to me. I also had to get used to being one of only five other Asians at my school! There had been a lot more diversity at my high school, but at Centre College, the majority of the students were white, though in the years since I graduated, the student body has diversified quite a bit.

The dean of the school was Dr. Ward, an older gentleman with white hair and a kind and gentle demeanor. He was friendly and approachable, and he made it clear right away that he would help us in any way he could—not necessarily academically. Incoming freshman had been invited to the president's home on campus. We also had a Meet and Greet with Dr. Ward, whose house was also on campus, and, apparently, open to us should there be anything we thought we might be in need of.

"The faculty here wants your college experience to be amazing," Dr. Ward said. "We want you to feel that we are your second home now. If you ever need to talk to me—and it doesn't have to be about school—just stop by my office. Or, you know where my home is on campus. Anything you need, if we've got it, we're happy to share. We're all like family here." I looked at him, trying to figure out if he really meant it, and was as approachable as he was saying. (That winter, when a few of us needed a sled to truly enjoy the freshly fallen snow, we decided to go to the dean's home and see if he really meant it— *Would he lend us a sled?* To our surprise, he had a few to choose from—some were saucers, some were long and narrow—and he gave us our pick and told us to bring them back when we were done, and oh—have fun!)

I found his words encouraging. The guy I was standing near looked at me and smiled. His name was Kevin, and he was fit and handsome, with his dark hair and stunning brown eyes, framed by long, dark lashes. I could tell Zita thought he was cute right away, because she immediately struck up a conversation with him. She made it seem so easy! I mostly stood there and listened, though Kevin did try to include me as they chatted.

As it turned out, Kevin and I were both in the same English class, taught by Dr. Mark Rasmussen, a Harvard graduate. He had thick, dirty blond hair and wore big plastic frame glasses. I was hopeful his class would help me continue to improve my English skills. I certainly felt at a disadvantage, having spent so much of my time in high school playing catch-up to my native-speaking peers.

But it quickly became apparent that I was going to have to play catch-up there, too.

When I got my first writing assignment back, I was shocked to see a big red C scrawled across the top, and, below that, many more red marks indicating all the ways in which I needed to improve. The fact that English was my second language was not going to get any special consideration from this professor. I looked at my paper in dismay.

I had never received such a low grade before. I felt like such a failure!

Kevin, who was seated across the room from me, must've seen the stricken look on my face, because he gave me that kind, genuine smile of his and, after class, asked if I was okay.

"I'm fine," I said quickly, even though I felt nothing close to fine. I had never gotten such a poor grade before, and I couldn't let this continue—I'd lose my scholarship if I did. I couldn't even let myself think that.

"Oh hey, I did worse than you," Kevin said, in such a light tone it was like he was asking me what my favorite movie was. He showed me his paper where the D shone like a beacon. I wouldn't have thought it possible, but it appeared that his paper had even more red marks than my own. I looked up at him, wondering how it was he could be so unbothered.

"Don't feel bad! English is my first language, and I did worse than you. Dr. Rasmussen has a reputation for being extremely tough, but I was told that by the time we finish his class, we will know how to write well. If you want to study together some time, let me know," he said. Was he serious? It was a little hard to believe this cute guy wanted to hang out with me.

"My grades might get better if I make myself sit down and study with someone," he added. "I need to improve my grades before my father cuts off all my money supply."

I agreed to meet with him in the library, starting a tradition that would continue throughout our time at Centre together. The first time we met, though, I was a little nervous, which there really wasn't any reason for, because Kevin had been nothing but nice so far. Perhaps it had to do with Zita and two other girls in our hall finding out that I was going to meet up with Kevin—they had all giggled about how cute he was, and how lucky I was to go study with him. The way they were talking it was like we were going out on a first date.

Which, of course, was not at all what happened.

We found a table near the back, in a quiet corner. Kevin was about a foot taller than I was, but still considered not that tall for a guy. The night we had first met at the Meet and Greet, I remembered overhearing him tell Zita how he had played football in high school, which he really enjoyed, even though he was "vertically challenged."

And that, I would come to find out, was one of the things I appreciated most about Kevin: his down-to-earth self-deprecation. He didn't let it hold him back from anything, but he wasn't afraid to admit when he found something challenging.

"English has never been one of my favorite subjects," he said. "I'm not smart like other kids, so I have to work harder."

I stopped writing midsentence, my pen hovering above the page in my notebook. Had he just said that out loud? English was his native language, yet he was speaking about his difficulties with it the way someone might describe the weather.

But I appreciated his vulnerability, even if to him it might not seem like that big of a thing to admit. Kevin appeared to be one of the wealthier kids at school even though he never disclosed it; I could tell just from the clothes he wore and the fact that he had his own very nice car and could come and go as he pleased. It was difficult not to feel significantly less than when I couldn't even afford to make a long-distance call home to talk with the Hearns.

I put my pen down. "English is hard for me, too. I've spent so much time playing catch up, I sometimes feel like I'm never going to make it."

"I bet it's challenging," Kevin said. "I can't even imagine what it would be like to learn a *second* language and get into a competitive school like this; I'm having a hard enough time with the one language I *do* know."

He smiled, and I returned his smile—how could I not? But he was also making me feel better about myself. Here was this young man, from a privileged family, being open about his struggles. His willingness to do so was an invitation for my own vulnerabilities to surface, and I found myself telling him a little bit about the Hearns, and how good they had been to me, and how I had resolved not ask them for anything once I was at college.

"They sound like good people," he said. "I think most parents want to help their kids if they need it."

"Oh, I know. It's just the Hearns have already done so much. They don't have a lot of extra money, either. Even if they did though—how could I ask them for anything else? I'm an adult now; I need to make my own way."

"Well, if you ever need a ride somewhere, just let me know, okay?" Kevin said. "I mean it."

It surprised me how easy Kevin was to talk to. I was never in fear of his judgment, never felt like there was a topic we couldn't discuss. We would continue to study together, but we also met up regularly for lunch in the cafeteria. Our relationship would grow during our time at Centre, and Kevin would become one of my closest friends. And he wasn't just making an empty offer that day when he said to let him know if I ever needed a ride anywhere—he was always more than happy to take me to Walmart if there was something I needed to get, or occasionally I'd join him and some of his friends to go out to eat, and he would often quietly offer to pay for my meal.

Kevin and I could talk to each other about anything, so I suppose it was only natural that other people would think we were an item. We were not—we never crossed the friend zone, which I think we were both happy about, because a possible romantic relationship was not worth jeopardizing the friendship we had.

Unfortunately, Kevin's family was not as open-minded as he was, which I experienced firsthand when I went home with him over a long weekend. The fact of our friendship seemed puzzling to his family, particularly when it became clear that we were not boyfriend and girlfriend. His parents could not seem to figure out why Kevin was friends with me, this person who looked so different from what they were used to, who was clearly from a different socioeconomic background. What was it that made Kevin so willing to embrace diversity when it was clearly something he hadn't learned at home? I would probably never have an answer for that, but it did nothing to diminish my gratitude for Kevin, and his ability to look beyond a person's physical appearance.

* * *

Jamie was another person I would meet at Centre who would become a close friend. He was from Louisville, the oldest of six kids in a big, Catholic family. Unlike my experience with Kevin's family, when I went to visit Jamie's home, everyone was more than welcoming.

They lived in a beautiful, grand home, with a wraparound porch. Their front yard looked out onto a wide, quiet road, and Jamie's siblings were often playing outside in that peaceful, tree-lined neighborhood. What I recall most was my shock at the amount of food they had, though there certainly were a lot of mouths to feed. The refrigerator was full of food and the pantry was overflowing—I didn't even want to think about how much their weekly grocery bill was. But they were such a loving and welcoming family, and the noise and chaos of all the kids running around just enriched everything.

* * *

Not all of my relationships at Centre were as easygoing as my friendships with Kevin and Jamie, though. Which I suppose is to be expected, when you get that many people together from such diverse backgrounds. That first year having Zita as a roommate proved to be somewhat of a challenge.

Our room had bunk beds, so I took the bottom bunk and Zita took the top. One night, as I was drifting off to sleep, I felt something fall onto my head, and when I turned to get it, it became entangled in my hair. I sat up, pulling, trying to free whatever it was. My eyes had adjusted to the dark just enough to be able to see that it was Zita's retainer—she must've spit it out while she was asleep!

Needless to say, after that incident, we decided to separate the beds, and she took one side of our small room and I took the other.

Zita was from California's Bay Area, and she was incredibly smart. The sort of smart that did not require her to do any real studying, yet it still seemed she aced all her exams and papers. Being her roommate, I knew she studied hard on top of being intelligent. My confidence was shot feeling like I was failing and having to catch up with someone like Zita, who was an over-achiever and English was her first language. It was difficult not to be envious of a person like that, doubly so when you shared a room with her.

And she certainly had some ambitious ideas.

Her major idea during our freshman year was to ride a bicycle across America.

"Why do you want to do that?" I asked her.

"It's a charity ride; I'm doing it for the American Heart Association. I've already had a lot of donors, but it's a big undertaking, and I'll need to get more."

I wasn't entirely sure what that entailed, but I was about to find out.

Our dorm room quickly became the one-woman headquarters for Zita's fund-raising efforts. It seemed that whenever I stepped into our room, returning from class or from a meal in the dining hall, Zita would be on the phone, explaining her upcoming mission and trying to solicit donations. She was enthusiastic and passionate about her future endeavor, and I did admire her tenacity, but I also wished it wasn't happening in our dorm room, seemingly all the time.

It made it impossible to study in my room. It made it impossible to do anything, really, other than listen to Zita talk about her plan, her charity, and how exciting the adventure was going to be.

In a way, Zita's constant use of the phone was a good thing, because it forced me to seek out alternative places to study. The library was the main place, and Kevin often accompanied me, but I also ended up hanging out with some of the other girls in my hall. There were Marianne, Sandra, Maura, and Christi: girls who were incredibly smart and took their studies as seriously as I did.

We'd study in the lounge or in Sandra or Marianne's room when their roommates were out. While most of our time was dedicated to studying, we also really got to know each other. Like me, Sandra, Marianne, and several girls in our hall were virgins, which I did find a little surprising since these young women were quite attractive. I had a certain idea in my mind of the way American kids were—especially those in college—and it felt good to connect with people who shared similar values. We jokingly dubbed our floor "the Virgin Hall."

Over spring break, Sandra invited me back home with her to Tennessee. "I've told my family all about you!" she said as we drove. "They're really excited to meet you. A lot of people in my family are!"

Sandra's family lived in a nice two-story house in a decent neighborhood. Her mother exuded a bubbly, vibrant energy, and when we went through the front door, she embraced me right away. She pulled me to her and hugged me tight.

"I'm so glad to finally meet you!" she crowed, releasing me from the hug and holding me at arm's distance for a minute, her smile shining down on me like sunshine. She had voluminous amounts of blond hair and these incredibly long, thick eyelashes, which Sandra would later tell me were fake. But Sandra's mom made me feel right at home immediately with her southern hospitality.

"So, Nhi," Sandra's mother said to me at breakfast one morning, midway through our trip. "We've heard from Sandra that you spent most of your time in high school studying. While that's great and all, it probably didn't leave you a whole lot of time to go out and do fun things, now, did it?"

"It didn't," I agreed. "I never went to any parties or anything; I just really felt like I had a lot of catching up to do."

"Well, I was hoping you'd like to have a little fun now. We were thinking of going to Dollywood; would you like to go? It'll be a blast."

"Sure!" I replied, having no clue what Dollywood was.

But oh, boy, would I find out.

Dollywood turned out to be not just a theme park, not just a resort, not just a festival . . . it was a living tribute to famous country singer Dolly Parton. I did not expect it to be an amusement park, and I did not know anything about Dolly until we got there. The family educated me about their Tennessee legend, Ms. Parton. Her photos were everywhere, and country music filled the air. Good thing I enjoyed country music! Sandra's family was beyond generous; knowing I didn't have any money, they graciously paid for everything that day.

"Just think of it as the experience you should have, above and beyond your college education," Sandra's mother told me. "Isn't this place great?"

I cheerfully nodded.

I had a fun time being with Sandra's family, and it made me happy to see that her mother was so warm and loving, not just to her daughter but to everyone. At the same time, it made me sad thinking about how far away I was from my biological family, and how there was no way we'd ever be able to go out all together and enjoy the day at some place as ridiculously over the top as Dollywood.

* * *

At the end of our freshman year, Marianne invited me to Fancy Farm, Kentucky, for a visit with her family. We listened to Reba

McIntire the entire six-hour drive, and Marianne enthusiastically sang along with all her favorites.

"I think you've killed my love for country music," I told her once we'd arrived at her house and were out of the car.

Like Sandra's family, Marianne's family welcomed me like I was one of their own. They lived in a more rural area, in a beautiful farmhouse with a large, manicured front lawn and abundant garden beds. It looked like something out of a magazine. Her father had fought in the Vietnam War but showed no resentment toward me at all. Marianne's mother was equally as kind and warm toward me, though I knew she drove Marianne nuts because she was concerned that Marianne was "sleeping around at school," as she put it.

"Is my daughter behaving herself, Nhi?" she asked. "You would tell me if she wasn't, right? Marianne, you're being a good girl at school, aren't you?" All I could tell Marianne's mother at the time was that her daughter was so smart and did well in school, but I could not tell her about our virgin hall. I laughed about their typical mother-daughter relationship—universal, it seemed, it didn't matter the culture.

On Friday evening, after dinner, Marianne's mother sat at the kitchen table with the newspaper open in front of her. Every so often, she would circle one of the classified ads, and then look at a map she had next to her.

"What are you doing?" I asked.

"Mom's doing one of her favorite things," Marianne said. "She's mapping out all the yard sales she's going to go to tomorrow."

"Yard sales?" I had never heard this term before. "What are those?"

Marianne's mom stopped writing, midcircle. She lifted her head and looked at me, eyes wide. "You've never been to a yard sale before?"

I shook my head. "I'm not even sure what it is."

"Oh, boy," Marianne said, laughing. "Now we're in for it."

Yard sales, as it turned out, were quite a thing in Marianne's family, and apparently, for many Americans in that part of the country. While I was certainly more used to the abundance in the United States, this seemed to be taking it to a whole new level. Some people had so much stuff, so many things, that they would hold a sale outside in their yard, things priced very cheaply.

"Well, then, Nhi, you girls are coming with us tomorrow. We leave at 6 a.m. I know that sounds early, but if you get there right when it starts, you'll have first dibs on all the good stuff, which gets snapped up real quick." She beamed. "Oh, this is so exciting. If you've never experienced this part of American culture, I will be more than happy to show you! Our entire family needs to go and educate Nhi."

The next morning, we were up early and out of the house right at six, just like Marianne's mother had said. Her easygoing father tagged along to make his wife happy. She consulted her map and her newspaper, and soon I found myself in someone's yard, where they had folding tables set up, displaying a wide variety of items. There were household items, like coffee cups, a stack of dinner plates, several copper pots and pans. Two coffee makers, one still brand new in the box, I overheard a woman say. There were large plastic bins overflowing with clothes, and I followed Marianne over to one where we picked through T-shirts, summer dresses, jeans, and sweaters. Several articles of clothing still had tags. A handwritten sign on the outside of each bin read: *25¢*.

I couldn't believe it.

And it wasn't just this first yard sale; we visited eight or nine different sales that day in nearby towns, and the one thing they all had in common was the sheer amount of stuff on offer. Toys, bedding, household furniture, power tools, jewelry . . . It seemed anything you might want could be found at a yard sale, and in many cases, for less than a dollar!

Marianne's family also took me on another experience I'd never been on before: attending Catholic mass. That Sunday, I went with them to church. One of the things that surprised me most was the fact that people there already knew about me and were so warm and friendly toward me. Apparently, Marianne's family had been so excited I was coming to visit that they had told their whole congregation. I was struck by the solemnity of the mass, but also the beauty in the hymns. I kneeled in the pew when everyone else around me kneeled, and near the end, when members lined up at the altar to receive communion, I started to follow, not entirely sure what was happening, what the priest was depositing in each person's hand, or, in a few cases, directly into their mouths.

"You don't have to go up," Marianne whispered before she exited the pew. "You can just wait here; I'll be right back."

I watched as she made her way up to the priest, received a thin wafer, which she put in her mouth, and then returned to the pew. Everyone kneeled until the last person in line received communion.

After mass, I had many questions about the service. Marianne's family was happy to explain the Seven Sacraments and the Catholic belief that Jesus had died for our sins. It was fascinating to learn about other people's beliefs, particularly because I was still sorting out my own—I wasn't sure what I believed, but I wanted to be as open and accepting about these things as I could, much in the way Marianne's family had been to me.

* * *

Perhaps the most important professor during my time at Centre was Dr. Clarence Wyatt. A tall, fit man who wore wire-rimmed glasses, he was a history professor and a Vietnam scholar. Even though I did not take Dr. Wyatt's history class, being one of the few Vietnamese students on campus, he had heard about me. During my junior year, right around the time President Clinton lifted the embargo against Vietnam, Dr. Wyatt approached me one day and told me he was considering taking his class to Vietnam for a winter semester.

"I heard you haven't seen your family in quite some time now," he said. "Would you like to see them? Would you go with us if I could make it happen?"

It was surprising to hear such a question. See my family again? I had always hoped I would but was uncertain how such a possibility could ever take place. But now, here was Centre's history professor making just such a proposal.

But it wouldn't be that simple, would it? "I would love to do that," I said. "But I'm not a US citizen and I don't have a way to pay for the trip."

"What if you didn't have to worry about those two things?" he asked.

"Well, of course I would love to go!" I just wasn't sure how it would be feasible.

Dr. Wyatt, though, had some ideas. "What if the school paid for you to go," he said, "and you acted as our interpreter?"

That was certainly something I could agree to, but it didn't take care of the larger problem of gaining US citizenship. If I traveled to Vietnam without it, I was putting myself at risk for potential arrest while over there, and there would be nothing anyone here in America would be able to do.

"I know you have a lot on your plate as it is," Dr. Wyatt said, "but if you could study up and pass the citizenship test, I think the school would be able to help get you naturalized as soon as possible, so you'd be able to go with us."

Never one to shy away from a challenging test, I agreed, though I still wasn't sure what the school would be able to do to facilitate a quicker process.

As it turned out—the school was able to do quite a bit.

I studied for and passed the citizenship test, where I answered a number of civics questions, like how many senators are there and what were the thirteen original states? Once I had passed the citizenship test, the school contacted one of their alumni who was a judge, and they were able to pull some strings. I went into court to become a naturalized citizen, which usually happened to a group of people at a time, but that day, it was just me with my family and friends who came to show their support. I wore a green dress, and I stood in front of the judge, right hand raised, as I pledged to renounce allegiance to Vietnam and that I would both support and defend the US Constitution. I wished my mother could have been there that day, because I knew that was what she had hoped for, all those years ago, when she was trying to save the money for me to try to escape.

And there I was, a United States citizen. I was thrilled to be officially recognized as a member of this country that had been so accepting and welcoming toward immigrants and refugees, a haven for those who could not safely live in their country of origin.

I could return to Vietnam without fear of being detained. But with the citizenship issue taken care of, I began to feel a bit of nervousness intertwined with the excitement at the prospect of reuniting with my family after not seeing them for seven years. Although I had been writing to my family regularly since my arrival in the United States, I wonder how Mother would feel about me. My life was so different than how it had been, and the last time my mother saw me, I was a twelve-year-old girl. Now I was a young woman. What would the reunion with my family be like, after all these years?

CHAPTER NINE
FAMILY REUNION

I never believed I would return to Vietnam, and certainly not with twenty of my fellow American classmates and a film producer named Michael Breeding, who recorded our trip. Later, our reunion was broadcast on Kentucky news channels and also released as a series, *Vietnam 101*, on the KET Network (a PBS affiliate).

My feelings were a tangled mess—I was so excited, scared, anxious, and still in disbelief that it was really going to happen. After Dr. Wyatt had given me the trip's itinerary, I wrote to Mother and told her the good news—I would, in fact, get to see her again, and it would be in Vietnam, because I was going to travel there with my school. Her return letter included lots of underlining and exclamation points—my family was beyond excited at the extraordinary opportunity I had.

We arrived in the north, in Hanoi. From there we would travel to the central part of Vietnam, Danang, with our final destination being far south, in Ho Chi Minh, where my family still resided.

The trip was exciting for all of us, for different reasons. Some of my classmates had never left the country before. The trip would allow them to gain a better understanding of a country that played a central role in the American experience, particularly for their parents, many of whom had gone to fight in Vietnam.

And for me, too, the trip would include seeing places I had never been to before, particularly up north, where we previously could not go because the country had been in chaos. Just being surrounded by people speaking Vietnamese was incredible—it had been so long since I'd last spoken it. The dialect of the people in the North reminded me of how the Viet Cong spoke, their accent different than those from the South. But to hear my native tongue again was like embracing an old friend.

I acted as an interpreter for my classmates, who now found themselves fully immersed in a culture that, up until that point, they'd only known through our history class and the pages of our textbooks. The streets of Hanoi were crowded, and I could tell how shocking many of my classmates found the chaos of Vietnamese streets. I recalled my own surprise when I left the airport in Kentucky and saw how orderly the traffic in America was; my classmates were now experiencing the reverse. Motorbikes, bicycles, pedestrians, the occasional pickup truck or van traveling in every direction, not following the traffic signals or street signs. There were vendors everywhere, selling all sorts of things—snacks, trinkets, handwoven baskets, leaf hats. One man even approached one of my classmates and tried to sell her American dog tags.

But all these people—they were just trying to make a little money, much like I had been all those years ago, trying to sell black market cigarettes. Though I was considered poor by American standards, it was not even close to the level of impoverishment that we were seeing right in front of us, on the streets—men, women, children, some with missing limbs or obvious mental disabilities. It was another stark reminder of how fortunate I was to have made it to America.

Christi, who had lived in the same hall our freshman year, found herself the center of much unwanted attention as we navigated the chaotic streets. At six feet tall, with bright red hair, she really stood out. Most Vietnamese people had likely never seen such a tall woman with such pale skin and vibrant hair. She was too tall for people to come over and try to touch her hair, but that didn't stop them from pointing, staring, and exclaiming when we passed by.

"I'm glad I can't understand what they're saying," she said. "This is awful, though, all this attention."

"People are not malicious. They're just not used to seeing a woman who is so tall," I said. "But now you know how I've felt living in Kentucky all these years, looking so different from everyone else." I had said it more out of solidarity than trying to make her feel worse, but I could tell when she frowned and didn't reply that she hadn't taken it that way.

We took a bus from Hanoi to Ha Long Bay. The trip was long, but it was nice to see the scenery and to escape the chaos of the city. Our travel was often hampered by animals and livestock crossing the street—the bus had to stop and wait many times for a herd of cows or a line of pigs to cross. We passed rice fields, dotted with farmers hard at work, humble village homes, and stray dogs trotting down the dirt roads. The journey took a while, and when we arrived at the coast, we were all eager to get off the bus.

Ha Long Bay is renowned for its stunning emerald green waters, but the fog was heavy on the day of our visit, and the water appeared only a few shades darker than the heavy gray clouds above us. Nothing could detract from the mystical beauty of the place, though, as we cruised around on dragon boats. Ha Long Bay is also known for the thousands of limestone islands that jut out of the water, and the mist really made them seem ethereal. As we approached, the closest islands would become visible, while the ones further away remained barely visible, shrouded in fog. It was chilly, but it was so beautiful we barely noticed the temperature.

As we made our way around the bay and took in the sights, I couldn't help but wonder why we would have so many wars in such an incredible country. In a way, I felt like I was seeing this place for the first time, or through a different lens—I had returned to my home country, yet as a visitor. Some of these places I was seeing for the first time, and it was impossible not to be struck by the sheer amount of natural beauty everywhere.

We were not the only boats out on the water. People would drive up on dilapidated motorboats and latch onto our boat for a little while, hoping to sell something. Many had baskets of shrimp or shellfish, though they also tried to sell us shells and pieces of coral. There were entire families living on these boats; they did not have a home on land to go to. They strung laundry lines from bow to stern, the clothes waving like flags in the wind. There were many children, and they would hop into a rowboat and easily maneuver their way closer to us, wanting to get a better look, hoping we had some sort of treat to give them.

On our last day in Hanoi, we went to Hoa Lu, which had been the capital of Vietnam in the tenth and eleventh centuries. We went to a small village and again boarded wooden boats where we followed the Red River past caves and jutting geological formations, quite similar to the ones we saw at Ha Long Bay. The sun was shining on this particular day—the first time it had come out since we'd arrived in Vietnam—and the surface of the water sparkled and everything felt so peaceful and serene.

* * *

We flew from the Hanoi to Da Nang, near where I was born. I had asked Mother to let Uncle Hong and Aunt Tien know that I would be in the area for that part of my trip, and they came to visit at the hotel where we were staying. My classmates had gone out to explore the area, which gave me some time alone with my family.

"You've come back to see us!" Uncle Hong exclaimed. "And your mother tells us you're now an American citizen."

"We weren't sure if we'd ever see you again," Aunt Tien said. "But we're so happy that things worked out for you. We're always so eager to hear news of you from your mother. Tell us about your life in America."

I filled them in. But then our conversation shifted back in time.

"It's a shame about your father," Uncle Hong said. "Your family went through so much and lost everything."

My father had died two years ago, in 1992. Mother had written to tell me, and it felt abstract; I had so few memories of him, and the last memories I had were awful. The last time I had seen Father, before he left to move back with his first wife, he had been beating my brother Cu.

"But you should be so proud of yourself, Nhi," Aunt Tien said. "We know your mother is. So much to overcome. But look at you now, coming back to visit us with your American classmates."

Uncle Hong smiled. "Do you remember the last time we saw each other?"

"Of course," I said, thinking back to that train ride I took all alone, after convincing Mother she needed to let me do it.

"You didn't want to leave."

"We weren't in the best situation."

"I know. But if we had let you stay with us, you wouldn't have made it to America. And you'll be seeing your mother after you leave here?"

"Yes, Ho Chi Minh City is one of the last places we'll visit before we head back to America."

"Your mother is so excited. She has been waiting for this moment for so long."

I did not share with my aunt and uncle how nervous I was to see Mother again. My visit with Uncle Hong and Aunt Tien had gone so smoothly, I hoped it would be equally as pleasant with Mother. So many years had passed since we'd seen each other; she remembered me as a girl, but now I was returning as a young woman.

We took a short flight from Da Nang to Ho Chi Minh City. The closer we got, the higher my anxiety went. My heart raced and my palms were sweaty, and I kept replaying the possible ways it might go.

We took a bus to the hotel where I was going to meet my family. The traffic was so congested, that for a moment, I wasn't sure if I was going to be able to get off the bus. But there they were—my mother, my brother Fourth, my sister Fifth . . . I almost couldn't believe my eyes.

There they were.

I managed to get off the bus and zip across the street, right into my mother's arms. Vietnamese people generally do not show displays of affection in public, but my mother wrapped me in her arms and kissed me. I felt my brother's arms around me next, then my sister's, and then my mother had me back in another hug. The tears flowed freely. It had been so long since I had last seen them, and I had come to believe we would never see each other in person again.

"You are so grown up, but still my little girl!" my mother said.

She also looked different, her hair dyed black again, no longer the white it had been. It seemed that she, too, could not believe we had been reunited; she kept looking at me, a smile breaking out on her face.

"I'm so happy," she said. "You're living the life I always dreamed for you. You are doing so well. Tell us more about what your life is like."

I was just so happy to be with them again I didn't even want to think about my life back in America. But they were eager to hear about it, and so I described college, and told them a little about Kevin, and I gave them updates on the Hearns, who they had already heard about in my letters.

Dr. Wyatt was kind enough to let me stay with my family, instead of at the hotel with the rest of the group. There was plenty in Ho Chi Minh City for them to explore, and this gave me a few days to just be with my family, here in the little room I'd spent part of my childhood in.

The room, though, had expanded, because Mother had been able to save enough money to build a floor over the filthy shallow creek and then add a room above it, so now there were two rooms. There was still the Helly Hole, though it was smaller than the old one because, as she told me, she used the money I sent to make this improvement. When Dr. Wyatt and my classmates stopped by for a brief visit, I was going to show them the Helly Hole, but Mother stopped me and pulled me aside.

"Please don't," she said. "It's such a humiliating thing for our family; don't further that humiliation by showing your classmates. They've probably never seen anything like it."

Something unexpected began to happen, then, in the final days of my time in Vietnam. After the initial shock wore off that I was really back, my mother began to treat me like the twelve-year-old girl I had been before I'd left, even though I was no longer a child.

"You've become too Americanized," she said to me. "I'm beginning to not even recognize you." She frowned at my Centre College sweatshirt. "And Nhi, I do not want you to date or marry a non-Vietnamese person."

I stared at her, unable to believe that she was somehow more concerned about my heritage than my actual life.

"But I live in America," I said. "The family who adopted me is American and most of my friends are Americans and I love them all regardless of their skin color." I tried to remind myself that my mother had never left Vietnam, had never been exposed to the range of diversity that I had found in America. "It's different in America. It is a melting pot, and there are people living there from all over the world. I will date and marry the person I fall in love with."

That was not the destiny she had in mind for me, though. "Then if there are people from all over the world there, surely you can find a Vietnamese man to date and marry."

"My school has only five Asians on the entire campus. It would be a challenge to date a Vietnamese guy in that environment. If the ideal man you envision for me happens to be Vietnamese, then great," I said. "I don't like it when you want me to exclude certain people in my life, such as my dear friend Kevin, just because they look different from us."

It was not the answer she wanted to hear. "I'm starting to question my decision to let you escape for a better life," she said. "It appears that I no longer know who you are and that I might have lost my daughter."

Her words were harsh, and I couldn't help but inwardly flinch. I loved Mother and didn't want her to feel like I was turning my back on the place where I was born, or the people I shared my youth with, yet I couldn't bring myself to fully explain to her that I was living a new life, a different life in a different culture—and that meant change. How much harder would things have been for me if I had rejected the new culture I was immersed in on a daily basis, and instead clung to what had been familiar? I knew that the change would be for the good, and I hoped and prayed that someday Mother would see that too.

"If you had stayed in Vietnam, you would marry a Vietnamese man," Mother said. "We would not even be having this discussion."

"But I live in America now, Mother. And there's a good chance the man I marry might not be Vietnamese. Are you really telling me you're not going to accept me if I marry someone who isn't Vietnamese?"

I felt as if she were making me choose—either marry a Vietnamese man, the way she wanted, or marry someone else and run the risk of her refusing to accept me and be a part of my life.

"You should marry a Vietnamese man. It is the right thing to do."

"The right thing to do is *not* marry someone just because they happen to be from the same place as you. I'm not going to tell you I'll do something if I don't plan on doing it!"

"So you're not going to marry a Vietnamese man?"

"Mother, I don't know. I'm not planning on marrying anyone right now. Can we please stop talking about this?"

Mother stared at me for a moment but said nothing and went into the second room, leaving me with my older sister, Sister Fifth. She had a glare on her face, directed right at me.

"What?" I asked, exasperated. Was she about to get on my case about marrying a Vietnamese man, too?

"How dare you talk to Mother that way? You were always Mother's favorite, and now you're breaking her heart! Your behavior is unacceptable!"

I opened my mouth but then stopped. It was not the end to the trip I had envisioned. Now Mother and Fifth were both mad at me.

Perhaps I should have expected it, but the trip had stirred up mixed emotions and a lot of pain about being back in the country I had escaped from years ago. I never wanted to forget where I came from, but I also had no intention of living in the past or with some sort of restrictive rules about what I could do and whom I could do it with. Mother was so adamant because she had never left Vietnam and didn't know what it was like in America.

I knew it would take time and lots of patience, but I hoped that someday Mother would understand why I was doing the things I was doing, even if she didn't agree with them. I was an adult now, and my choices needed to be my own—for better or for worse.

Her criticism hurt, and though it was uncomfortable to admit, by the time the trip was over, I was relieved and eager to get back to America. I felt as if I were lying when the camera was on me and I was being asked how the reunion went. "Incredible!" I replied, even though "a complete emotional roller coaster" would have been more accurate. But I knew the angle the producer was going for. It was supposed to be a positive story of triumph, not the painful reopening of old wounds.

When I left Vietnam for the second time, I wondered if I would ever truly want to come back again.

CHAPTER TEN
LIVING ABROAD

My senior year of college, I decided to head to Europe as part of the study abroad program in Strasbourg, France. I had heard so much about France growing up, because the French had occupied Vietnam for nearly one hundred years. The program provided me an apartment to live with several other young ladies, and Centre also sent two professors to oversee the students and be our guides. While I had an opportunity to graduate early, instead, I jumped at the chance to participate in the program instead—I really wanted to experience life.

I suppose some might say I'd already experienced plenty of life, but so much of what I'd been through were the sort of things you wouldn't wish on your worst enemy. Thanks to my life in America, I was slowly amassing more "typical" experiences, and I was eager to add to that whenever I could.

But before I headed to France, there was someone from my past I wanted to reconnect with.

Before I had left the Minors Center, Bridget, who had recognized the distraught look on my face and saved me from the continued abuse at my half-brother's hands, had written down her home address in Michigan and told me I could write to her whenever I wanted, though she might not get back to me right away because she hoped to continue to travel to different countries. She had since returned to the United States and was living in New York, and it seemed like the perfect opportunity for a quick visit before heading to France.

What would have happened to me if it hadn't been for Bridget? I didn't want to think about it. She was working in Manhattan, and we met up at a little café near the airport. Her husband, George, accompanied her. I learned she had met him while working at the camp. Bridget, as it turned out, had not been a nun as so many of the children at the Minors Center suspected, but a lay missioner working with a Catholic charity called Maryknoll.

"I'm so happy to have the chance to tell you in person how thankful I am for you," I told Bridget. "You were so kind and helped so many of us."

She smiled, and it was the same kind smile I remembered from when we had first met. "You kids changed my life."

There were so many of us in the Minors Center; most of us Bridget would never see after we left. Yet she had always been so generous with her attention, so compassionate and kind-hearted, and that was exactly the sort of thing I wanted to carry with me, to treat others in my life the way Bridget had treated us kids at the refugee camp.

* * *

While studying in Europe, I took some easy classes Tuesday through Thursday, so that I could explore France and travel to different countries on the train Friday through Monday. Because the French had occupied Vietnam for so long, I recognized much of the architecture in the beautiful buildings around me. Yet it was also completely beyond anything I could have imagined to see in person, places like Versailles and Notre Dame Cathedral. I had thought my college, built in 1819, was old, but I realized while I was in Europe that comparatively, the United States is quite young!

It was great to be able to travel so freely after being prevented from moving around much in Vietnam. I took full advantage of this opportunity. I would often travel with my two friends from the program, Rob and George. During these days, it was easier to travel with a small group, as it was before GPS and cell phones, so we had to figure things out on our own. One of us would read the map, another would watch the road signs, while the other was thumbing through our well-worn *Let's Go to Europe* guidebook. We went to Greece, the Czech Republic, and Poland, and I got to learn about other cultures and to expand my worldview.

On the train on our way back from Greece, George turned to me and said, "I have an adopted Vietnamese sister."

I laughed. "Very funny."

"No, I mean it," he said. "My sister is Vietnamese. She's adopted, but she doesn't know much about her heritage, but the rest of our family is white."

"Oh," I said, surprised. "Your family adopted a Vietnamese child?"

"Yes. My dad's a doctor and my parents decided to adopt a Vietnamese baby after the war."

"My dad was a doctor, too," I said. My mother's previous comments about me being "too Americanized" drifted through my mind. I wondered about George's sister, who, if she had left the country when she was just a baby, would probably have no recollection of where she was originally from at all.

George and I spent the rest of the train ride talking about Vietnam. Rather, he asked me questions and I tried to answer them the best I could, and I wondered if he might share some of this information with his sister when he got home. Who would have thought that on our trip to Europe I would find out I shared a Vietnamese connection with one of my schoolmates?

* * *

I didn't always travel in a group; a few times I went alone, and one of those solo trips I made was to Germany. I didn't know anything about the Holocaust until I took a world history class during my junior year; when I had the chance to go to Germany, I visited several Holocaust museums and memorials.

Learning the history of what happened and visiting an actual concentration camp shocked me. The barbed wire and the stark, empty buildings reminded me of the reeducation camp my own father had been in, similar to the sort of place we would have ended up had it not been for my mother's quick thinking.

I looked at photographs of Jews in their gray- and blue-striped prison uniforms, herded together like cattle, bands bearing the Star of David on their upper arms. Big groups of children, their eyes wide with fear. I learned that it wasn't just the Jews who were targeted but also Roma, gay people, and those who were either physically or mentally disabled. It made me sick to my stomach to learn about it. How could people be so hateful? How could others have just stood by and done nothing?

* * *

It was during my visit to Germany that I called my half-sister, Tuyet-Em, who had been sponsored by her two older siblings who immigrated to Germany after the war.

"You're in Germany?" she asked. "Who are you with?"

"I'm by myself this time," I said. "Sometimes I travel with friends, but I took this trip alone. I'm studying abroad; I'll be going back to America after this semester is over."

"I can't believe it," she said. I paused, waiting for her to elaborate. "You're *alone*? You traveled alone? And you're not scared?"

"Well . . . no," I said. After all the things I'd been through, traveling alone through Europe was thrilling. "I'm having a really good time, actually."

"I'm glad to hear it, but . . . I just don't know how you can do it alone. I don't know if I'll ever have the courage to travel far away like that on my own."

"It's really not that bad," I said. Tuyet-Em invited me over for a visit, an offer I accepted though I was a bit hesitant, because I knew it was likely that her brother, Thuy, would be around, and I never wanted to see him again. Yet I also wasn't the scared little girl he probably remembered. I realized after I hung up the phone that there was still a part of me that resented her for not trying to do more to protect me from her brother.

When I arrived at Tuyet-Em's, she hugged me and exclaimed over how much I had grown up. "The last time I saw you, you were just a little girl!" she said. "Now you are a grown woman." She smiled. "But still little."

I did end up coming face-to-face with Thuy, who lived nearby with his wife and two young children. For so long I had tried to forget the horrors he had inflicted on me, yet there we were in Europe, in the same room. He looked as if he could be any regular father, a normal person, certainly not the sort of man that would abuse a young girl.

I had always felt so much shame and anger about being molested and physically abused, and seeing Thuy was bringing all of those feelings back to the surface. I wanted to scream. I wanted him to hurt as badly as he had hurt me. I wanted to tell him just how much I hated him.

But I did none of those things.

Instead, I wondered how he treated his family. How would they feel about him if they knew what he had done? It was strange to think that this person who had caused me so much anguish might have a loving family, people who looked up to him, people who felt safe in his presence. Tuyet-Em would later tell me that he and his family were on welfare, and he had trouble keeping a job. And I admit—it made me feel good to know that I was in a far better position than he was.

I looked him right in the eye, something he had forbidden me to do when we were in the camp together. I held his gaze until he was forced to look away. Yet he did not seem remorseful, or fearful that I might say something about what he had done. I wasn't going to do that, but I wanted him to know he didn't scare me anymore. He couldn't control me.

But was he controlling me in a way? I wondered. Even though I could now make eye contact and was no longer fearful of him, the negative energy I associated with him felt like poison coursing through me. Did I want to carry these feelings with me for the rest of my life?

No, I didn't. I knew that, in order to be able to truly move on and have peace, I needed to forgive him. I inwardly bristled at such a thought, but he was clearly a sick person, unable to control his desires or feel remorse for them. I knew I needed to replace my hatred with forgiveness. It would take time, but seeing him at Tuyet-Em's was like the catalyst to begin the process. I'd repeat a mantra to myself: *Thuy is sick. I am a good person and that is why the Hearns love me and will continue to love me.*

And really, it was the Hearns' love and humanity that allowed me to heal, to forgive my half-brother for what he had done, and to absolve myself of the shame of his actions.

* * *

Tuyet-Em and Thuy were not the only people from that time in my life that I would see while in Europe. In Switzerland, I was able to connect with some of my old friends from the refugee camp. We had kept in sporadic touch over the years, and I knew they had gone to Switzerland.

Nhieu had been one of the girls I had waved a tearful goodbye to when I boarded the bus to leave the refugee camp in Thailand. She was thrilled to hear from me, and even happier to find out that I was traveling and could meet up with her in Geneva.

"It'll be like a reunion!" she said, her voice brimming with excitement and enthusiasm. "I can't believe I'm going to get to see you! You're really traveling alone?"

Apparently, no one could believe that I was traveling around Europe alone.

Nhieu met me at the train station and brought me back to her apartment. Nam, another refugee who had been at the camp with us, came over, and for the next several hours, the three of us hung out, reminisced, and marveled at just how far we all had come.

The last time I had seen them, they were still behind the fences at the refugee camp, and I was boarding a bus to places unknown. We were scared children then, but look at us—Nhieu was studying to become a nurse, and she was married with a new baby, and Nam was studying at the university to become an engineer. And they were equally happy for me, that I had been adopted into a loving family, that I was about to graduate college, that my life in America was good.

It wasn't long, though, until we started reminiscing about the bad old days. "Nhi, do you remember that time you shared your food with us? We were starving, that's one of things I remember most, just how hungry I often was as a teenager. Your family would send you care packages—you were one of the lucky ones. And they sent you the dried squid that one time, and I don't think food has ever looked so good." Nhieu smiled, wiping at her eyes with the back of her hand. Even after all these years, it could still be so heart-wrenching to talk about— even the fond memories. "It really meant so much," Nhieu said. "I don't even recall if I thanked you at the time; I was salivating seeing that snack; it reminded me so much of home! It meant so much to us—you didn't have to do that."

I was impressed that these friends became successful and was touched hearing them thank me, so many years later, for sharing that last bit of my food with them. Funny how certain things can stay vivid in our memory. There was a part of me that didn't want to leave when it was time, but I had to get back, and soon, return to America. But knowing that the three of us, against all odds, had escaped Vietnam, found our way out of the refugee camp, and had managed to create lives that were busy and rewarding, filled me with a buoyant gratitude. Things had worked out. And as we said our goodbyes at the train station, I hoped that things would continue to work out for all of us and I anxiously wondered what would be waiting for me in my next chapter of life after Europe.

CHAPTER ELEVEN
THE COLD CALL

After I graduated from Centre in 1996, something amazing happened. I was sitting at home, drinking my morning tea, getting ready to continue on my job search by calling around to companies for which I thought I might be a good fit.

I picked up the phone and dialed the next number on my list, for a company called Lucent Technologies, located in Louisville, Kentucky. They had posted a classified ad in the jobs section of our local newspaper, looking for a telecommunication consultant. While it's true that was a very male-dominated industry, I was not going to allow that to deter me. The phone began to ring.

The person who picked up the phone had a strong, deep voice. Later, I would learn that this person, Gene, rarely, if ever, answered his assistant's phone. But on that particular day, at that particular moment, and for some magical reason, the branch manager answered the phone and spoke to a woman who had a thick accent, inquiring about the job that was posted in the newspaper—and that woman happened to be me. While speaking on the phone, it was clear that Gene liked what I was saying and how I was saying it. He asked if I would come in that Monday for an interview, and I got the job.

So, there I was, just out of college, going to work at a telecommunications company that employed primarily white men. Never mind that the majority of these men had worked with Gene for twenty years or more. Something else I would later find out was that one of Gene's long-time employees had died unexpectedly and that he was frantically looking for a replacement. He was also under tremendous pressure from the corporate office in New Jersey to have a more diverse workforce, and what better way to satisfy two of those requirements—a woman *and* a minority—than by hiring me? So the stars just seemed to be aligning in my favor on that particular day.

At six and a half feet tall, Gene towered over me, but I could tell, from my very first day at work, he was impressed with not just my knowledge but also my work ethic. I did not know about the telecommunication industry as much as his veteran employees. Yet, I had no fear picking up a stack of thick manuals to read and study, the same way I did in the refugee camp. As a result, I moved quickly through the ranks to become one of only five women on his exclusive team. I was also the youngest woman in management at the Kentucky office after Lucent split from AT&T. Not knowing at the time whether it was fate or just dumb luck, Lucent's corporate requirement for more diversity within its company had benefited both of us.

My job was to consult with big corporations like Toyota, Ford, Nabisco, and many other Fortune 500 companies. After the sales team sold our product and services, I would meet with the company executives to determine what their needs were with their telecommunication systems. Then, I would design, customize, and work with our engineering team to implement the system. I was eager to learn and ready to work as hard as I could in my new position.

Gene assigned me a mentor, a man named Marvin who had worked for him for years, and who had no qualms taking me under his wing and really showing me the ins and outs of my new job. In the beginning, he accompanied me on the client assignments I went on, though he would never try to take over, even when the clients tried to address him instead of me.

"This is a very male-dominated industry," he said. "As I'm sure you know. And in this area of the country, there's not a whole lot of diversity, so that's why some of these people are trying to act like you're not even in the room."

And he was right. At that early stage in my career, many clients questioned whether I was the right person for the job. Several company executives even called Gene to demand someone else, because they refused to work with me. It was not an isolated event, and it was frustrating because I knew it had nothing to do with my work ethic or my abilities—it was solely based on appearance and narrow-minded beliefs.

But Gene proved to be unwavering in his support of me.

"They think they're paying an outrageous amount of money and don't want an inexperienced young woman—and probably, an inexperienced young non-*white* woman, if I'm to be honest—coming in and telling them what to do," he told me one afternoon in his office. "They're saying they want me to send them someone with more experience; though what *more experience* really means is someone who looks like them."

Perhaps ironically, Gene's phone beeped and his assistant came on the intercom. The executive from the company I had just met with yesterday was on the line and wanted to speak to Gene right away.

I started to get up, but Gene motioned for me to stay. So I remained in my chair on the other side of his large executive desk, and overheard his entire phone call.

They exchanged greetings, and then Gene was silent for the most part, except when he'd occasionally nod his head and say, "I see."

I could not hear what was being said on the other end, though I knew the executive was phoning in with the same issue some of the others before him had. I was too young, I was too inexperienced, I was a woman, I was Asian.

"I appreciate you sharing your concerns," Gene finally said in his deep, rumbling baritone. He had his elbow propped on the desk, forearm up, holding the phone to his ear. "And yes, I can agree with you on a few points there. She is young, and she might not have the years of experience some of my other employees do. However—she is one of the best! She knows what she's doing, she's got impeccable work ethic, and I'm telling you that even though I have many seasoned twenty-years-plus employees working for me. Give her a chance and she'll show you that she deserves the billable hours we proposed to you!"

There was perhaps another minute of conversation, and then Gene hung up the phone. "Well. That's all set." He smiled, but I could tell from the way he had just spoken to the person on the phone: this was a conversation he'd had before. And would likely have again, the next time I met with a new client. "Can I give you a little advice, Nhi?"

"Yes, please do." Gene was generous with his time and his advice, and I valued his wisdom. Still, I wasn't sure if there was going to be anything he'd be able to say that would help in convincing our clients I was more than capable at my job.

"I've received these phone calls regularly with executives complaining about you looking inexperienced. I have daughters and I also understand that many people might be prejudiced and discriminate against you, especially since we're in the South. Never mind being a young woman in a male-dominated industry. People discriminate against other people because of their differences. It can be over race, religion, sex, politics—it doesn't actually matter *what* it's over, but the fact that people are treating you differently is based on false perceptions. So, when you first meet with new clients, you might want to address their concern right away."

I nodded, but wasn't quite sure what he meant. "Okay, but how do I do that?"

"Address the client's objections—even if they don't bring it up—within the first few minutes of meeting. Get it out of the way. You might consider saying something like: 'I know I look like a teenager with no experience. And it doesn't help that I'm a minority, a woman in the telecommunication industry. If you give me only ten minutes of your time, I will show you that I'm very good at my job and can help your company. If you're not happy after ten minutes, then I will ask my boss to send you someone else who looks older.'"

I took Gene's advice to heart and used this method moving forward. And it worked well. After talking with me and hearing my ideas, clients realized that I knew what I was doing. Gene stopped getting those calls from concerned executives. Thanks to Gene's great advice, I always won our clients over with my expertise, knowledge, and determination, and I did it in the first ten minutes of meeting them.

Even still, my desire to learn had not abated since I was done with school, and I wanted to continue to learn as much as I could at my job. This meant going in early, staying late, and sometimes going in on the weekends, when everything was quiet and no one else was around. Occasionally, though, Gene would show up and was always surprised to see me there.

"Nhi," he would say, "you show up even when you're not asked."

One Saturday afternoon, I was sitting on the floor, technical manuals scattered all around me, when Gene came by. At that point, I would have thought he'd be a little more used to running into me there on the weekends, but on that particular day, he seemed to be looking at me a little differently than usual.

He smiled. "Nhi, you've really opened my mind about embracing immigrants and new young talent. You have exceled since the first day on the job. I've been telling everyone what a trailblazer you are. Because of you, I've started hiring more young people, and I'm glad to have you working for me." It felt a little surreal, this gentle giant of a man, who took a chance on me, almost a year ago, but at the same time, it was an amazing compliment and a huge vote of confidence.

* * *

The following week, I would find out myself just how much Gene meant what he had said to me. I had gone into the break room to make some tea and a few of my coworkers were there, including the six-foot-tall account executive, Sue Dee.

"Gene has a new pet in the office," my coworker, Bill, said.

"He does?" I asked, not understanding the idiom. "What did he get? A dog or a cat? Is it here?"

Bill, Sue, George, and the rest of them started to laugh. "It's you, Nhi!" Sue said.

"Me?"

"Yes. It's just a phrase. If you're someone's pet, like a *teacher's pet* or something, it's that it seems you can do no wrong."

I still didn't entirely understand, though. They thought I was Gene's pet?

"You've set a new work standard around here," Sue explained. "Don't think we didn't all hear about it when Gene caught you here on Saturday, with all those manuals scattered around you. Everyone else was doing who knows what with their weekend, but here you are, always trying to improve and learn. What boss wouldn't love seeing an employee unexpectedly go to work just to get things done? You can do no wrong."

That, of course, was not true. I did do some things wrong, and that was perhaps no more apparent than the time I was sent to a rural area of Kentucky to consult with the owners of a chicken farm about their communication network. This was before GPS, so after looking at physical maps from AAA and trying to figure out how to travel through rural roads outside Paducah, I made it to the meeting, dressed in high heels and a business suit.

Did I mention this meeting was at a chicken farm?

I had not done my homework prior to the meeting, at least in regard to appropriate clothing. Yet there I was, having to walk around the farm in high heels, inspecting their telecommunication network and current technology while chickens swarmed me, cooing and clucking and pecking the ground. The farmyard smell was pungent, and my heels sank into the mud almost up to the sole of my shoes. The two owners of the farm were nice, but I felt foolish being so inappropriately dressed.

It was when we walked inside the barn where they raised the chicks under a special light that I suddenly remembered a chicken I'd kept as a pet, back in Vietnam. While I stood there among what must have been thousands of chicks, in my business suit and high heels, I could recall the buff-colored feathers, the amber eyes, the red wattles. This was when my family and I lived in Ho Chi Minh City and we didn't have enough food to eat. Mother wanted to raise a chicken, hoping to get eggs when it got older. What she wasn't expecting was that I would develop a bond with this chicken, who I called "Precious," and decide she would become my pet. "Precious" did grow up and produce eggs. But, as she got older, the eggs stopped coming, and my family decided to kill my pet for food even though her meat would be very tough. I begged them to let the chicken live, but in the argument of full bellies versus pet, I would not win. I sobbed when my pet was killed, while it was being cooked, and when the rest of my family devoured a nice meal of chicken and rice soup, I could not even bring myself to eat a mouthful.

It was more than likely the farmers had a good laugh over my outfit after I left, and a few of my coworkers jokingly inquired as to how the visit to the farm went and how much my dry-cleaning bill was going to be.

"Very funny," I said. "But from now on, I'll always remember to do my homework before I go meet with a client and make sure I'm dressed appropriately. I don't think I'm going to eat any chicken for a while, either."

* * *

Not long after my visit to the chicken farm, Gene sent me for software training with a female instructor named Angela. She stood out, and not just because of her vibrant red hair—she had a great smile and such a warm, loud, infectious laugh that whenever she started, anyone else in the room soon found themselves laughing, too.

Angela was an internet and web development engineer at UPS, but she also had a side gig teaching computer applications, which was how we met.

"I have to say," she told me, "you don't look like the person I was expecting, seeing as you're coming over from Lucent."

"I don't?"

She shook her head. "No, ma'am. But I think it's great. Did you know I didn't meet a nonwhite person until I was *sixteen* years old? That's what you get when you're raised in certain parts of Kentucky, I guess."

"I can see why that might happen," I said with a smile.

"I've tried to make up for that, though," Angela said. "Working for UPS makes it easy, too—for certain positions in the company, I get to fly for free all over the world. Now, I know you said you just started working at Lucent, so you're probably going to stay put for a while, but if you ever decide to take a trip somewhere and want a traveling companion, you just let me know." She gave me a grin and a wink. "We'd have a blast."

I appreciated Angela's offer, and her willingness to be friends. For a girl who had led a sheltered life in Kentucky until she was old enough to go off on her own, she seemed so worldly, so carefree. I hoped there would be an opportunity, at some point in the future, for us to take a trip somewhere together, because she was right—we'd have a great time.

* * *

Though my career was going better than I could have imagined, I did find myself feeling lonely when I wasn't working. I couldn't just get on a plane and go somewhere for a few weeks and have a fun adventure with Angela; work took up much of my time and I didn't want to slow my pace of learning. But there were still the weekends, if I didn't go in to do more work on a Saturday, or the quiet hours after dinner, when it was still too early to go to bed.

The Hearns were no longer in Kentucky; Mary Lou had inherited a farm in Virginia from her aunt, and instead of selling it, the family decided to move there. My sister Second still lived in town, but we were not close and had little contact. With the Hearns gone, I had no family members close by, though I was fortunate that my two college pals, Kevin and Jamie, stayed in the area.

Jamie, especially, always seemed willing to drop everything if I needed him. I even used a few of my vacation days to take a road trip with him and Kevin to drive to Niagara Falls, or to Toronto, Canada, all the way from Kentucky, just because it seemed like a fun thing to do.

And it was—the three of us made great traveling companions, if you ignored the part where they both snored like freight trains.

"My family would really like it if you came by for a visit," Jamie told me when we got back to Kentucky. I was more than happy to accept the invitation, particularly since the Hearns were in Virginia.

Though I had always been "one of the guys," a few of my girlfriends sometimes told me of their suspicions that Jamie had feelings for me that went beyond our friendship. I always brushed it off; Jamie and I were good friends, but that was it. Jamie's father would confirm those suspicions, pulling me aside when Jamie was preoccupied with his younger siblings.

"I think my son is in love with you," he said. "And our entire family loves you. Why are you two not dating each other?" He caught me off guard with that comment.

The short answer was that I hadn't met anyone that I really felt a deep, romantic connection with; the long answer was, after my experience with my crush in the refugee camp, I was so afraid of opening up my heart only to get crushed emotionally. I was scared to love and possibly lose it, which certainly went against the adage "It is better to have loved and lost than never to have loved at all," but why subject yourself to such pain if you didn't have to?

But I didn't want to get into my past with Jamie's dad—or anyone, really—so instead, I tried to keep it lighthearted. "I love your son and your family, but I know your son likes women with big boobs and someone who's willing to put out, and neither of those things describe me."

Though I doubted Jamie's dad knew this, my close guy friends knew that I was not going to have sex until I was married. Being "one of the guys" meant we could be open with each other about such matters, and my guy friends felt so comfortable around me that they would talk about anything, sometimes more than I wanted to hear. Likewise, I could be as blunt and honest with them about anything—except my past. Both Jamie and Kevin knew that anyone who made it to the third date with me would get "the talk," which went something like: "I like you, but I want you to know that if you are just hoping to find an Asian woman to have exotic sex with, then I'm not that person and please don't waste money taking me out. I'm saving myself until I get married!" Perhaps it should come as little surprise that my dates disappeared on me after getting that talk, though I refused to budge on it, even after both Kevin and Jamie told me it was crazy to think that any American guy would put up with such a requirement. I laughed and told them if I hadn't found that special guy by the time I turned thirty, I'd give myself permission to start having all the sex I'd been missing out on in my twenties.

Which, of course, was not something I was about to reiterate to Jamie's father, even if he was probably right that his son had feelings for me.

"Well, listen," Jamie's father said. "Even if you don't date my son, or marry into my family, we still consider you family, and want you to know that you can call us any time you need anything."

With the Hearns so far away now, Jamie's father said exactly what I needed to hear. Sometimes, it's just knowing that there are people out there who show they care that makes all the difference.

* * *

Working under Gene's leadership and within the amazing culture that he'd created in his Kentucky office was an incredible gift. Most of Gene's employees had been there for at least fifteen years, and there was never any employee drama; I never heard anyone talk badly about anyone else.

During my annual performance review, Gene asked, "What do you want to do long term with the company?"

I timidly replied, "I'd like to be transferred to France for a few years while I'm still single and have all the freedom to travel. I really enjoyed living there during my semester in college."

Gene said, "I like that about you, Nhi. You're not afraid to dream big. Someday, we could look into doing that for you. But not right now. You have to put in your time with the company before you can even make the request for international transfer."

My face grew hot, though Gene's tone was kind and I had the feeling that if it were up to him alone, he'd be more than happy to transfer me, if that was what I wanted.

"But," he said, "it sounds like maybe you'd like a change of scenery. Would you have any interest in flying out to Denver for new software training?"

I had never been to Denver before. "Sure," I said.

"I think it'll be a good experience for you."

I appreciated Gene's willingness to work with me, and even if he couldn't have me transferred to France at that point, he could still find a way to get me on an airplane to go somewhere new. Little did I know that that chance trip to Denver would again set my life on a completely different course.

PART THREE
BECOMING

CHAPTER TWELVE
THE CHANCE ENCOUNTER

Imagine being stuck in a line of passengers, waiting to move down the aisle to get your seat, the people in front of you trying to cram their carry-on in the ever-shrinking available space in the overhead bins. Well, that was me on my business trip to Colorado. As I stood there, getting jostled from behind, looking up at the bin that was crammed full, I wondered if Gene's idea to send me on a trip had been such a good one after all.

And even if there was some free space in the overhead bins, at four foot nine, it wasn't likely I was going to be able to lift my heavy, stuffed suitcase that high anyway. I'd been fortunate to be one of the first to board on the first leg of the trip, which took me from Kentucky to a layover in Chicago, but now, for the second part, it looked as if things were not going to go quite as smoothly.

It was late, around 11:00 p.m., and the flight had been delayed, so I think it was fair to say that everyone on board was suffering from varying degrees of irritation. Some of the passengers who had already found their seats were sitting there, eyes closed, like they were envisioning the flight being over with. I looked back up to the bins, casting my gaze further down the aisle. Colorful suitcases, purses, and duffle bags filled the area, and there did not seem to be even a wisp of available space left. If that was the case, they were going to make me gate check my luggage, which would just delay things even more.

And that's when I saw him.

The people in front of me had found their seats, so the aisle was clear, my sightline unobstructed as I looked further down the aisle and saw this guy waving in the back. No, he was motioning, at first I thought for someone else, but then realized that it was me.

"You can use my luggage space," he said, pulling a heavy-looking backpack from the bin. "I think I can get this to fit underneath the seat in front of me."

"Thank you," I said.

He smiled. "Here, let me get it up there for you." He easily lifted the suitcase and it fit into place like a puzzle piece.

I thanked him again. "No problem," he said graciously.

I went back to my seat, part of me hoping this incredibly kind person would be seated next to me, but, alas, no such luck—he was seated a few rows in front of me. Still, I would catch glimpses of the back of his head whenever he would shift in his seat, and every so often he would crane his neck around just enough to make eye contact. Each time he did this, I would smile politely, and I must admit, I did spend the duration of the flight quite impressed by his kindness, compassion, and eagerness to help me.

After we landed at Denver International Airport, he helped me take my suitcase out of the overhead bin, and I did have a moment thinking he was cute. As I entered the airport train, there he was again.

"Thank you again for giving up your luggage space for me," I said.

"You are welcome! Are you here on a business trip? Are you working for Lucent Technologies?" he asked.

"I am," I replied in shock, not knowing how he'd figured it out.

Seeing my expression, he smiled and said, "Your gear shows your company name!" I was happy that he felt the need to talk again. After all, he was very cute and I loved his smile!

"I never got your name," he said. "I'm Jeff."

"My name is Nhi."

"Are you staying here in Denver?" he continued.

"Yes, in the Denver Tech Center."

He nodded. "I know the place." He cracked a smile. "I hate to be the one to tell you this, but where you're staying isn't the most exciting place, and you certainly won't really get to see Denver. If you get bored, I'd be happy to be your tour guide and show you around."

"That'd be great!" Was he flirting? Or just being nice? I didn't have much personal experience to go on, so I wasn't sure. But he gave me his business card and repeated that I could call him, so it looked like perhaps I would find out.

* * *

Prior to departing for Denver, I had called Angela and asked if she wanted to meet in Denver, since I was going there for training but would have some downtime and we could hang out.

"I love Denver!" she told me. "Let's do it." She took care of booking the hotel and told me to just give them my name at the front desk and they'd give me the key.

It was two in the morning when I finally arrived, and Angela was fast asleep. I was so excited, though, that I had to wake her up.

"Is everything okay?" she asked blearily, sitting up. The side light I had turned on shone through her hair and made it look like it was on fire. "Are you all right?"

"You won't believe what just happened! My flight was delayed, and I met the cutest guy on the plane! And he was tall, good looking, and *so* nice."

Angela yawned. "I'm so happy to hear that! You'll have to tell me tomorrow. I need to sleep. I bet you do, too! But I'm glad you made it safely, and I really want to hear all about this guy. In the morning!"

Over breakfast the next morning, at a diner near our hotel, I told her how kind Jeff had been when no one else seemed like they could be bothered, and that he had offered to show me around while I was in Colorado.

"What a gentleman!" she said. "They don't come around every day, Nhi. This sort of thing is rare. *Very* rare."

"I can't stop thinking about him," I admitted. He was on my mind as I drifted off to sleep, and the first thing I thought about before I was even fully awake. I'd never had that sort of experience with someone before, and that, coupled with the happy fluttering feeling in my torso, made me think that maybe there was something more to this.

That's silly! I thought. *You don't even know this person!*

Angela took a sip of her cappuccino and licked the foam mustache away with the tip of her tongue. She grinned. "So . . . you're going to call him, right?"

I hesitated. Angela laughed, shaking her head. "Girl, he gave you his number and offered to be your tour guide. You just said yourself you can't stop thinking about him. Take the man up on his offer and give him a call!"

She made it sound so easy.

Feeling like an anxious teenager, I decided to do it after Angela left me and returned to Kentucky. I held Jeff's business card and nervously dialed, fighting mightily against the urge to hang up before the call went through. The phone rang.

He picked up on the second ring.

"Hello."

For a second, I was certain I had called the wrong number— the person who had just answered did not sound friendly or at all happy to be answering the phone. I learned later that during work hours, it was all business for Jeff since he was on billable hours as a consultant.

"Hi," I said. "Is this Jeff?"

"Yes." His voice was cold, abrupt. "This is Jeff. Who is this?"

Obviously, Angela had been wrong—calling him had been the wrong thing to do. He didn't even remember me, and he certainly did not sound like he wanted to be on the phone. "This is Nhi—we met on the flight to Denver and you gave me your phone number."

There was a pause, and in those moments of silence, I thought that maybe I should just hang up. He'd been so nice on the plane, but now he sounded like a different person. But right as I was about to say never mind, he asked me if I enjoyed hiking.

"Hiking? Um, yeah, I like hiking." I couldn't remember the last time I'd been on a hike.

"Okay. There is a great hiking trail at a mountain near my home. Would you like to go with me?"

In Kentucky, when a strange man asks you to go hiking in the mountains, you might never come out of the woods alive. I did not want to become a cautionary tale, a story on the evening news: *Kentucky woman on business trip vanishes after accepting offer to go hiking with psycho masquerading as kind gentleman.*

"How about you come to my hotel lobby and we'll figure out where to go then?" I asked.

"Sure," he said.

I told him where I was staying. "I'll be there after work," he replied. "Around 5:30. Since it's summertime and it's bright out much later, we can go for a hike and maybe get something to eat." He hung up.

I stared at the receiver, seriously wondering if I had just made a huge mistake. Would he even bother to show up? Maybe it would be better if he didn't—he had been so cold on the phone.

But, the next day at 5:30 on the dot, Jeff showed up. He picked me up in one of the ugliest cars I'd ever seen. It was a beat-up, brown Delta 88 and it looked like a big boat on wheels. It had a white top, a smashed-up passenger door, and red velvet seats that were about a decade past their prime. It reminded me of the sort of car you might see in a gangster movie, after it crashed and got shot up, that is.

The Jeff who picked me up at the hotel was the Jeff who had been on the plane—he was kind and more than a gentleman. He opened the dingy passenger door for me, quickly pushing away empty beer cans off the seat, mumbling that they had been there for six months and that he did not drink before picking me up.

I couldn't help but wonder, as he shut the door behind me, whether that little bit of extra information was meant to put my mind at ease that he wasn't a raging alcoholic, or that he wasn't always a slob. It didn't really matter, because it was my first red flag. I cast a longing glance at the hotel as we pulled away—was going with him a huge mistake?

He immediately turned on the car stereo, clearly the most valuable part of the car. He probably paid twice as much for that stereo system than for the car. It felt like I was about to be sonically blasted out of my seat as some sort of raucous rap music poured from the speakers.

"It's the Beastie Boys!" he replied, when I managed to shout over the music, asking him who it was. The bass reverberated so much I could feel it vibrating every cell in my body. Jeff appeared to be right in his element, though, rocking out to the music as the car sputtered down the highway. I bit my lip to keep from laughing. Clearly, he was just another white man trying to act "cool" and pretend to be a black rapper like the ones I'd seen on TV.

Red flag number two.

It was around that time that I began to question my judgment. Sure, he was good looking and had a great smile, and he was kind enough to give me his luggage space on the airplane. But judging from his decrepit, ugly car he was also probably poor, an alcoholic, and his taste in music was more than questionable. Even if the volume hadn't been set to ear drum shattering levels, I still would not have been able to understand a word of what these people were saying. It was hard to believe he was the same guy that I couldn't stop thinking about! By that point, I was willing to bet that our first date would be our last, and all I had to do now was try to get through it without too much awkwardness.

No sooner did I think that than Jeff reached over and changed the music. Not only did he change what was playing, he turned the volume down, and the sweet, uplifting sound of a violin filled the car.

"This is Vivaldi," he said. "But if you don't like it, I can put on another composer."

"This is great," I said. "I didn't realize you liked classical music."

"I was in band in high school. I like a lot of different types of music."

"I can tell," I said.

"So, I got the feeling that maybe a hike up the mountain wasn't exactly what you had in mind. There's a nice little park over here we could take a walk around, and then, if you'd like, we could get a bite to eat."

No hike through the mountains at dusk? "Sounds great to me!"

A stroll through the park was a much better idea, and put me at ease. There were plenty of other people—walking dogs, riding bikes, and playing Frisbee on a flat, grassy expanse.

After our walk, we went to a casual Italian restaurant, full of families and older couples, and we were given a table near the back where it was a little quieter.

"So do you like living in Denver?" I asked, after our server had taken our order.

"Oh, it's great," Jeff said. "And having a dog now makes it even better."

I reached over and took a sip of my water. "What is your dog's name?"

"Zoe. She's still a pup; I just adopted her. I wasn't even necessarily planning on getting a dog, I was just going to the pound to look, but then she gave me those puppy dog eyes and I knew I had to bring her home."

His eyes really lit up as he talked about it! Which was sweet, I supposed, but it also seemed a bit strange to hear someone go on and on about a dog, as they weren't that popular in Vietnam. Some people in Vietnam ate dog meat, which I suspected Jeff had no clue about.

Since I'd been living in America, I'd seen plenty of instances where dogs were beloved pets, in some cases like regular family members. Though Jeff hadn't had his dog for long, he was clearly smitten.

"She's so great at cuddling," he said, and I took a deep breath and wondered just how long one person could go on and on about his dog. Quite a while, apparently. "And she'll hop right up into bed with me."

I widened my eyes. Sleep *in bed* with him? Never mind the previous red flags—this was an obvious sign of some serious misjudgment. In Vietnam, dogs were considered filthy animals that should be left outside, not sleeping in bed with their owner.

"Your dog sleeps in bed with you?" I asked, wondering how he might feel if I told him I had a pet pig that slept next to me.

Jeff smiled and nodded happily. "Yeah, isn't that great?"

Yes, if by "great" you mean "disgusting!" The thought appeared in my mind, but I kept quiet. How could I get a word in edgewise, anyway, with him going on and on about his dog?

Things didn't improve until after we'd eaten, our plates had been cleared, and the waiter's offer of dessert declined because

I couldn't bear to hear another thing about his dog. I was counting down the minutes until I would have to get back into that boat of a car and be dropped off at my hotel. I had taken a chance in calling and going out with him—a mistake, yes, but thankfully, a mistake that was soon to be over.

As we were about to wrap up our dinner, I asked Jeff about his work and he told me about the environmental engineering and remediation work he had been doing in Ohio. He'd been returning to Colorado when we met on the plane. I learned about the required training and knowledge for him to oversee the major remediation sites around the United States. I also discovered that he was smart enough to receive his undergraduate in Civil Engineering from the University of Connecticut and a Master's in Environmental Engineering from the University of Colorado in Boulder. He impressed me with some of his knowledge. Perhaps he was much smarter than he appeared to be.

After we left the restaurant, we decided to walk around another local park. My hand brushed up against his arm. We made physical contact for only the briefest moment, but I swear I felt a jolt, like a little surge of energy between us. He looked at me right as it happened, though he said nothing; he paused and started holding my hand as we continued our walk.

He didn't try to kiss me before I got out of the car, but he did ask if he could see me again before I went back to Kentucky. I even surprised myself a bit when I replied, "Yes," though the truth of it was—I kept thinking about that feeling when my hand brushed against him. I'd never felt anything like that before: it was like we were energetically connected, like we recognized each other on a deeper level. That touch was more charged than any other contact I've ever had—and that *had* to mean something, right?

* * *

Jeff and I would see each other one more time before I returned to Kentucky, and our second date, I am happy to report, was much better than the first. I knew it would be the moment he showed up at the hotel to pick me up, because he hadn't brought that ugly car of his—instead, he arrived on a big Honda V65 Magna motorcycle. He wore this tough-look-ing tan leather jacket, underneath which were his nice pro-fessional work clothes. He had two helmets, one of which he held out to me.

"I took my motorcycle into work today and then just headed here right after." He smiled. "Want to go for a ride?"

Now, I was used to seeing mopeds zipping along the streets of Vietnam, but that bike was a big, burly thing. *What is up with this guy and all the weird surprises?* I thought. But I couldn't stop thinking about that connection I felt I had with him, and I wanted to explore it further.

"Sure," I said, holding my hand out for the helmet. It felt big and clunky on my head, and I probably looked a little silly, but the bike sure looked like it could go fast, a lot faster than any moped.

So I hopped on the back of the bike and put my arms around Jeff's waist. We had a blast! We went all over the place, and though it was hard to have a conversation because of the wind, just being this close to him, flying down the streets on his big bike, was exhilarating.

Part of me wished the night could've continued forever, that I could've just stayed on the back of Jeff's motorcycle, and we could go anywhere. But I was leaving to go back to Kentucky the next day, and I had an early flight to catch.

"I'm really glad you called me and let me show you around," Jeff said.

I smiled up at him. "You were a great tour guide. Thank you."

For a moment, neither of us said anything. Would we ever see each other again? Yes, we had an undeniable connection, but we also lived in two different states, and it wasn't like either of us was just going to uproot our existence, at least at that point.

We embraced, and it was a full-body hug, the sort that I could've gotten lost in forever. Being held in his arms like that made me feel as if I had found the home I had always been looking for but hadn't realized. I didn't want him to let go, and he didn't, not for a while anyway. When he finally did, he leaned down and kissed me, his hands on either side of my face, and I trembled as I kissed him back, fully knowing it could be both the first and last time it happened.

"Goodnight," he finally said, breathlessly, when we pulled away. "Safe travels tomorrow."

"Thanks," I said. "Goodnight." I watched as he walked away; it felt like he was taking part of me with him. He glanced over his shoulder as he walked, and I waved. Yes, I had only just met this man, but there was no way I could deny I had a connection with him that I'd never felt with anyone else before.

Whether or not I would be able to explore it further still remained to be seen.

CHAPTER THIRTEEN
MOTHER, MEET MY MOTHER!

Not long after I returned from my Colorado trip, I was headed out on a different trip—that time with Mary Lou in tow. Because of my success at Lucent, I had the resources to take Mary Lou with me on a special trip to Vietnam. Not only would my American mother be able to see where my journey began but she would also be able to meet my Vietnamese mother. And Mother, I hoped, would be happy to meet the woman who had been so instrumental in helping me have a good life in America.

We spent the first few days in Hong Kong, which was a new experience for me as well. But after dealing with the cultural and language barriers in the United States, I found the adjustment to Hong Kong to be quite easy, this Asian culture with its heavy British influence. Mary Lou spent her time in Hong Kong adjusting to the Asian culture and learning some basic skills, like how to use chopsticks. She did try to ask for a fork at the first couple of restaurants we went to, which always resulted in the same response: "No, we don't have that."

"Welcome to Asia," I told her, after our waitress denied Mary Lou's request for silverware. "If you want to eat, you'll either have to learn how to use chopsticks, or use your hands. You made me learn how to use a fork in America, and it's now your turn to learn how to use chopsticks." I laughed.

We were eating lunch in a small, noisy dim sum restaurant. Mary Lou tried valiantly to use her chopsticks to pick up the small steamed dumplings, but more often than not, it fell on the table before making it to her mouth. She laughed and then brutally stabbed the dumpling with her chopsticks and then said, "Yay! I can finally get it into my mouth!"

A few times, it was painful for me to watch her picking up one rice grain at a time with her chopsticks. Yet, she burst into laughter and said, "I'm dropping more food than I'm eating with these chopsticks. At the very least, it'll be a great way for me to lose weight!"

Suddenly, Mary Lou found herself as the foreigner, the person who looked different. Needless to say, our visit was as amusing as it was adventurous. Despite all that, I couldn't stop thinking about that geeky white rapper with the ugliest car on planet earth. Which was quite strange, because there I was, in Hong Kong with my adoptive mother, who, in a few days, I would introduce to my biological mother, and I couldn't get Jeff out of my mind.

We had just gotten some curry fishballs from one of the many food stalls Hong Kong is known for, and were taking a stroll down the bustling street.

"I have to tell you something strange. I recently met a young man on an airplane. I know we will not see each other again, but I just don't understand why I can't stop thinking about him," I said to Mary Lou and shared with her my story. "He always seems to be on my mind."

She smiled. "You'll figure it out," she said. "But, if he's in Colorado and you're in Kentucky . . . that's quite a distance. He sounds like a perfectly nice gentleman, and I'm glad someone was there to help you with your luggage, but it sounds to me that nothing will probably come of it. I just don't want you to get your hopes up and then get your heart broken."

I knew she wasn't trying to be dismissive, and when I considered the situation the way she worded it, I had to admit, she was probably right, but I just couldn't believe this *feeling* I was experiencing would end up amounting to nothing.

After we finished our snack, I decided to buy a postcard and write to Jeff. If I didn't do anything, then Mary Lou certainly *was* right—nothing would happen. (And as it would turn out, Jeff was writing me an email on that very same day, though I wouldn't discover it until three weeks later.)

I kept it simple: *Greetings from Hong Kong! I'm thinking of you. ~Nhi*

I mailed it off before I had second thoughts as to whether or not sending it would be a good idea.

We popped in and out of shops and walked through an open-air market, and when I saw the colorful painting in a small gallery, I knew I had to buy it for Jeff. Using a blend of broad watercolor strokes interspersed with black ink accents, it was a cheerful, happy painting. You could look at it and see any number of impressions: the flight of a butterfly or a bird of paradise. Unmistakably, though, were two hearts, each their own shape but connected. You could have the artwork customized, if you wanted, and I chose to have Jeff's name written on it, across the bottom in English, down the right-hand side in beautiful Chinese calligraphy.

"That's beautiful," Mary Lou said, her eyebrows raised. She didn't have to say anything else for me to know what she was thinking: I was acting so out of character! And it was true, but something in me refused to forget about him, and I even began to wonder if it was fate that brought us together—even though I didn't really believe in such a thing.

Whether it was fate or whether I would never see him again, it was really the side story to that summer in 1998, when I would finally witness my two mothers meet.

After a few days in Hong Kong, Mary Lou and I flew to Vietnam. My family met us at the airport, and it was here my two lives intersected. I hugged my mother, but then stepped back so she and Mary Lou could embrace. There were a lot of tears and laughter as they hugged.

"I'm so grateful to be able to be a part of Nhi's life," Mary Lou said, which I translated to my mother. My mother thanked Mary Lou for not just taking care of me but also loving me. And there I was, with these two women who were both so important to me, whose decisions and guidance had shaped the trajectory of my life. We were all together, and though I knew we wouldn't stay like that forever, in that moment, the love was palpable and true happiness was possible.

Mary Lou and I took a taxi back to my family's house, since there wasn't room on their mopeds for our luggage. The house, though improved some from what I remembered, still had a hole in the ground for a toilet. I decided to rent a room at the motel across the street for Mary Lou and me.

I did spend some time at my father's altar. He had passed away in 1992, during my freshman year of college. There was a framed photograph of him, as well as a porcelain bowl to burn incense; around the bowl my mother had arranged fruit. My family had never been religious, but they did strongly believe in family values, ancestor worship, and filial piety. Filial piety was a common practice in Asia, where children were expected to not only respect but also be obedient to their parents—obviously not always my strong suit. Ancestor worship took that a step further—reverence and honoring your parent did not stop once they died—it was to continue through worship at a family altar where the deceased loved one's photo would be displayed, along with incense holders and daily offerings of fruit.

I looked at my father's picture. In the photo he was handsome and youthful looking, his dark hair thick, his skin smooth and unlined. It was the father from my childhood, at our house on the lake. To be honest, though, I had few memories of him. And he looked nothing like the broken man I remembered seeing for the last time, when he had been released early from the reeducation camp.

Who were you? I wondered as I gazed at the photo, this man whose DNA I shared, yet I felt I had barely known him at all. So, though I stood there in front of his altar, I chose not to pray, burn incense, or bow in front of his altar. The clearest memory I had was when I'd visited him in prison, a barricade of barbed wire separating us, and the few times he'd visited us in Ho Chi Minh when Mother tried to protect us from his abusive behavior by putting a distance between him and us kids.

"You are not going to pray or burn incense?" my mother asked when I turned away from his altar.

"No, Mother," I said.

She frowned. "You are disrespecting your father's memory. You are his daughter. You dishonor him by not at least burning some incense."

It just wasn't something I felt comfortable doing, but I knew such an explanation would not satisfy her.

"You're too Americanized," she said. "You don't even care about your parents. Well, you care about your American mother, that much is obvious."

After a few days watching Mary Lou and me together, my mother started showing some growing bitterness about my relationship with Mary Lou.

But I wanted us—*all* of us—to have a good time together, and that included my two mothers. I took both of them to a spa for a little pampering. As we sat in the tranquil waiting room, several of the massage therapists came out, all clamoring to be the one who got to work on Mary Lou.

"Look at that white skin!" I heard them whisper. Fortunately, Mary Lou didn't understand what they were saying, though it became rather obvious when they only gave her a small hand towel to cover herself with. Mary Lou ended up getting quite the deluxe treatment, as all six of the massage therapists surrounded her and somehow managed to get their hands on her, so they could touch her pale skin themselves.

"I feel amazing," Mary Lou said after we left. "That was easily the best massage of my life." She paused and burst into laughter. "Well, I think that was the *only* massage I've ever had, and all those therapists got to see more of me than they should since they only gave me a tiny hand towel that was barely large enough to cover my bottom!"

I rented a twelve-passenger van, with a chauffeur, so we could all travel together—Mary Lou, my mother, and my two siblings, Brother Fourth and Sister Fifth, and their spouses and kids. Not only did I want to show Mary Lou more of Vietnam but I also wanted my family—and myself—to be able to see more of the country. I had gone to many new places when I'd come back with my classmates from Centre College, and I was eager to have a similar experience now with Mary Lou and the rest of my family. We left Ho Chi Minh City, on our way about 270 miles northeast to the coastal city of Nha Trang. Along the way, though, we made several stops to visit extended family I had not seen in years.

Our first visit was with Uncle Ninth (he was the ninth kid in his family), who worked for the communist party and had sponsored my father for his early release from the prison camp. Only four years had passed since President Clinton lifted the US embargo, and the communist regime could still be hostile toward Westerners, as we would find out. But I was surprised at how warm Uncle Ninth was toward Mary Lou, welcoming her into his home as if she were just another family member he had not seen in some time.

But not everyone was as friendly as Uncle Ninth had been, and nowhere was it more apparent than when we tried to check into a hotel. After we left Uncle Ninth and continued on our way to Nha Trang, we stopped and explored some ancient temples along the way. Many of the temples and pagodas had been built centuries ago, some as early as 600 AD. To see such structures was breathtaking, even though they were not very well preserved because the government did not have money to maintain them.

That evening, we tried to check into a nearby hotel. It was a modest place, nothing fancy, and I think we all went in there not anticipating a problem. But the man working behind the desk narrowed his eyes at us before we could even request a room.

"You have to leave," he said, shaking his head at Mary Lou. He spoke in Vietnamese, so she had no idea what he was saying.

"We just need a few rooms for the evening," I told him.

"No," he said. The look on his face relented a little. "I'm sorry. It's not that we here at the hotel have a problem with it—we're in the hospitality industry, after all. But the police will give us a hard time if they find out we let an American stay at our hotel."

There was no point in arguing, so we left and went to another. After a nearly identical experience, I asked Mary Lou if she would mind waiting in the van while I went in and booked the rooms.

"Is everything okay?" she asked. I hadn't told her why the first two hotels had turned us away.

"It's because you're American," I said. "And white. And the people who own the hotels don't have a problem with it, but they're afraid the police or government officials will give them a hard time if they let you stay there."

"Oh," was all she said. I went into the third hotel, bribed the receptionist with some money, and was able to book us a few rooms without any issue.

Later that night, Mary Lou sat down next to me on the bed. It was almost time to go to sleep, and we had both changed into our pajamas. My mother and siblings were in the next three rooms.

"I'm having a really good time," Mary Lou said. "But it's also been quite eye-opening." She paused. "I finally understand what it's like for you being a minority living in Kentucky."

Her experience wasn't all bad, though. At some point during our trip, Mary Lou began to refer to herself as a "dumpling."

"I feel gorgeous in this country!" she proclaimed after getting so much attention. "I'm a rich and beautiful white dumpling! They are all the features that Americans don't like, but the Vietnamese consider beautiful!"

And it was true. In America, Mary Lou was the target demographic of places like Weight Watchers, but in Vietnam, carrying some extra weight was a good thing, because it meant you could afford plenty of food. Likewise, the lighter your skin, the better—only those with money in this country did not have to toil out in the rice paddies under the hot sun, which turned their skin dark and weathered.

Nha Trang was a coastal resort city, boasting long, white sandy beaches and turquoise water, perfect for swimming or diving. The green mountains in the background made the place feel every bit like the vacation destination it was, and for a few days, that was exactly what it was for my family and me.

We spent those days relaxing on the beach, exploring Tran Phu Street, which was the main street that ran parallel to the beach. It was a picturesque, tree-lined promenade that was home to many bustling shops, restaurants, and museums.

"I can't get over how beautiful it is here," Mary Lou said. "It doesn't matter if we're in a rural area or the city—everywhere is just so magnificent. I never would have known if I hadn't come here. Everything I thought about Vietnam had been from whatever I'd seen broadcast on TV about the war." She shook her head. "But there is so much more to it than that."

From Nha Trang, we drove up the coast to Central Vietnam, to my childhood hometown, Ha Lam. There, Mary Lou got to meet my Uncle Hong, who helped my mother hide some of her assets when the communists took over our property, and Aunt Tien. Aunt Tien was Mother's oldest sibling—she was seventy-eight, but she certainly wasn't the sort of person who would let age slow her down. We witnessed this when watching her tiny body climbing straight up a towering coconut tree barefoot to get coconuts for us. When we walked down the streets in the small village where I was born, children would gather around Mary Lou and ask for permission to touch her. Most had never seen a white woman with blue eyes before, or had the chance to be so close to one. Mary Lou was more than a good sport about it; I think she even reveled in it a bit.

* * *

We left Ha Lam and headed south again, to Tam Ky, where my father's first wife and her family lived. I met several people I hadn't met before, including a man who appeared to be a young version of my father.

"Who is that friendly man?" Mary Lou whispered. We were sitting in the modestly furnished living room with concrete floors, on a wooden bench, my mother on one side, Mary Lou on the other.

"I'm not sure," I whispered back. I leaned toward Mother and asked her if she knew who he was.

"He is one of your father's unclaimed sons," she said in a low voice. "After your father passed away, the wives decided to claim a few of his kids including that man, and another daughter from a different mistress. Kids born out of wedlock often feel terrible about themselves and are not treated well. So we decided to accept a few of them into our family."

I nodded. So, another half-brother. Much older, though. I leaned back toward Mary Lou and reiterated what Mother had just told me.

Mary Lou's eyes widened and she started to laugh. "Boy, your father was one ACTIVE man!" We both giggled, though I stopped when I felt Mother's disapproving gaze on me.

These little instances had been common throughout our trip—Mary Lou and I would share a laugh over something, and I would immediately sense Mother's jealousy—she'd give us a look or whisper furtively to whatever family member was closest. I didn't need to be privy to her exact words to know what she was saying—it was hard for her to understand and accept the close bond Mary Lou and I had created, even though she was happy I had another family who loved me.

I tried to be understanding. I recalled how it had been Mother's greatest dream that her children escape Vietnam for a better life in America. Only Sister Second and I had managed to do so, yet now Mother seemed to think it had been a huge mistake. I thought maybe it would help if we were able to talk about it, just the two of us.

Tam Ky is also home to many beautiful beaches, so we took a walk on the beach together, with the frothy, white-capped waves gently licking the shore before receding.

"I'm glad you and Mary Lou were finally able to meet," I said.

Mother didn't say anything.

"It was your biggest dream, remember?" I continued, hoping she would be able to recall how strongly she had wanted her children to be able to grow up in America.

"I didn't think you'd become so Americanized," she said. "But it's like you're a different person. I thought things would have remained the same between us, like all those years you were away wouldn't matter, because you're my daughter. But . . ." She paused. "I feel like I've lost my daughter for good."

I understood why she would hope we could just pick up where we left off, like we hadn't been apart all those years in between. But those had been some of my formative years, and of course it was only natural Mary Lou and I would form a bond.

"Mother, you sent me away to have a better life," I said. "You even told me we might never see each other again. And now that you get to see me, you feel jealous of my relationship with my other mom."

"I can't help it," she replied. "I can't help it!"

I would learn later that she was telling family and friends about how much she hated seeing the beautiful bond her daughter and Mary Lou had formed, that she couldn't understand why I would prefer to sleep in a room with Mary Lou and not with her.

Luckily, Mary Lou didn't know about all the drama since she didn't speak the language. Mother could say anything she wanted in front of Mary Lou and, unless someone translated, there would be no way for Mary Lou to know what was being said. But my American mother did pick up on the fact that it was emotionally difficult for me. Toward the end of our trip, when we had returned to Ho Chi Minh City and were sharing a hotel room across from my family's house, Mary Lou asked why I seemed so sad.

"Are you sad that we're leaving soon?"

We were lying on the bed together; the TV on the bureau was playing a show but the volume was low and neither of us was paying attention to it. I told Mary Lou how I felt about the reunion and how hard it was to hear that Mother felt like she had lost a daughter. It was so easy to talk to Mary Lou, even when what I had to say wasn't easy to discuss.

"I can only imagine what your mom must be feeling," Mary Lou said. "I'm sure she's got a lot of feelings about it, and some of them probably contradict each other. She will always be your mother, though, and you will always be her daughter, and nothing will ever change that."

I tried to keep that in mind. I was eager to leave Vietnam, though, and glad that our trip would be over soon. To be honest, I wasn't sure if I'd ever want to return, and I wondered if I was setting myself up to have to pick one mother over the other.

CHAPTER FOURTEEN

THINKING ABOUT JEFF

Going to Vietnam had proved a good distraction from Jeff. Despite the fact we'd only spent a brief period of time together, I couldn't rid myself of the feeling that there was something more there, something worth pursuing. Sure, we lived in different states, had hung out only twice, and I still really questioned his taste in both music and automobiles, but there was no way I could simply shut down my feelings for him.

Upon returning home, I discovered that Jeff, too, had been thinking about me, when I checked my email and saw that he had sent me a message while I'd been in Asia. The message's time stamp actually showed he had sent me the email the same day I had written him the postcard and bought him the painting, which I still had and hoped to be able to give to him.

I know I met you for only a short time, his message started, *but I don't know why I cannot stop thinking of you. Will you call me when you get back from Asia?*

Just reading his words gave me a fluttering feeling that I had never experienced with anyone else before. I'd been considered "one of the guys" in college, and that had continued on in the male-dominated industry I worked in, yet I had never encountered a man who made me feel the way Jeff did.

How can two people be connected mentally this way? I wondered. I had done so many things that were out of character for me when it came to Jeff—sending him the postcard, buying him a gift, and talking about the whole situation with Mary Lou— that I decided the only way to see if my feelings were right and there really was something more to it was to invite him to Kentucky. He accepted the invitation.

* * *

When Jeff showed up at my apartment, he discovered that I lived on the campus of the Southern Baptist Theological Seminary in Louisville. Because I was living by myself, I thought I would be in a much safer place if I lived near pastors-to-be and their families. But because I wasn't a student there, I'd been required to make a special request, which included getting verification from my employer. At first, Gene had seemed almost a bit indignant. "Why on earth are you applying to live on the campus of a theology school?" he had asked. "I just got a call from the apartment manager there. I pay you well enough to live anywhere you want!" But after I explained my reasoning with him, he understood.

If Jeff seemed surprised by my living situation, though, he didn't show it. I decided to take him out to a little Korean restaurant right near campus. There was a small population of Korean families living in the area so they could attend the school and return to South Korea to spread the Christian faith.

"Do you like Korean food?" I asked Jeff.

"I haven't had it before," he said. "But it smells great."

I wondered, though, as I watched him eat, if he might change his opinion. His forehead glistened with sweat as he worked his way through a bowl of *bibimbap*, a hot and spicy mix of rice, seasonal vegetables, meat, and eggs. But then he looked over and saw me watching him and he grinned. "This is delicious," he said. "Really. Maybe a little spicier than I've had before, but it's really great."

And yes, I was a bit in awe of a white guy who not only could tolerate the spiciness but actually seemed to be enjoying it. I'd yet to meet a man in Kentucky who enjoyed international food, especially when it came with a side of extreme heat.

Jeff stayed at my apartment during his visit. On our second night, we went on a riverboat for a dinner cruise on the Ohio River. It was a glorious late summer evening, the day's earlier humidity having dried out, so the night was comfortable with a refreshing breeze off the water. Any apprehension I had about Jeff's visit and perhaps the feeling of mine being wrong disappeared once we were together again. I felt as if I could just be myself with him—a good thing, certainly, though it also meant I didn't hold back when it came to the amount of food I ate that night.

I weighed about eighty-five pounds at the time, but I could eat as much as Gene, my six-foot-five boss, who once asked me how it was possible that I could use up my entire food allow-ance—sixty dollars a day—when going on business trips. After Gene and I had a few business lunches together, he had his answer, and he never questioned my appetite again.

The dinner cruise had a buffet with things like crab legs, flat iron steak, several types of green salad, roasted potatoes, corn on the cob, and green beans. I piled my plate high with crab legs and steak, and carefully carried it back to our table. Strings of tiny white lights hung above us and twinkled like fireflies. When my plate was cleared with empty shells of crab legs, I looked over at Jeff, who was still working on his. After he finished, I asked if he wanted to go back for seconds.

He leaned back in his chair and stretched, as if he were making room for a second round. "Sure," he said. "It was delicious."

He took less food the second time, though I probably took about the same as I previously had. Yes, it was a little baffling as to how someone as small as myself could eat so much, and I knew he was probably thinking that, particularly when I asked if he wanted to go back for thirds, to which he hesitated, but then grinned and said, "Sure."

Would this man ever want to be with me again after this dinner? Would I scare him off with the amount of food I was able to eat?

He reached over at one point and took my hand, and when I looked at him, it was as if I could feel the love in his eyes. I learned later that Jeff loved seeing me feel comfortable with who I am and that I ate so much without worrying about his judgment. He said he went out on dates previously, and women typically just got a salad and were usually concerned about being judged (even when he knew they were hungry).

"I'm so glad you invited me out here," he said. "I have to be honest—I haven't been able to stop thinking about you." He paused, still looking deep into my eyes. "Do you believe in fate? In soul mates?"

I laughed. "No, that's a bunch of bullshit. I don't believe in that kind of stuff."

The question had caught me off guard, and I responded without thinking about how he might take it. No, I had never believed in soul mates or fate, but then again, why would I? Life had been a series of choices and chances—some truly awful, some beyond wonderful—but I had never believed any of it was preordained.

Jeff sat back, looking deflated, but only for a moment, before he waved it off. "I was just curious," he said, smiling.

Even though we were on a romantic dinner cruise, I still found it too deep of a conversation to have about fate and soul mates, with other couples around us, laughing, chatting, and having a good time. My feelings for Jeff were confusing because I'd never experienced such a strong connection before, yet that didn't change the fact I was not used to being vulnerable, especially around someone I was still getting to know. I was happy to drop the subject and just enjoy the rest of our evening.

When Jeff brought me back to my place, though, it was clear there was still something that was on his mind. At first, I thought maybe he needed to talk about my large food consumption and that it turned him off. Or maybe he was considering leaning in for that goodnight kiss, which would have been more than fine for me. We were sitting in the living room, and there was a lull in the conversation, and for several long moments, he sat there, just looking at me. Perhaps it was the connection we had that I wasn't quite ready to fully admit yet, but I knew there was something he wanted to say, something even more important than whether or not we should kiss.

"Have you ever dated . . . ?" He paused. "I mean, I have something to tell you."

"What?" I asked warily. *Was he gay? Or already married to someone else?*

He took a deep breath. "Have you ever dated a Jewish man?"

"What's that?" I said. "I mean, I know what it is, I just don't know that much about it, other than what I learned about the Holocaust when I was in Europe. I don't know anything about Judaism. Is there something wrong with being Jewish? By the way, have you ever dated a Vietnamese woman?"

"No," he admitted.

"And, I have to tell you—I'm not having sex until I'm married."

He blinked. "Marriage? . . . Sex?"

"It's just something I like to let the guys I date know so that you wouldn't have to waste time and money on me."

"Are you dating other guys?"

"No. Not at this moment."

He looked relieved. "That's fine," he said. "I'm in no rush."

"Good," I said. "So it sounds like we'll both be having a new experience, which is fine by me. We can just learn about each other as we go, can't we?"

Jeff smiled. "That sounds like a great idea!" he replied, just before kissing me goodnight.

* * *

Two months after Jeff visited me in Kentucky, I invited him to visit my American family's home in Farmville, Virginia. The home is located on eight hundred acres of land with the

beautiful Appomattox River running right through the property. Though stunning, I considered it too far from civilization.
When you drive the property, you could turn on the radio and
hear about how Robert Lee and his army retreated during the
Civil War and marched right through the area. To get to the
grocery store was a thirty-minute drive, and Walmart was "the
place" for shopping.

It was Thanksgiving and the first time I ever brought a boyfriend home to meet the family; so clearly, it was something of
a big deal, not just for me but for Mary Lou, Lewis, and the rest
of the family. They were as warm and welcoming to Jeff as I
knew they would be.

The farmhouse Mary Lou had inherited was about two hundred years old, a true piece of Americana. It was also quite
drafty and cold, so Jeff and I spent quite a bit of time snuggled
together in front of the big fireplace in the family room.

One evening, Lewis pulled me aside while Jeff was talking
with Mary Lou and helping her clean up after dinner. "How do
you feel about Jeff?"

It was impossible for me not to smile when I talked about him,
so I answered my American father with a grin on my face. "I
don't know exactly how I feel," I said, "but I do know I can't stop
thinking about him all the time. And that I want to be with him."
It did feel strange to be so candid with Lewis—with anyone,
really—about feelings like that. "And it hurts to keep it all inside."

Lewis listened intently, and then nodded. "You know what
I think? I think it's called love. Has Jeff told you how he feels?
From the look in his eyes, it's obvious that he loves you."

I thought back to that conversation Jeff had tried to initiate
when we went on the dinner cruise. Fate? Soul mates? I had

laughed and called it bullshit. But it seemed the opposite was true. "No, we haven't really talked about that yet."

"I think the reason for that is less that he doesn't have these feelings and more that he's scared to tell you because you are the sort of person who is not used to opening your heart and letting people in, especially when it comes to men. Guys can sense it and might be afraid to share their feelings with you. Jeff probably doesn't dare to tell you for that reason."

I wanted to believe that he was right, and that I could trust the feelings I was experiencing. But there was still a fear of being vulnerable, of admitting out loud, to him, my true feelings.

"You shouldn't do anything until you're ready, of course," Lewis said, "but it's obvious to everyone here that you are already in love."

The sides of my face flushed and I looked down at the well-worn planks of the hardwood floor. Just hearing it—*in love*—made me smile even more.

"Now, Nhi, I know you're an adult, and I know you're very smart, but as any good parent should, I just want to make sure that you'll use protection if you—"

"That's enough!" I interrupted, inwardly cringing. I couldn't have asked for a better father in Lewis, but I didn't need to be having that particular conversation with him any time soon, or ever, really. "Don't worry about me getting pregnant! I'll wait until we get married."

Lewis looked at me in surprise. "Wow," he said, shaking his head. "Are you sure he's not gay?"

"What do you mean?"

"Actually, I know he's not, I can tell by the way Jeff looks at you," Lewis laughed. "What I'm trying to say, and I guess I'm not doing such a good job is—unless a guy is head over heels in love with you, he's not likely to stick around if you're not . . . well, how should I say this? Putting out."

Was that conversation really happening? I just started laughing, because what other choice did I have?

"This conversation took a turn I didn't expect," Lewis said, looking a bit chagrined.

"I'll be honest," I said. "If I tell Jeff how I feel—that I love him—what if he rejects me? I would be devastated. Every time I think of telling him, I think of how awful it would be if he didn't feel the same way. So it's better not to bring it up and just enjoy each other. "

Lewis smiled. "I understand why you would feel that way. But can I give you a bit of advice?"

"Please," I said. "As long as it's not about safe sex."

"Don't be afraid of vulnerability—it can be a good thing. If you tell him how you feel and he rejects you, then you know where he's at. You'll know the truth. Yes, rejection always hurts, but it's not going to be the end of you. Think of everything you've been through, everything you've overcome. You've taken so many chances throughout your life, and I know it hasn't always worked out, but if you don't try, if you don't ever take the chance, you will never know. If you had been too afraid to leave Vietnam? You wouldn't be here right now. You never would have met Jeff in the first place. If Jeff doesn't feel the same way about you, at least you'll know the truth. You took a chance. If you love him, then tell him how you feel before it's too late. Not often do you get to meet an amazing guy with such patience."

I knew Lewis was right, but still—knowing and doing are two completely different things.

* * *

I wouldn't work up the nerve until a few days before Jeff and I were to leave. He asked if I wanted to go for a walk to see the full moon, so we held hands as we walked toward the Appomattox River. The moon bathed everything in a milky light that cast shadows and made the need for a flashlight unnecessary—we could see perfectly clearly.

We came to an old bridge and walked across it, so we could lean on the railing and look down at the water, which trickled over some jutting rocks. The temperature was milder than it had been the past few days, and I couldn't help but feel it was as romantic a setting as I'd ever been in. In other words—the moment I had been waiting for. I could hear my father's advice from a few nights ago: *Don't be afraid of vulnerability.*

"This is the last full moon before the winter solstice," Jeff was saying. "It's also called the Beaver Moon or the Mourning Moon because—"

"I think I love you!" I blurted out, my eyes immediately filling with tears. It was the very first time I'd ever told a man that I loved him, and now that I had done what Lewis had encouraged—be completely open and vulnerable—I wasn't sure I would be able to bear it if Jeff told me he didn't feel the same way. But there was also some relief, because I *had* been forthright with him, and I had finally spoken word to the feelings I'd kept under wraps for so long.

Jeff gazed at me for several seconds, not saying anything, though the look in his eyes communicated all I needed to know. He leaned down and kissed me, a long, open-mouthed kiss that I felt I could've gotten lost in for eternity. But then he pulled back gently and brought his hand up to the side of my face.

"I love you, too," he whispered.

* * *

Not long after he'd gone back to Colorado, Mary Lou and her best friend, Yulane, went on a road trip and found themselves in Colorado. What a perfect opportunity for them to spend some time with Jeff and see how he lived. Jeff was more than gracious in opening his home up to them, and Mary Lou made sure to give me regular reports.

"Jeff's an organized guy, but he does not see dust. So, we helped him out in that area," she told me over the phone. She started to laugh and I could hear Yulane cracking up in the background. "Also," Mary Lou continued, once she'd gotten her laughter under control, "Jeff has a big crack in the front of his toilet seat, which can be dangerous for guys. Maybe he didn't realize this, or it didn't bother him enough to change it, but we bought him a new toilet seat and changed it while he was at work." I laughed, too, imagining Jeff returning home from work to a completely transformed bachelor pad.

"Don't worry, we're not getting too crazy here," Mary Lou said. "What's most obvious is that he's a good-hearted person and someone we feel you'll be safe with. That's the most important." Though there was a part of me that felt a little bad about all the scrutiny Jeff was enduring, I was also thrilled that he was so willing to put up with it, and that the people closest to me all thought he was as wonderful as I did.

* * *

Mary Lou and her best friend were not the only people who
wanted to check Jeff out. There was one more group of people
that were eager to assess whether Jeff was a good match for me,
and that was my group of guy friends. Kevin, Jamie, and Joe
from college were also eager to meet Jeff. I think they could
pick up on the fact that he was something more than a guy who
would disappear after I had my third-date talk with him.

"So, you're still seeing this guy?" Kevin asked me one
evening. I had met him and Jamie after work for a bite to eat.

"Still seeing him," I said.

"The guy from the plane?" Jamie said.

"Yes. Jeff."

Kevin grinned. "So, I have to ask then—have you had 'the
talk' with Jeff yet?"

"Actually, I have," I said.

They exchanged surprised glances. "What?" Jamie said.
"And he's still interested?"

"Yes. So it would appear your longstanding theory that no
American guy would be able to abide by that is wrong."

"Well," Kevin said, "it sounds like we need to meet this mys-
terious man."

"Yes, this guy has unbelievable patience. No sex until marriage. Something doesn't sound right. We want to meet him,"
Jamie said, though he looked decidedly less enthusiastic about
the prospect.

But the next time Jeff came to visit me, I made sure to introduce him to my friends. Jeff walked into a restaurant and was
surprised to meet my group of friends—all guys: Kevin, Jamie,

Chris, and Joe. All of them were friendly and curious; Jamie, however, looked Jeff up and down a few times, sizing him up. He was a bit more formal and at points, his questions to Jeff started to sound a bit like interrogations.

"What were you doing in Ohio?" Jamie asked.

"Traveling for work."

"What do you do for work?"

"I'm an environmental engineer."

"Do you travel a lot? Do you meet many people on planes?"

Jeff was speechless at that one.

It was obvious Jamie was in overprotective mode, but I understood—we were good friends and he wanted to make sure the guy, who, yes, I met on a plane, was okay. Good enough for me. Which clearly he was, and after a little while, Jamie seemed to relax and we were able to hang out and enjoy ourselves for the rest of the evening.

* * *

What I had never told anyone about was the image I had always had in my mind of the person I would end up with. He was a tall white man, someone who was kind and caring, and would be understanding of the fact that I was saving myself until we got married. I could never quite make out the person's face when I imagined him, yet there was Jeff, who seemed to check all the boxes. In addition—he was sublimely attractive. My heart skipped a beat every time I saw him. I was so drawn to that sexy man and had to use so much control just to keep my hands off him. There was a part of me that wanted to just for-get about the whole saving myself until marriage, but the fear of ending up pregnant and possibly a single mother eclipsed my desire to sleep with him just yet. I had been through so much, and come so far, that I was not going to throw it all away because I had to give into my lust.

It was a common story, especially in Kentucky—a single mother, no family close by for support. There would be no more travel for work or pleasure—or, if there was, it would be significantly complicated with a baby in tow. It would also bring shame and dishonor to both of my families. At times, it felt like I was being torn in two different directions, my desire for Jeff felt great, but I had worked so hard to get to where I was. I did not want a simple lapse in judgment to jeopardize it all. Did I want all the horrors I had been through during my escape to be for nothing if I ended up alone and pregnant? Absolutely not. And that fear was able to override even the strongest flares of my desire.

I had also learned through research that even with various contraception methods, there was still a 7 to 23 percent failure rate. Based on my survival experience, I didn't want to take that risk with something within my control. Watching Sister Second with three young kids at age twenty-two and her struggle was the best natural birth control method for me.

CHAPTER FIFTEEN
MEETING THE FAMILY

The first time I met Jeff's family was in Washington, DC. The patriarch of the family, Jeff's uncle Bob, was having a big sixtieth birthday celebration, which meant I would have the chance to meet most of Jeff's family in one place. A bit intimidating, though I decided to ignore any anxiety I felt about it and instead just be myself.

Uncle Bob was a very successful real estate agent in the DC area. He was average height for a man, but he had a presence that could certainly be intimidating, though he and I hit it off right away. He was easy to joke around with, which put me at ease. In fact, I think some of Jeff's family was a little surprised that Uncle Bob and I had such an easy rapport.

"You've got spirit!" he said, "I like that. So Jeff tells us you work for Lucent?"

"Yes, I'm a telecommunications consultant."

He furrowed his brow and regarded me for a moment. "You

know," he said, "I know we've only just met, but I can tell—you've got the personality of a sales person."

"I do?"

He nodded emphatically. "Oh yes you do. Perhaps you should consider getting into sales. Real estate. Something along those lines. It's a very lucrative and rewarding industry. You don't have to make any decisions now, of course, but maybe think about it. And if you have any questions, I'm more than happy to talk with you about it."

Jeff later told me that having Uncle Bob's approval meant the rest of the family would most likely follow. Once word got around that Uncle Bob approved, the rest of the family welcomed me like I was one of their own. Except for Jeff's mother, Gloria, who was beautiful, elegant, and immaculately dressed. I understood why she might be a little standoffish toward the petite woman from Vietnam whose relationship might not go much further with her son since we had a long-distance relationship.

"You know," she said, "my son always dated tall women."

I smiled. "And were they blond or brunette?"

Though her comments were a little off-putting, I understood why a mother might feel a certain way to a woman she suspected her son was very interested in. And over time we would grow to love each other.

I really clicked with Jeff's father, Richard, right away, though, after getting to know him, it was apparent that anyone he met would feel that way. A tall man with such a genuine smile, he exuded warmth and made me feel like part of the family right away.

"We've heard a lot of good things about you from Jeff," he said. "And I'm so glad we get to meet you now in person. He just radiates every time he talks about you. And to think you met on an airplane!"

"I know, what are the chances? If my seat had been closer to the front, or if I'd taken a different flight . . . . "

"You never know how you meet people. I heard that he was a gentleman and helped you with your luggage. His mother, not me, did a great job raising him." Richard smiled. "His mother and I were a little worried about how he might turn out when he was a teenager. . . . Did he ever tell you how he used to make beer in our basement?"

"No!" I said, laughing. "I didn't know he knew how to make beer."

"We didn't either," Richard said dryly. "Let's see, he was probably fourteen, fifteen years old at the time—so, way under the legal drinking age, too. He kept a keg in his bedroom closet—don't ask me where he got it from—and I kept hearing these strange sounds whenever I'd go into his room . . . sort of like *blurp blurp*. But whenever I asked him about it, he'd just deny it and say I must have a hearing problem." Richard laughed. "And once Gloria and I came home from vacation early to find out Jeff had thrown a huge party . . . I think every kid within a fifty-mile radius was there."

"I didn't realize Jeff was such a naughty teenager."

"Well, he's come a long way from hiding a keg in his bedroom closet. And he's always had a great work ethic. When he was at UConn, he had a full load of classes and then worked at a restaurant every night, and somehow managed to get by on just a few hours of sleep." Richard looked across the room, where Jeff was talking with a few of his cousins. "I can tell you make my son very happy. And that makes us happy."

The rest of Jeff's family seemed genuinely curious about me and interested in hearing about all the details of how Jeff and I met. When they heard it was on an airplane, they wanted to know where I was living.

"Kentucky," I replied, watching as some of his aunts and uncles exchanged quizzical looks.

"But, Jeff . . . you're still in Colorado, right?"

"Still in Colorado," he said.

After everyone learned that Jeff and I lived in two different states, it seemed that the general consensus was they wouldn't be seeing me at any more big family events—after all, how many long-distance relationships were really that successful over the long term?

* * *

Although Jeff and I had both said *I love you* to each other, it wasn't enough. Having a long-distance relationship was agonizing for both of us.

We could only see each other once a month if we were lucky and every time we felt like we were on our honeymoon, only to have it end with a painful goodbye.

Once, Jeff made another trip to Ohio for work. So that we could see each other, we agreed to meet halfway in Ashland, Kentucky—the same town where my friend Angela had grown up and not seen a minority until she was sixteen years old.

Well, not much seemed to have changed in Ashland! Jeff and I only had a few days to spend together, but whenever we went out, we received quite a few unfriendly, and even hostile, looks. It felt like everyone stopped to stare when we entered a restaurant or walked into a store. No one specifically *said* anything to us, but I recalled what Angela had told me, and later, when I mentioned it to her, she laughed and said Jeff and I together must've been quite eye-opening for those in her hometown; they'd probably never seen an interracial couple before.

Meeting up in a strange town or having to wait a few months before seeing each other again was stressful and frustrating, though I didn't realize how serious Jeff was about things until he said one day, "I'm sorry to tell you this, but to make this relationship work, we both need to live in the same town. Either you move to Colorado, or I'd sell my house and move to Kentucky. What would you like to do?"

I loved Colorado, with its abundance of natural beauty and the active lifestyle that could be had year-round . . . I couldn't imagine why anyone would want to leave Colorado for Kentucky. There were some people, though, who didn't want me to go, especially my close friends, in particular, Jamie.

"Are you sure you want to move away to be with a guy you only met on an airplane?" he kept asking.

"I've given it a lot of thought. This isn't just some whim. I mean, maybe it will end up being a mistake, but I've got a good feeling about it and want to take my chance."

"If it does not work out, just call to let me know and I'll be there for you," Jamie said. He paused. "I wanted to give you something." It was a James Taylor CD, which had the song "You've Got a Friend" on it.

"Thank you, Jamie," I said.

* * *

Not long after our trip to Virginia to meet my family and to Washington, DC, to meet Jeff's, I approached Gene and asked if perhaps he could transfer me to Colorado. I still hadn't put in the time required to go to Italy or France, as I had originally requested, but I didn't want to go to Europe anymore—I wanted to be near Jeff.

Gene gave me a curious look. "Did you meet somebody when you were in Colorado?"

"No," I lied. "But I loved everything about it there. It's so beautiful. And the mountains are really something else."

Gene raised an eyebrow. "The mountains," he said. "I'm not quite sure I buy that. I think you met someone special."

"It's a really nice area. And I wouldn't mind a change of scenery."

"Before I do the paperwork," he said with a grin. "I want to meet this guy. I have daughters and I can tell you just met someone."

Okay, maybe it was more obvious than I thought. "You're right," I said. "I did meet someone, on the plane on the way over, actually."

"Well, you know all of us here are going to want to meet him. When will he be here next?" I wasn't exactly sure, but I knew if I gave him an exact date, Gene would put it on his calendar for the interview that it was clearly going to be.

But Jeff handled it perfectly, not the least bit intimidated by Gene, whose stature alone made him an imposing figure. Joining him for this hour-long interview-disguised-as-lunch was Sue, who, at six feet tall, could herself be an intimidating person. They grilled him about his background, where he went to school, and what he did for work. Toward the end, Gene asked, "How would you feel if I offered you a position here in Kentucky? I've got just the thing in mind."

Jeff caught my eye and gave a tiny smile before looking back at Gene. "Thank you," he said, "but I think I might be too expensive and you wouldn't be able to afford me."

Everyone laughed, but inwardly, I breathed a sigh of relief—I wouldn't want to work with my boyfriend if we were going to be living in the same town.

After meeting Jeff, Gene agreed to fill out the official request to transfer me to Colorado. It would be a big change, but it felt as if there were forces larger than myself propelling me in that direction.

"I know you'll still be working within the company," Gene said, "and I can just tell how crazy Jeff is about you. But sometimes I wish I had just sent you to France like you had asked."

"But Gene," I said, with a smile, "if you had done that, I wouldn't have met Jeff."

"I know," he said. "I'm just feeling sorry for myself. You've taught me so much. It's a huge loss to us here, but Jeff is a great guy and it's clear you guys have something special."

He was right—it was, most surprisingly, turning out to be the perfect love story, and I wanted to start the next chapter and see where it would go.

"Thank you, Gene." I thought back to that day, sitting at the kitchen table, making cold calls, hoping that I would land a job. There was a good chance my career at Lucent never would have even started if Gene hadn't been the one to answer the phone. Had something steered me in that direction, some omnipresent force? I didn't think I believed that, yet the serendipitous moments in my life would not allow me to fully discount such a notion.

* * *

A year after Jeff and I met, Gene completed the transfer request to send me to Colorado, to Bell Labs, which, only a few years ago, had been spun off as part of Lucent. Not only was I looking forward to moving but I was also excited to work at such a prestigious division of the company. It felt like I was making a move in the right direction.

However—despite moving to Colorado to be closer to Jeff, I didn't want to be *too* close, not at first, anyway. I found a place about thirty minutes from where he lived, closer to my work, just in case our relationship didn't work out. I figured if that happened, I didn't want to be running into him at the grocery story. But I also didn't want to go from a long-distance relationship to being right under his nose all the time, falling into a rut and annoying each other before we actually had a chance to form some strong bonds. (The annoying would come later.)

I went so far as to limit the amount of time Jeff could see me—he could visit me once a week, which meant I had plenty of time to study for my master's degree in telecommunications engineering, while working full-time at Lucent. I never wanted Jeff to consider me a burden, but more importantly, I always wanted to have the resources to be able to take care of myself.

The other thing was—Jeff was already living with someone.

No, not another girlfriend, but a housemate who had found him by way of a classified ad Jeff had posted in a newspaper. His name was Tim, and at six foot three, he was even taller than Jeff and just as fit. They were quite the pair, the two of them, those outdoorsy and athletic bachelors with their two dogs, Jeff's Zoe and Tim's Sierra. When I'd go over there for my weekly visit, Jeff and Tim would be in the kitchen, cooking up some elaborate meal the three of us would then sit down and eat together, the two dogs sitting faithfully near their respective owners, still as statues, except for their eyes that would follow each morsel of food as it went from plate to mouth.

"This chicken's really good," Tim said. "I think we got the seasoning just right."

The food *was* always quite good, particularly for two bachelors, though having both worked in the restaurant industry in college, they had picked up some good culinary skills. They might not have had an ounce of decorating ability between the two of them, but they actually did know their way around the kitchen.

"This is so great," Jeff said one night over a meal of roast chicken and asparagus with saffron risotto. He looked at me, then Tim, then the two dogs, beaming. "How lucky am I? I find a great friend and roommate from a classified ad, an awesome dog at the pound, and the most amazing girlfriend on an airplane. My life is almost perfect."

But as I sat there, enjoying the delicious meal they'd concocted, seeing just how happy Jeff looked in that moment, I wondered if I might someday be living in that house with the two of them *and* their two dogs.

* * *

Five months after I moved to Colorado, my friend Jamie flew in from Kentucky to visit. "I can see why you'd want to move out here," he said. "It's really nice." He was staying with me at my place, and we hadn't seen Jeff yet. I could tell that he wanted alone time with me like the old days in Kentucky. Thankfully, Jeff was never jealous of my friendship with any of my guy friends and suggested I should spend quality time with Jamie—without Jeff being around. Though the night before Jamie was to leave, when we were hanging out on the couch, talking about our good old college days, he abruptly said, "You seem serious about Jeff. If Jeff asks you to marry him, what would you say?"

"I would say yes," I said instantly, a big smile on my face just at the thought. "I am so in love with him. I've never felt this way about anyone before." But I tried to temper my delight when I saw Jamie's reaction, or lack thereof. Instead of being happy, the way you would expect a good friend to be at such a confession, his expression remained impassive, and he just gave the briefest of nods.

"I'm probably going to go to sleep," he said. "I've got to get up early tomorrow."

"But . . . I thought your flight wasn't leaving until the afternoon."

"It's not, but I want to make sure I get there with plenty of time."

Perhaps it should not have surprised me to receive a letter from Jamie not long after he returned to Kentucky. It was a long letter, and one he had clearly put a lot of thought into. But its contents broke my heart. He could no longer continue to be my friend; he felt like our friendship had largely been a one-way street, where he was always there for me, yet I never reciprocated. I was so driven and focused on myself and my career and he was tired of it.

I read that letter over and over again, at first not wanting to believe it; maybe he was right, that I was selfish and obsessed with opportunities and success in America. But had it really been a one-way street? I had never been there for him? I realized, though, that was my defensive initial reaction, and after I'd had time to think more about what he said, I could understand why he would feel that way. Though Jamie himself had never come out and admitted to having feelings for me that went beyond just being friends, it would seem that was the case. But why hadn't he ever just come out and admitted it? Maybe Lewis was right that I had not been vulnerable and willing to open myself up romantically.

I did end up showing the letter to Jeff. "I'm not surprised," he said, once he was finished reading. "I had a feeling that Jamie has feelings for you that go beyond just being friends. I kind of knew that the first time I met him."

"You did?" This surprised me. And if so, why hadn't he brought it up? "How?"

Jeff shrugged. "I don't know, it was just how he looked at me. I feel for the guy, though. That's hard, and I hope he's able to move on." He nodded to the letter. "I think that's part of what he's going to do to cope with the situation, which I know is hard for you, because you've always considered him a dear friend."

"I didn't want anyone to get hurt."

"I know. I didn't either. And honestly, I appreciate him for always being there for you and for loving you. We just can't control how we feel sometimes."

The pain of losing a friend is never easy, and even to this day, Jeff and I still think fondly of Jamie. Sometimes, Jeff will still call him to wish him a happy birthday. At the time I shared my sadness about Jamie breaking up our friendship, though, I didn't mention to Jeff the conversation Jamie and I had right before he left that was likely the impetus for his letter—whether I would say yes if Jeff asked me to marry him.

* * *

Jeff and I took a week off from work in the middle of February to go visit his parents in Connecticut. It was cold and snowy, and aside from the fact that there weren't any mountains, it didn't seem much different than Colorado. On Valentine's Day, we took a drive through the quaint town of Woodbury, and he asked if I wanted to walk over to the gazebo on the village green, which wasn't green at all, at the moment, because it was covered in snow.

I laughed. "No way," I said, looking down at my nice suede shoes. "I'm not ruining these shoes just to go check out some gazebo."

"It's really beautiful, though, you should check it out."

I could see it in the distance, a turret-shaped octagon, encircled by a white railing with a cupola sitting atop the center of the roof, like a hat. Perhaps it was stunning in the summer, when everything was lush and green and in bloom, but at that moment, it looked a little stark, the ground covered with snow, and very cold.

"I don't want to ruin these shoes."

"I'll carry you," Jeff said.

This must be some really special gazebo, I thought.

So he carried me across the snow to the gazebo. We went up the four steps and it was then I noticed that Jeff had started shaking.

"Are you cold?" I asked. A gazebo in the middle of winter was probably not the best place to go to get warm.

But he didn't answer. He came over to me, and then got down on one knee, taking something out of his pocket as he did so. It was a ring. "I am so in love with you, and I want to spend the rest of my life with you. Will you marry me?"

I opened my mouth to say *Yes!* but before I could, he continued, "If you don't like this ring, I'll get you a different one."

"Yes, of course I'll marry you!" I exclaimed. "And the ring is beautiful."

He slipped it onto my finger. It was a little big, but it was gorgeous—an emerald with small diamonds around it. He stood up and we embraced, and then kissed.

"Why did you think I wouldn't like this ring?" I asked. "I would like anything from you."

He gave me a sheepish smile. "Well . . . I've had quite the time trying to find an engagement ring. . . . This ring was actually a gift my dad gave to my mom twenty-five years ago. When I went to the jeweler's, the sales rep there told me that I better get at least a one-carat diamond or you'd say no."

I raised my eyebrows. "Oh, really? Do I know this sales rep?"

"No, but he said that since you were Asian, if it wasn't at least a one-carat, you'd say no."

"Jeff," I said, "you should know me better than that. I put up with you and your ugly car. I would've said yes if you proposed to me with a plastic ring from the Dollar Store."

He gave me another kiss. "Well, you have just made me the happiest man alive. But . . . I do have one more question."

I looked up from admiring the ring on my finger. "Yes?"

"Would you consider converting to Judaism?"

CHAPTER SIXTEEN
I DO

Working full-time and studying to get a master's degree does not leave one with much free time to focus on planning a wedding. Jeff and I were both eager to get married as soon as we could though, since we had held off living together until we tied the knot. Because of that, I decided to ask Mary Lou if she would take care of the wedding plans for me.

"I'd be happy to!" she exclaimed. "Do you guys have a date in mind? A venue? If you don't, I think getting married here on our farm would be lovely."

"That'd be great! What's the soonest you could put together a wedding, if we don't have to worry about booking a venue? Like two or three months?"

"Two or three months?" She paused. "Is there . . . is there a big rush?"

"Jeff and I aren't going to live together until we're married, so, yeah, the sooner the better."

She let out a breath. "I see. The thing is, Nhi, people might think you're pregnant. That this is a shotgun wedding."

"A what?" I asked.

"It's just a term for when people get married real quick. Usually because the woman is pregnant. You're not, are you?"

"No! We're not even living together yet. And honestly, I don't care what other people think—this is about Jeff and me, and we are ready to start our lives together."

"Then I'll get started right away. What about the end of June? That's a little over three months away. That should be plenty of time."

"Perfect. And we'd like a small wedding, like forty guests or so."

"Of course."

The eight-hundred-acre ranch would be the perfect place—I knew it the second the words were out of her mouth. Summer would be just getting underway and the landscape would be lush and fertile—everything a rich, verdant green, the air fragrant with the scent of day lilies, flowers, and trees in full bloom. It would be the perfect place to have a wedding.

Other relatives proved a little more skeptical about the wedding date, set so soon after our engagement, but I was quick to clear up their unspoken and incorrect assumption: "In case you are wondering, I'm not pregnant; Jeff and I are more than ready to be married and don't see the need to wait any longer."

And that was the truth. Jeff was the right man for me and it made sense to have our wedding as soon as possible so we could begin our life together.

* * *

Just before our wedding, on June 24, my future husband did a beautiful thing for me.

When Jeff turned thirteen, he became a bar mitzvah, meaning he was seen as accountable for his own actions in the eyes of Jewish law. This is a coming-of-age ritual for all Jewish children, and Jeff had received a number of government bonds as bar mitzvah gifts. Those bonds grew over the years and he decided he'd cash them in and use the money to fly my mother and my brother in from Vietnam for our wedding. I was floored that he would do that, and thrilled that my mother would be able to share the special day with us.

Mother and Fourth flew from Vietnam to Kentucky, where they stayed with Sister Second and her family. Then they all drove from Kentucky to Virginia. Mother pulled me aside two hours before the wedding ceremony and said, "We had a layover in Los Angeles. An old Vietnamese friend met us and we showed him your wedding invitation. He told us that Jeff's name looks Jewish. Is he correct?"

I had not expected such a question right off the bat. My heart was thumping when I reluctantly told her "Yes." I had not wanted a dramatic explosion right before my wedding, yet it was not something I was going to lie to my mother about.

But her response surprised me, especially after our previous disagreement in Vietnam when she insisted I marry a Vietnamese man. "I heard that the Jews have great work ethic, like us," she said. "So, I think Jeff will not sit around expecting you to work and take care of him. As long as he takes good care of you, then I'm fine with him being Jewish."

Relief flooded through me. At least *that* was one thing I wouldn't have to worry about.

To be honest, though, I really didn't have much to worry about at all in regard to my wedding, which is something not every bride can say. The whole Hearn family really stepped it up when it came to planning my wedding; Mary Lou was mainly in charge, but my brothers were also helping by planting new flowers and doing some landscaping in the side yard where the ceremony would take place. Mary Lou had also enlisted the help of her new best friend and neighbor, Phyllis, who became known as "The Sergeant." She was a no-nonsense sort of woman who had a knack for organizing events and people.

And there ended up being quite a lot of people. Originally, we had thought there might be around forty guests; in reality, it was more like 140. The day before the wedding, I drove to the nearest town, which was about thirty minutes away. I had a few minor errands to run, nothing pressing, but I wanted a few moments by myself, away from the busyness back at home. Downtown Farmville was a quaint area with a small-town feel. I stopped into a coffee shop to get a cup of tea and use the bathroom. While I was in the bathroom stall, several women came in, chatting, clearly out-of-towners with their Yankee dialect.

"This place is so far! How many hours have we been driving? And I can't believe how remote it is," one of the women said.

I was done in the bathroom, but stayed in the stall.

"Who is this girl he's marrying? This is farm country. Doesn't he live in Colorado? How on earth did he meet this girl and have a wedding in this part of the country?"

"Speaking of, where is that map? We're definitely going to need the map if we're going to find that place. Talk about *remote*. Should we ask for directions?" Their conversation continued as they washed and dried their hands and then left the bathroom.

Yes, I could've exited the stall and introduced myself, but it seemed a little strange to be meeting for the first time in a

public restroom, and, chances were, they'd ask me for directions, and I didn't want to be blamed if they got lost on country
roads that probably all looked the same to them.

When I returned to the house, a truck was just leaving, having dropped off several Porta-Potties.

"What are those for?" I asked Phyllis.

"I don't think Mary Lou's three bathrooms are going to be
able to accommodate 140 people. You don't want your wedding guests having to wait in long lines to use the bathroom, do
you?"

"140?" I asked. "You mean forty."

She shook her head. "No, you heard me right. This is going
to be quite the celebration! Mary Lou has gotten word that people from all over will be here. So, we need the Porta-Potties."

And she was right. People I hadn't even expected came from
all over.

Sister Second and her family drove with Mother and Fourth
from Kentucky, as did my old college friend Jamie and his
father. I think the letter Jamie had written to me about ending
our friendship had been cathartic for him, and allowed him to
move past the feelings he had for me, at least to make it to the
wedding.

My two friends from college, Kevin and Marianne, were
going to be a groomsman and a bridesmaid. My old friend I
met from the Governor's Scholars who also went to Vietnam
(during my college trip), Rebecca, was my maid of honor.

After Rebecca met me and went to Vietnam with me on
the Centre College trip (she attended a different university and
received special permission from my college to join our program in Vietnam), she met both my Vietnamese and American

families. She told me that somehow, I influenced her tremendously. Upon her college graduation, she spent two years in Vietnam teaching English to college students, where she learned the language and became fluent in Vietnamese. It was hilarious to watch the tall skinny white woman speaking Vietnamese with the northern (communist) accent.

Mary Lou's brother-in-law, Bob, came in from Ohio. Uncle Bob was a professional singer and he was going to sing during the wedding. Other members of the Hearn family arrived from Georgia, Kentucky, and North Carolina, and Jeff's family came down from New England. Since it was before GPS, more than a few of them got lost trying to find the farm.

But everyone eventually found their way. The weather that day was stifling, full sun and high humidity. My dress was sleeveless, but Jeff and the poor groomsmen were sweating in their dark suits. Still, they all looked so handsome.

The 140 guests were seated in the backyard, and unfortunately, the only shade was the wooden arbor that Jeff and I stood under to exchange our vows. But the grass had been mowed just the day before; two of Jeff's groomsmen maybe had a little too much fun taking the ride-on lawn mower out to mow the acres of grass that made up the front, side, and backyard.

My wedding dress was simple but elegant, sleeveless with a darted bodice and a gently flowing skirt, the hem of which just barely brushed the ground as I walked. Mary Lou and my mother both wore dresses in the shade of cyan; Mother wore a traditional Vietnamese outfit with long sleeves and embroidered white flowers; Mary Lou's was short sleeve and had muted patterns in different shades of blue-green. They wore matching white-rose corsages.

Lewis escorted both of them down the aisle—Mary Lou on one side, my Vietnamese mother on the other. Jeff stood underneath the wooden arbor with the justice of the peace who would marry us. He looked so handsome in his tuxedo. I watched as Mary Lou and Mother took their seats. They were all there— my three families: my Vietnamese family, my American family, and now Jeff and his family that I was marrying into. All these people gathered there to help us celebrate. I reveled in the bliss of the moment.

After my mothers were seated, Lewis came back to escort me down the aisle. He held his arm out and I slipped mine through his.

"Ready?" he asked, smiling down at me. He gave my hand a pat. I nodded.

Off we went.

As we slowly walked, and everyone turned to look at us, Uncle Bob began to sing "Sunrise, Sunset," the well-known song from *Fiddler on the Roof*. Uncle Bob had a beautiful voice that he projected powerfully as I made my way toward my soon-to-be-husband. I saw that Jeff's mom had tears in her eyes, and I knew Jeff had been right in his claim that every Jewish mother loves that song, and I was glad we had included it.

As I stood there in front of a crowd of 140 people, looking up at Jeff as we recited our vows and exchanged rings, my sheer happiness was also intermingled with overwhelming gratitude for every person who had been a part of my life to get me where I was. The little girl selling counterfeit cigarettes in the slums of Saigon had somehow managed to make it there, where I was about to cross the threshold and become a married woman. The love that radiated from Jeff's eyes was the sort you might expect from a fairy tale, and in a way, that is exactly how it felt. I had lost one fairy tale existence after being run out of my childhood home, but I had come to find it again in Jeff's love.

After we said our vows, we broke glass wrapped in white linen napkins. Perhaps the most widely recognized part of a Jewish wedding, the breaking of glass was a reminder for temperance even in the times of immense happiness, and also symbolic of the fragility of our human relationships.

And then—it was time to kick back and enjoy some good music and excellent food. Though roast pig was not on the menu, there was a huge buffet table set up underneath a big white tent. There was barbeque chicken, beef, all types of pasta and green salads, and a variety of delicious homemade pies. Uncle Bob sang several more slow, romantic songs and then his two daughters, Beth and Tina, got up to join him and the music changed to rollicking country that got pretty much everyone out of their seat and dancing—even those who didn't usually dance.

There wasn't just good food and dancing for entertainment though, not when you live on a farm. One of my brothers got the big tractor going and gave hayrides to anyone who was interested, which turned out to be many of the out-of-town guests and even a few of Mary Lou's neighbors, who had surely been on plenty of hayrides before.

Still to this day, I feel so touched whenever I think back to my wedding day, and how people from three different families from different parts of the country—and the world—had come together to celebrate Jeff and me. The following day, Jeff and I would leave for our honeymoon on a cruise to the Bahamas. And from there, it would be on to a new chapter: life as husband and wife, living together for the first time.

* * *

We returned to Colorado after our honeymoon. My mother and my brother had gone back to Kentucky with Sister Second after the wedding, so when we got back, we flew them out to stay with us for the remainder of their time in America. Having never lived together before, perhaps inviting others to stay with us right away wasn't the smartest idea, but I wanted Mother and Fourth to have the chance to see Colorado before they left, and to be able to spend some more time getting to know Jeff. And Tim, who was still living there.

"Who is this other man?" Mother asked. "He's so tall."

"It's Jeff's friend, Tim."

"So you're going to live here with two men?"

I shrugged. It was starting to look that way. "They're both really good cooks."

Mother looked like she didn't believe me. "We'll see," she said.

They only stayed with us for another week, but it felt like months. Nearly every day, Mother was able to reduce me to tears with her criticism over my relationship with Mary Lou.

"I'm glad we were able to come to America and attend your wedding," she told me one afternoon. Jeff and Fourth had gone to take the dog for a walk, and I was hoping that Mother and I would be able to spend a little quality time together before they left the next day. "It was a beautiful ceremony and you have a husband who is not only a hard worker but he also cooks!" She shook her head in amazement. She still couldn't believe that Jeff knew his way around a kitchen and had cooked several meals for all of us. Mother smiled. "Do you remember when you were little, you'd insist you didn't need to learn how to cook and that you would never cook for a man just because you are expected to do it?"

I had a clear recollection of myself declaring such a sentiment and the way my family would shake their heads over it, like they couldn't believe I would be so stubborn. "I remember," I said.

"And you were right! This is incredible! I've never seen a man cooking in a kitchen before. We all wondered who you'd marry, because who on earth would put up with a woman who doesn't know how to cook? But here in America, you've got men who cook. And Jeff, his food's not bad. I can't wait to share this story when I get back home—Nhi's husband in the kitchen cooking for her. People might think I lie."

Her smile slowly vanished. "But it makes me sad to see the way I have lost you to your American family and your American way of life."

"Mother, please," I said. "I know how you feel. And I disagree with you that you've lost a daughter, because you haven't—I'm right here! I know my lifestyle is different than if I had stayed in Vietnam, but *you* were always the one saying how great America was! How you wanted to send all of us here because it's the greatest country in the world."

"I did not expect to lose you like this, though."

"One of the last things you told me before I left was that we might never see each other again."

"Yes, because that was certainly a possibility! But now I don't know, this might be even worse. Because I don't even know you. I haven't been a part of your life for so long, it's like I lost a daughter, but she's still here."

"How can you say that?" I asked, unable to keep the anger out of my voice. I had always tried to be understanding and empathetic to her position—she had made the ultimate sacrifice by sending me away for a better life. "I have worked so hard to try to succeed and have a good life. I could've slept around and gotten pregnant, or flunked out of school because it was too hard. I could've not stayed in touch. I did none of those things, but you still criticize me! Why can't you just be proud of what I've accomplished?"

I had hoped that my success in school and in my career and now in my personal life would be able to eclipse Mother's feelings of jealousy, but that didn't seem to be the case at all. In fact, I felt the only thing that would assuage her feelings would be if I announced I was never going to have anything to do with the Hearns again.

"I would like it if you would sponsor me so I could also live in America," Mother said suddenly, which caught me completely off guard.

"I'll need to talk to Jeff about it," I said, even though I already knew what the answer was going to be. The week that Mother had been with us after we returned from our honeymoon had felt like a month—and not in a good way. I couldn't tell her this, but there was no way I could bring her into my life when she felt the way she did about my relationship with Mary Lou. I would tell her before she left that Jeff and I were simply not in the financial position to sponsor her at that time.

I felt relieved the next day when we took Mother and Fourth to the airport. Jeff and I were newlyweds and should be enjoying our time together, not to mention we were acclimating ourselves to finally living together. Having Mother and her jealousy and criticism over my being "too American" made me constantly feel on edge.

"I'm really glad your family was able to come out here for the wedding," Jeff said, as we drove back to our home.

"I am, too. Thank you again for making it happen."

Jeff glanced at me. "Everything okay?"

I hesitated. Part of me just wanted to put the whole thing behind me. I had no idea when I might see Mother again, and dwelling on her disappointment would only upset me more. But I knew Jeff could tell something was bothering me, and I wanted to be upfront with him about everything.

"Well," I said, "for starters, my mother is very impressed that you can cook so well."

Jeff smiled. "Phew. Glad to hear that."

"What she's not so impressed with is how Americanized I've become." Jeff was quiet while I told him some of the things Mother had said. "It's like she wants me to be the same twelve-year-old girl who left Vietnam. But that's impossible. She makes me feel like I'm going to have to someday choose one family over the other."

"I thought things seemed a little tense between you guys at times," Jeff said. He took a deep breath. "It's a hard position for your mom to be in. I'm sure she knows she did the right thing sending you away. That sort of thing is any parent's worst nightmare. But she sent you somewhere she had only heard about, somewhere she was able to imagine in her mind. And now she's here and sees the reality of your life, and how American it is. And there's nothing wrong with that! You live in America. I can tell your mother is happy for you. I don't think she secretly wants your life here to fall apart so you move back to Vietnam. But it's also hard for her because she missed out on so much of your life and now she sees how you've assimilated into another culture. And married a man who practices a different religion!"

"She was surprisingly approving of the fact you're Jewish," I said. "I didn't mention that I was going to look into Judaism myself." I sighed. "That will be a conversation for another day."

It was hard not to think that Mother would accept the news graciously, but I couldn't let her fears and insecurities hold me back from living the life that I wanted to.

* * *

With Mother gone, Jeff and I were able to start settling into our new life together. Tim, as it turned out, had been a bit overwhelmed finding himself living not just with me but also my mother and my brother for a week, and he informed Jeff that it was probably time for him to move out, which I knew saddened Jeff, but would also be a good thing, I hoped, as Jeff and I got used to living together.

Because we hadn't lived together before, it was an adjustment, and right away, there were a few things that needed to be changed.

Jeff's beloved dog, Zoe, continued to claim her spot in the middle of the bed for the first few weeks. It was basically a Zoe sandwich, with Jeff on one side, me on the other, and the dog in the middle. Every night, without fail, I would be awakened by Zoe, stretching her legs out, pushing her claws into me, and nudging me closer and closer to the edge of the bed.

"I need to talk to you," I told Jeff one morning at breakfast.

"Is everything okay?" he asked. He looked at me more closely. "Are you sleeping all right? You look tired."

"I'm so glad you noticed!" I exclaimed. "That's exactly what I wanted to talk with you about. No, I am not sleeping well at all."

"Is the mattress too firm?"

"No. No, the mattress is fine. What's not fine is I'm sharing the bed not just with my husband, but also his *dog*." I shook my head. "Jeff, if we want this marriage to work, the dog can*not* sleep in the same bed as us. It'd be like if I had a pet pig and brought it into our bed every night."

"I see," he said. "I'm all set with sharing the bed with any livestock. I'm sorry; Zoe's been sleeping in the bed since I brought her home and I thought it would be big enough."

"Well, it's not. What if I bought a special bed just for Zoe, and she can sleep near our bed. That way, she's still close."

"I'm fine with that," he said, though he looked skeptical. "I'm just not sure Zoe will want to sleep on it, is all."

"I'll train her. That's one of the great things about dogs, right? You can train them."

"Yes, but . . . "

I went out and bought Zoe a bed that day. I set it up at the foot of our bed, and that evening, when she tried to hop up into her usual sleeping spot, I called her down and had her lie in the dog bed. I gave her a treat to sweeten the deal.

"Stay," I said.

Zoe did not stay. She finished her treat and then jumped back on the bed.

"Do you know anything about training dogs? It's hard to train my dog because all she's able to learn is sit down, lie down, stay, and come here," Jeff said, after watching me lure Zoe back to her dog bed for the seventh or eighth time.

"I'll get some books," I said. "But for right now, I'm just winging it."

The very next day, after awaking refreshed because I no longer had to share the bed with a canine, I got a few books about training dogs from the library. While Jeff might have taught Zoe how to sit patiently at the corner of the table while he ate, the thing Zoe seemed to know best was how to destroy furniture. I don't know how many pillows and couch cushions met their demise in the jaws of that dog, but I was not going to dedicate time and money sprucing up the former bachelor pad to have a dog ruin it the next time she was left alone.

Consensus from all the books I read was clear: to be successful, you had to let the dog know who was boss. For Zoe, a German Shepherd and Border Collie mutt, that meant not allowing her to ignore you when you issued a command.

Zoe was smart, and she learned quickly. She was highly motivated by food, and one day, I got an idea.

"Sit," I said. She sat. I took a treat from the plastic pouch, and Zoe's ears immediately pricked at the sound of the bag. "Stay," I said firmly. She held perfectly still, only her eyes moving to track the treat in my hand. I placed the treat on her nose. She tried to eat it, but I grabbed it before she could gobble it up.

"*No*," I said. I balanced the treat back on her nose. This time, she remained still, her eyes nearly crossing as she tried to look at the treat. "Stay."

She held still for a few seconds and then I clapped my hands. "OK!" Zoe bounced her head back and caught the treat in the air. I laughed. It really wasn't so difficult at all.

That evening, when Jeff got home from work, I had him come into the living room and sit on the couch. I called Zoe, who came trotting over to me.

"Sit," I said. She sat.

Jeff nodded, smiling like a proud parent. "That's great," he said.

"That's not all."

I ran Zoe through all the commands she had and I had mastered, both in English and Vietnamese, saving her final trick for last. Out of the corner of my eye, I could see the disbelieving look on Jeff's face as I balanced the treat on his dog's nose. I counted to fifteen, and then clapped my hands and said, "OK!" She tipped her head back and caught the treat.

Jeff's mouth fell open. "All right, then," he said, after giving himself a moment to recover. "I guess you know how to train dogs."

* * *

One Saturday morning, I was inside making tea when I heard Jeff start yelling and cursing like a sailor. He had just gone outside to mow the lawn, but it didn't sound like much mowing was happening.

I hurried to the back door, afraid that he might've somehow injured himself. He was really yelling!

"Jeff?" I said. His back was to me and he was fiddling with the lawn mower. Okay, good, there didn't appear to be any blood or missing limbs. "Jeff!" I had to really raise my voice so he would hear me.

He turned, his face red. "Are you okay?" I asked.

"NO! This stupid thing keeps cutting out. It's got gas, I replaced the spark plug not long ago . . . What the hell is wrong with this piece of crap?!"

Knowing nothing about lawn mowers, I retreated back inside.

But that was something I had noticed about Jeff, that I hadn't noticed before we were living together—when he got upset with something, his default mode was to start yelling. And, as anyone who was raised in a traditional Asian family can tell you—that's not how we would handle our problems. No, we withdraw into silence. I had been taught not to scream or yell or raise my voice, which, apparently, was the opposite of what Jeff had been taught.

"Yeah," he said, when I brought it up to him later. "I do yell when I get upset. It's East Coast style, though."

I blinked. "Excuse me?"

"East Coast style," he repeated. "You know, the yelling, cursing and stuff. It just helps me get my frustration out."

"I see," I said slowly, wondering about the family I had married into. I couldn't ever see Richard or Gloria yelling like that. (Later, I would mention this to them, and they both looked at me and laughed. "We don't do that," they said, confirming what I had always known to be true.)

But what was also true was the fact that Jeff and I had two very different styles of communicating when we got upset, and I knew that could spell trouble for us down the road if we didn't learn how to fight nicely.

We began to work with a man named Todd, who was a therapist and someone Jeff and I would continue to see throughout our marriage. In our early meetings with Todd, he would help us better understand our different communicating styles, though often, the issue was about something like a disagreement over that one-dollar hot dog we got to share at Home Depot. Jeff had offered me a bite and I wanted more.

"And the issue arose because I thought he did not love me enough," I said, "because he didn't want to share more of that one- or two-dollar hot dog."

Todd appeared to be trying to suppress a smile. "Okay, a hot dog," he said. "So, it sounds to me like you two need to be clearer with your communication. Nhi, you could have said, *Let's split this evenly.* Or, Jeff, you could've told Nhi you were feeling hungry and wanted to split it more 60/40."

"OK, we'll be clearer with our communication when it comes to sharing food," I said.

Todd let his smile break free. "Well, the good news here is that most people who come to see me are on the verge of divorce and can hardly stand to be in the same room with each other. You two are fighting about food."

Both Jeff and I knew disagreements are a healthy component of any relationship, but the important—and often overlooked—part is that many couples don't know how to argue productively. I didn't want Jeff and me to fall into that trap, especially if we were going to have kids.

* * *

I also wanted to honor the commitment I made to Jeff, so we decided to take an "Introduction to Judaism" course, offered through the Rocky Mountain Rabbinic Council. After successful completion of the course, many students would receive a certificate, which was a requirement if they decided they wanted to convert. I still didn't think I was going to convert, but I was excited to learn about something that had played such an important role in my husband's life.

Though the course itself was eight months long, I spent the next four years immersed in learning about Jewish culture and history. It was striking to realize how much my own history and the struggles of the Jewish people had in common. I came to discover that, in Judaism, I was free to challenge certain texts or messages from the Torah, and I would not be judged or looked down upon. I was surprised to learn that there are Jews who are also Buddhist or even atheist.

What also helped me along were the people I met during the course. Jeff and I were not the only interracial—and at the moment, interfaith—couple in the course. Some of the people we met would go on to become dear friends—there was the stunning Marisol from Venezuela, and her husband, the quiet and calm Rob. The woman with beautifully smooth dark skin and tightly curled thick black hair named Sharon, from Nicaragua, was engaged to Gregg, a handsome physician. And there was a Catholic lawyer named Monica, who was to be married to the nice, kind, and gentle soul Dan. While I had expected to meet others in the class who were new to Judaism, seeing these other interracial and interfaith couples really helped me feel like I fit in, like I wasn't the only person who was interested in exploring the faith.

Sharon and Monica were attending the program as part of the conversion process in order to have a Jewish wedding, which was common for interfaith couples who wanted to have a traditional Jewish wedding. Because Jeff and I were already married, I did not feel the pressure of converting and instead was able to focus on enjoying the process of learning.

For the next four years I continued to learn and be part of the Jewish community. It was during that time that I realized just how important the Jewish faith had become to me. I loved the fact that Judaism can be viewed as more of a cultural way of being than a religious belief, and at some point over the course of those four years, I went from simply honoring my commitment to learn about the faith, to actually loving and embracing many aspects of it. In my heart, I knew that raising my family in a Jewish household was what I wanted to do. I was ready to convert.

I called Mary Lou to share the news with her. "I've got some news to share with you." I paused. "But . . . with you being a Christian, it might not be what you'd like to hear."

"What's going on?" she immediately asked.

"How would you feel . . . if I decided to convert to Judaism?"

She was quiet for a moment. "Well, many Christians might not like to hear of your decision to convert since the Jews don't believe in Jesus Christ as their Savior. They might pray for your soul because they'd think you'll go to hell. You and your family might also get discriminated against, which you are already familiar with being a minority in America. But for me, I'm happy for you in whatever you decide. I think your decision will reduce a lot of future conflicts when it comes to raising children together under one household."

"When we have kids, I don't know what they'll be. Maybe Jeff and I would call them Jewitnamese," I added quickly.

Even though she was Methodist, Mary Lou was unwavering in her support of me. Yet I wasn't sure how my Vietnamese mother would react. Even though she didn't mind that Jeff was Jewish, she sure had a problem with me becoming too Americanized. How would she feel after she found out her daughter was going to convert to Judaism?

CHAPTER SEVENTEEN
NEW LIFE, NEW JOB

Not long after the wedding, I realized something—I was lonely. Not in my home life with Jeff; rather, at work. I had gone from working at Lucent in Kentucky, where I consistently had support from a huge team of wonderful people, to spending most of my time in a large building on a huge campus, surrounded by other employees who were super smart, but didn't have much time or use for socializing. My boss, no longer with a corner office in the same building as me, was located across the country in New Jersey. I felt very much on my own.

In an attempt to challenge myself, I started programming and automating my work, which eventually had the opposite effect I was going for, as it cut my work time by half. Radio Frequency Identification (RFID) was a new technology at the time, and after I'd been trained by the person whose position I was taking over, no one else seemed to know much about what my job actually entailed or how to support me. My boss, John, was a great guy, but he was in New Jersey and didn't seem to understand that I could take on more work.

After several attempts to get more work were ignored, I got permission to work from home and leave early on the days my work was completed. The days I left early, I'd get a few errands done or relax on the hammock—there was ample time for that sort of thing. I felt guilty though—there I was, getting paid a full salary, while only working half the time I should be. It wasn't like the work wasn't getting done, but having automated much of it, I still felt like I was stealing from the company.

"You've got the dream job," Jeff said to me one day when he got home from work. "I would love it if my work day included a nap in the hammock!"

"Don't get too jealous," I told him. "I'm probably getting pretty close to automating myself out of a job. When that happens, I guess I'll have to fire myself."

One weekend, I ended up talking with Jeff's dad on the phone when he called. "Jeff says you've got quite the sweet job situation," Richard said.

"I'm very well rested. But I don't feel good not being challenged."

He laughed. "Since we first met, I've felt this about you—your personality is really best suited for sales, not engineering. Have you ever thought of getting into the mortgage industry?"

"I have not. I don't know anything about it."

"Has that ever stopped you in the past?"

He did have a point. "No, but . . . " I trailed off, not sure why I was resisting the suggestion. I was dealing with machines and equipment, which, though it paid well, was not something I was passionate about. What I loved was working with people and making a difference in their lives.

"You should explore the mortgage industry. It's financially rewarding and you'd make a difference in people's lives." My ears perked up at that.

"Well, you're making it sound pretty good," I said. "But I know nothing about the mortgage business. In Vietnam, if people wanted to buy a home, they had to pay cash; there were no mortgages from the bank."

"But you're not in Vietnam," Richard said, laughing. "You're here in America. And the truth of it is—the financial industry loves to get people in debt. You have a master's in engineering and a bachelor's in mathematics. You have a head for numbers, and a personality to go with it. You should at least think about it. You don't have to make any decisions right this second, but if you ask me, I don't think you have anything to lose. Let Jeff take care of things while you get started. I believe in you and think you'll be great."

From the first time I met him in Connecticut, Richard had made me feel as if I were part of the family, and he had become someone whose suggestions and opinions carried a lot of weight. I had a discussion about it with Jeff, and then, with Richard's encouraging words in my mind, I decided to change careers.

That meant leaving a six-figure salary with five weeks of paid vacation and working completely on commission as a loan officer. Instead of working with machines, equipment, and networks, I was helping people through assisting them with the process of getting a loan to buy a house. Home ownership was one facet of the quintessential American Dream, and it made me feel good that I could play a role in helping others get there.

* * *

As expected, I didn't make much money at first, despite working six days a week. I think I made twenty-four thousand dollars that first year, which, when you considered how many hours I was working, was certainly nowhere near what I had been making at the Bell Labs.

But the work itself was so rewarding. I hadn't realized how much I missed being able to really interact with people; at Lucent I had helped our clients with their telecommunications systems, but as a loan officer, I was working directly with all sorts of people who were eager to own their own home.

Jeff was happy to support me as I acclimated myself to my new career, but it was really my father-in-law who became my personal cheerleader for the endeavor. In the early stages, Richard would call daily to encourage me to hang in there. He was a safe place for me to vent any frustrations or doubts I had about whether or not I had done the right thing—I admit, it was difficult to go from making six figures and napping on the hammock at midday to working six days a week and making not even a quarter of what I had been.

"Keep working hard, kid, as you always have been! Put in your hours now and it will pay off later," Richard would say. "It'll be tough going at first, but give it two years of hard work and I promise you'll see results, if not sooner."

"I just don't know if this was the right choice," I said. "I barely made anything."

"You knew that was going to happen at first. And you know what? That's about how much I made my first year, too."

"Really?"

"Yes. But after that two-year mark, I began to make considerably more. And you will, too, if not sooner. You just have to

hang in there. Don't get too discouraged. Channel your dis-
couragement into diligence, and in another year, you'll see a
big shift."

And wouldn't you know it—he was right.

* * *

We had been married for two years when Jeff told me he'd like
to go to Vietnam with me.

"I'd like to see the country where you were born," he said.

"Really?" I asked, surprised that he was so intrigued about
my place of origin that he would want to go there.

"Of course," he said. "I feel like I would know you even better than I do, to see where you grew up, where you came from."

I was excited to go back to Vietnam with Jeff. To be able to
share such an experience with him meant a lot, but it was also
a reminder of how far I had come.

People in Vietnam were surprised to see Jeff and me together.
Interracial couples there are rare, so we got lots of attention
whenever we went out. It was not uncommon for strangers to
approach and ask if we were married, and, once finding out we
were, did we have children yet? Yes, we were married, no we
didn't have kids yet, though that was a path we would eventually
go down. In Vietnam, though, if you're serious about somebody
then you're going to have children with them right away.

We backpacked around Ha Noi and Da Nang, before we
headed down south to Ho Chi Minh City to see my family. In
the center of the country, Da Nang, I brought Jeff to my childhood home, which I hadn't seen since that day Uncle Hong
had taken me. It was the rainy season in Vietnam, and it was

raining heavily that day, the lake overflowing and flooding the surrounding roads.

"This is where I grew up," I told Jeff. "Though it wasn't a police station then."

There was a part of me that wanted to go over to where my house used to be, but I knew that was an unwise idea; it wasn't my home anymore, and the Vietnamese police probably wouldn't like to hear "I used to live here" as it also meant "You guys stole my family's home." The water lilies still bobbed on the surface of the lake as the rain poured down.

Jeff and I also stopped to visit my father's first wife in Tam Ky, the only place in Vietnam we really experienced any discrimination.

"I remember getting these looks when we met up in Ashland, Kentucky," Jeff said, as we were walking down a crowded street. He stood head and shoulders above many of the people, but it wasn't his skin color or height that caused them to shoot such nasty looks our way—it was the fact we were an interracial couple. Tam Ky, full of Viet Cong during the war, still had a strong communist belief against foreigners, and it was the same place Mary Lou had been discriminated against, when we had tried to check into a hotel, and I wondered, as we left, if the area would ever become more accepting.

Jeff and I stayed with my family when we made it down to Ho Chi Minh City. My family still lived in the same building, but had been able to expand from their two rooms and spruce the place up quite a bit. Mother lived there with my brother Fourth, his wife Koi, and their child. Though renovations had been done and the place was in much better shape than when I lived there, there was still a hole in the ground for the toilet, and there was no air conditioning to remove the heat and humidity from the sultry air.

When my Vietnamese family first met Jeff, they regarded him for a moment and then asked, "Can this white boy eat hot and spicy food?" in such a tone that clearly indicated they did not think he would be able to do such a thing.

Little did they know that Jeff *loves* spicy food, so I felt more than confident in telling them "Yes." What I declined to add was that I'd already had a little pep talk with Jeff, where I laid the ground rules for ensuring my family would fall in love with him. "Just eat whatever they put in front of you," I had told him, knowing that they were going to test him. Though they took it a bit further than I expected.

Jeff was bombarded with all sorts of spicy and exotic food, some of which even I wouldn't eat. He ate the raw hot pepper like he was snacking on apple slices, and I watched as my relatives' faces lit up—he had passed the initiation test, as if he were pledging a fraternity.

Then came eel. Followed by some dried fish, spicy shrimp, and even pork, though I had told them Jews did not eat pork.

"Okay, they don't eat pork," my cousin said. "But let's have some pig meat!"

Someone had even gone out and procured some grasshopper and scorpion, two foods I *knew* no one in my family ate; I think they just wanted to see how far he would go. And wouldn't you know it, that white boy who they assumed couldn't handle his spicy food ate everything they put in front of him, except the fried scorpion. But I don't think anyone in my family would've eaten it either—probably a good thing, because if it wasn't prepared exactly right, the poison could kill you.

After seeing Jeff eat everything they put in front of him, my family came to a consensus. "This white man is unexpectedly unique," they told me—in Vietnamese, so Jeff had no idea what they were saying—"We like him and think you'll be happy together."

* * *

A few days before we left, Jeff and I took Fourth and his wife out for dinner while Mother stayed at home. My brother and Jeff had really hit it off during the trip, and Jeff and I had started to talk about possibly sponsoring them.

"Is that something you'd be interested in?" I asked. "Immigrating to America?"

They both nodded immediately and emphatically. "Yes!" Fourth said. He had a good job, working in management for Unilever, but I knew both he and his children would have so many more opportunities in America.

"I have family in California," Koi added. "I would love to be closer to them."

Jeff and I looked at each other, smiling. "It's something we're more than happy to look into," I said. "I would also really like it if you guys would keep it confidential for now. These things can take a long time, and I don't want to cause family drama." I could hear my mother asking me not too long ago if we would sponsor _her_. "We just can't afford to bring the entire family over."

After returning from Vietnam, Jeff and I continued to discuss sponsoring my brother and his family. It was a lengthy process that involved getting all of their Vietnamese documents and birth certificates translated to English and notarized. We also had to show the immigration office paperwork including tax returns and bank statements that showed we could financially support and care for five additional family members. We also had to sign documents stating we would not seek any assistance from the government for at least five years, until they became US citizens. There were a lot of hoops to go through, a lot of red tape to navigate. Not to mention the reality of when they finally arrived—we would be welcoming five new people into our family. It would be challenging, yes, but it was a challenge both Jeff and I were up for. I was now in a position where I could pay it forward and help bring some of my family to America, as Mother had always hoped. Little did we know that it would take well over a decade for them to finally arrive.

CHAPTER EIGHTEEN
JEWITNAMESE

"I think I'm ready to officially convert," I said to Jeff one morning. It was 2004, and I was pregnant. If our children were going to be considered Jewish from the get-go, they needed to be born to a Jewish mother; otherwise, they would have to go through the conversion process themselves.

But my desire to convert was not because our family would be expanding—I'd been studying Judaism for four years. I'd made friends, participated in many different community events, and volunteered with Hadassah, a volunteer organization for Jewish women in America, founded over one hundred years ago, before Israel was even a state. Hadassah promotes positive social change and advocates empowerment for women and girls.

While it had started as something that I had promised my husband I would explore, during my years of study, Judaism had become something I embraced and felt from the heart.

"That's great," Jeff said. "It is a bit of a process, converting."

"Yes, I know."

We were sitting at the kitchen table, just finishing breakfast. Zoe sat patiently at the corner by Jeff, ears pricked, hoping an errant crumb might find its way to her.

But then Jeff pushed back from his chair and stood up, leaving his plate on the table. He left the room and then returned a moment later with a piece of paper, which he handed to me.

"What's this?" I asked, scanning the page.

"Well, if you want to join the synagogue, you have to donate a percentage of your income every year."

I continued reading. "Wait a second—they want to automatically withdraw the money from our account every month?" I knew it was common for people to donate money to the church they worshipped at, but I had never heard of it being automatically deducted, like a car payment or something.

"Yep," Jeff said. "I think it might be ten percent of our income. Well, if you officially convert, you're expected to donate. There's a chance we might have to show our tax returns if asked."

I put the paper down. "What?" I said. "Are you serious?"

He gave me a loving smile. "Honey, it's expensive to be a Jew. You are expected to pay until it hurts."

I found this idea so off-putting that I didn't bring up converting again for a few months. But it was something I couldn't fully avoid if I wanted my children to be born Jewish.

The money wasn't the only hurdle I'd have to get over—those rabbis really want to make sure that you're serious about converting, and one of the ways they do that is by rejecting you three times. Now, I knew it was a tradition and happened to everyone who expressed a desire to convert, yet even knowing your rejection is preordained doesn't always make it easy to take.

Jeff and I shopped around for the right synagogue. There were a number of synagogues in Denver, some reform, some conservative, a few Orthodox. We decided to join one of the conservative synagogues, because I liked the people I met. The rabbi, though, reminded me more of a businessman than a rabbi; he was not the sort of extroverted, warm and friendly type of person that you might expect from a religious leader, on first impression, anyway. He would be considerably more welcoming to me in later years, but when I first showed up hoping to convert, I certainly felt he was being rather standoffish.

"So you think you're ready to convert," he said one day, a few months after Jeff had informed me I'd need to donate part of my income to the synagogue.

"Yes," I said.

He eyed me from behind his desk but said nothing. I took a deep breath. "I made the commitment to my husband to explore Judaism after we got married. I didn't go into it with any preconceived ideas about converting—I told myself I would only do it if I came to truly believe in the Jewish faith. Which I have."

"You cannot even be considered for conversion until you have completed the Intro to Judaism course."

"I have," I said.

"Then you need to make your home kosher."

To keep a kosher home meant adhering to dietary requirements outlined by traditional Jewish law. The three main kosher food categories were meat, dairy, and pareve, which included anything that wasn't meat or dairy, such as fruit, vegetables, eggs, and fish. Only certain types of meat were permitted, and the animals had to be slaughtered by a *kosher* rabbi who was specifically trained according to Jewish laws. Other parts of keeping a kosher home included having specific utensils to be used only with meat, as well as not serving meat and dairy together.

What a headache! I could already hear the arguments Jeff and I might get into if I messed up this kosher law and mixed meat with milk or used the wrong utensil to cut something. It seemed like a minefield of potential marital conflicts awaiting us.

Now, the thing was, many Jews I knew didn't have a kosher home, and I knew that I would not be keeping one, either. I looked at the rabbi. "I could lie to you—and myself—by telling you that I would turn my home kosher, but that would be extremely difficult, as I've spent a lifetime eating food that is not kosher. I sure love shrimp, crab legs, and lobster and you want me to give them all up? That seems impossible!"

The rabbi frowned. "This place is not for you, then. Maybe there is a synagogue down the road that might take you. One of those reform ones. You should go talk to them."

"We checked out different synagogues and like yours the most."

"Then perhaps you are not yet ready to become a Jew."

It was frustrating to feel like I wasn't being taken seriously, even though I knew that converts must go through the rejection process. I had, after all, taken my Judaism studies quite seriously. I was not going to be deterred, though. I continued to go to services at the synagogue and stood out like a sore thumb because I was the only Asian there. I would often see the rabbi, and though he didn't say much, I could tell that he took note of my presence and the fact that I had not taken his advice to go to the synagogue "down the road."

Months later, we went back to the synagogue for a meeting with the rabbi. Before we went in, Jeff took my hand.

"Listen," Jeff told me, "this is just my assumption, but I don't think many Jewish leaders want to have kids who don't belong to the community just because their mothers aren't Jewish. I looked into it a little bit, and interfaith marriages of American Jews have been over fifty percent since the 1990s. That's a lot. And just think—if leaders don't accept the parents or their kids, then they won't join the synagogue, and the synagogue won't get dues because those people aren't members."

"That's a good point," I said, mulling it over. Perhaps the rabbi might not be so quick to dismiss me this time, if he knew I was pregnant. "Is it really all about the money?"

Jeff smiled. "No, of course not. But we are not much different than you Asians. Money is always a part of it, even when running a synagogue."

The rabbi greeted us coolly, and didn't give any indication that he remembered us from a few months ago, or that he'd seen us at regular services, which we had continued to attend. He also could not find my file in his cabinet; Jeff and I suspected that he threw it in the trash after hearing my comment about how much I loved shrimp and crab legs.

"I'd like to convert," I said. "We had visited with you a few months ago, and you told me I should go down the road, but, as we said before, we really like this synagogue. You also said we needed to turn our home kosher before I could convert."

"You don't need to convert to participate in the Jewish community, as you've been doing these past years," the rabbi said. "You can live a rewarding life without converting. Why would you want to be Jewish?"

He gave me a pointed look and then his gaze went to the door, as if he was expecting we would just get up and leave. Perhaps this was the second of my three rejections. Perhaps he really thought I couldn't handle such cold treatment.

"After I've studied Judaism the last four years, I finally feel it in my heart and want to be part of the Jewish community. If I wanted to fake the conversion, then I would have done it prior to us getting married so that we could have a Jewish wedding. I knew from the beginning that a conversion that does not come from the heart is empty and meaningless."

"You turned us away the last time," Jeff chimed in. "And we made some adjustments."

"We are COMMITTED to having a kosher home," I added, not wanting to start off the conversion process by lying to the rabbi about having a kosher home.

"My wife is extremely committed to the Jewish community and she wants to raise our kids Jewish," Jeff said.

At the mention of the word "kids," the rabbi looked up, first at Jeff, then at me. "It's your call whether you want to convert her and let our kids be part of the community. If not, we'll walk away. Just so you know, we are expecting a baby."

As we stood up, the rabbi said, "OK, OK. I'll work with you on your conversion."

* * *

Because I had already spent years studying Judaism and being a part of the community, once the rabbi agreed to my conversion, the process was relatively quick. The day of my conversion, I was called before the *Beit Din*, a Rabbinic court comprised of three people: the rabbi, and two other observant members of the synagogue who are knowledgeable about the conversion procedure. In this case, it was a gentleman named Albert Cohen and the rabbi's assistant, Joyce Perlmutter.

The three of them sat behind a small wooden table facing me, the rabbi in the middle, Joyce and Albert on either side. I sat across from them, knowing that Jeff was waiting for me just outside the room.

"Why did you choose Judaism?" the rabbi asked. "The path of the Jews is not an easy one. Jews have been persecuted, forced to flee their homeland; life as a Jew is not easy. Still to this day, Jews are discriminated against and must overcome obstacles that gentiles do not."

"I was not brought up with organized religion. But I have always wondered if there was something more out there, something bigger than myself. And when I read about the struggles that the Jews have gone through, I see parallels for things I have lived through. People in my home country were persecuted. I had to flee my homeland, and I found myself in a country where I look different and have been discriminated against because of it. While it's true that my initial motivation for exploring Judaism is because the man I love is Jewish, it has evolved into more than that, and become something I feel in my heart. I am dedicated to raising my children Jewish, in a Jewish home. It is not only what my husband and I feel is right for our family, but what is natural."

Our conversation continued for about another half an hour, with the rabbi asking me questions about my commitment to Judaism and the Jewish people. I answered truthfully and from the heart.

When the meeting with the *Beit Din* was complete, it was time for the mikveh ceremony, one of the last steps in my conversion process. This immersion was a symbol of transforming from one state to another—in my case, becoming a Jew. Jeff came with me, though he would not be present during the immersion; only the mikveh attendant, Joyce, would be in the room to watch me submerge. She showed me the preparation room where I had to shower first and then wrap myself in a towel. I would fully submerge myself in the mikveh three times, and I had to be completely naked, including no jewelry or makeup.

I followed Joyce into the room, both the floor and the walls covered in tiles in variated shades of earth tone. The pool was rectangular and small, very simple. There were three steps leading down into the water and a metal hand railing.

I slowly walked down the three steps into the mikveh. The water's temperature was a few degrees above lukewarm, so not unpleasant at all.

I lowered myself into the water. Once submerged, I lifted my feet off the tiles so I was fully suspended for a moment, floating weightless. I did this three times. And then—

I arose from the water, a Jew.

I only had a second to really revel in the fact before I was interrupted by a knock at the door.

"Honey?" Jeff called. "Did you remember to bring the checkbook? I need to write a few checks to pay for all of today's fees."

"It's in my purse!" I yelled back.

I guess Jeff was right—it really was expensive to be a Jew.

From the beginning, almost everyone in Jeff's family had made me feel welcome. But I knew just how much converting to

Judaism would mean to them, so even though it was something I was doing for myself, something that I had to genuinely feel within my own spirit, it made me happy to know how much it would mean to his family, as well.

I wasn't who my mother-in-law envisioned when thinking about the nice Jewish girl she hoped her son would eventually marry, but our relationship has grown and evolved, and today, we both love and respect each other a great deal. Richard, on the other hand, I would say was smitten with me on day one and that goes for Uncle Bob in DC, too. Both Richard and Uncle Bob were not shy in letting me know just how much they considered me part of the family. My father-in-law would often tell me how lucky he felt that I was a part of their family, and that he viewed me as a daughter, not a daughter-in-law, which meant a lot to me, because I felt like he was the father I never had.

Jeff's older sister Amy is like a sister, a friend that, over the years, I have found to be someone I can talk to and know she'll listen without judgment—a true gift. And Uncle Bob, while he was alive, for his part, would call our house every so often and leave a message if we weren't home, usually something along the lines of: "Hi Nhi! It's Uncle Bob. I just wanted to call and say hi. Also wanted to check to make sure you're investing some of your money in real estate."

If Jeff heard these messages, he would raise his eyebrows and shake his head, smiling. "It's great that my family loves you, but can my uncle at least mention my name in the voicemail as well? After all, I'm his nephew." But I knew that he was joking, that deep down he was as happy as I was that his family accepted me as one of their own.

Sometimes, my memories take me way back to when I was a scared, skinny kid in the refugee camp, feeling completely adrift and alone, wondering if I would ever have a family again to love me. It had seemed hopeless then, but then there were the Hearns, and now my husband and his family—my Jewish family. A family who accepts me for who I am and allows me to love and cherish them in return.

* * *

On June 24, 2004—our fourth wedding anniversary—our son, Max, was born. A year and a half later, in early November, we welcomed Sarah into the family. Jeff's family and both of my families were thrilled, yet being so far from us meant we could not rely on them much for support in those sleepless early days.

Adjusting to parenthood was a challenge because we didn't have any family nearby. It was such a busy, chaotic time; I did not take any maternity leave, and instead did as much work from home as I could while the baby was napping. It became clear quite quickly, though, that if that was going to continue, I would need some help around the house.

I placed an ad in the classified section of a magazine looking for a nanny. We had a number of applicants, and I interviewed a few of them before Kim walked through our door. Kim was forty-eight, a patient, kind, caring woman, who had come to the United States from Vietnam five years previously.

A smile lit up her face the moment she laid eyes on Max and she held her arms out for him. I handed him over and just knew once I saw how she cradled him and the loving expression in her eyes that she was the one. Not wanting to seem too eager too soon, I took my time and explained to her the situation.

"I'm able to work from home quite often, so I'll be around, but I do need to spend some time each day during the week doing work. So I'll just need help with cooking, cleaning, and taking care of the baby. Especially when I'm on the phone with a client; I don't want my clients to hear a baby crying in the background."

"I'm here to help," she said, looking up at me with such genuine care that I couldn't help but think of my own childhood nanny, who had been so abruptly removed from my life. Was it mere coincidence, then, that decades later, a different version of my beloved nanny would find her way to my own home to help me take care of my own children?

"You're hired," I told her as she sat on the couch, rocking Max. "Can you start tomorrow?"

"Absolutely," she said. "Though I am only available for a few months. I'm planning to do something else after that."

"Oh," I said, crestfallen but trying not to show it. "Well . . ." A few months were better than nothing. "A few months it is, then. I guess I'll have to look for someone else after that."

Perhaps someone else would have chosen to hire a person who was available for the long term. I did question whether hiring Kim for only a couple months would be smart—it would be hard to say goodbye to her once those few months were up. But then she started to sing a lullaby in Vietnamese, one I wasn't familiar with, yet the language, the cadence of her voice—I could've been transported back to my childhood, my own nanny singing me to sleep.

Kim was a true blessing. She would show up in the morning, as Jeff was on his way out the door. Once acclimated with the layout and where things were kept, she proved to be as hard a worker as I was.

"I'll take care of that," she would say—one time referring to the dishes on the table that needed to be cleared, another time it was a diaper that needed to be changed.

But a few months has turned into over fifteen years—Kim is still in our lives, though the family joke is that she's no longer the children's nanny, but mine!

* * *

Having two young children might not seem like the ideal time to change careers, but that's just what Jeff decided to do. After Max was born, I continued to work, managing to juggle a new-born's erratic sleep schedule and on-demand nursing by working from home. I'm not sure I could have managed without Kim, particularly because Jeff worked long hours and was away from us for most of the day.

"I feel like I'm missing out," he said. "The kids are just getting bigger, and my work hours are brutal . . . " I could see the frustration in his eyes.

"What if you switched careers?" I asked.

"Switch careers? I don't think now is the right time for that. And what would I do?"

"You could work in the mortgage industry, with me," I said. "You carried things while I was getting started. And now I can do that for you. Because you won't make much money at first."

He gave me a skeptical look. "We've got kids to think about. It doesn't seem like this is the right time."

"It's probably never going to seem like the ideal time. But if you want to be around more—and eventually making way better money—then I think you should do it."

"But what if I don't end up making any money?"

"Jeff," I said. "I doubt that would happen. If it did, though, then you can always go back to being an engineer, or you could do something else. You have options, and if you want, I think you should explore them."

Jeff decided to give it a try, and it didn't take long before he realized he loved the change as much as I did. Which is not to say it wasn't difficult—that whole time was really a blur, having the two young kids and carrying the load for the entire family while Jeff found his footing.

But I was so happy that I had the ability to do so. It was hard work, but it was rewarding, and we reaped the benefits of that in many ways. We both appreciated the flexibility our schedules afforded us. Working in the mortgage industry exposed both of us to new opportunities we likely would not have been aware of if we stayed in our previous careers.

Even though working together as a couple had many benefits, it also had its challenges, as Jeff and I found ourselves together much more than we'd previously been used to. We had to really work to improve our communication and reduce misunderstanding. We began to see our therapist Todd on a regular basis, both as a personal and a business counselor. One of the best things Todd suggested was, in order to protect our marriage, Jeff and I should have our own offices to create space during our work hours, hopefully creating a better work/life balance.

* * *

Jeff and I had talked about raising the kids both Jewish and Vietnamese, which meant I only spoke Vietnamese to them. Yes, they'd be growing up in America, but we both wanted them to have a strong understanding of their Jewish and Vietnamese identities.

As Max grew into a toddler, he was still not speaking at all. Like any new parent, I at first found it concerning that Max could not talk compared to other kids his age. It didn't mean he couldn't communicate—he was fluent in all sorts of guttural sounds he'd employ to try to show me what it was he wanted, but he still was not speaking any actual words. But to be honest—all his squawking drove me crazy and gave me nightmares.

The pediatrician assured me, though, that Max was right on track developmentally, and many bilingual children are slower to talk at first. Thankfully, not long after his second birthday, Max said his first word to me—*mẹ,* which, in Vietnamese, means *mom.*

"He said his first word!" I exclaimed to Jeff when he got home from work. Relief flooded through me that the pediatrician had been right. "*Mẹ.*" I looked at Max, who was sitting on the floor, playing with his blocks. He looked right at me and said it back.

"That's wonderful!" Jeff exclaimed. "Although, that's not his first word. I'm pretty sure he called me *da* this morning."

Though we'll never know for sure whether Max said *mẹ* or *da* first, once he uttered those words, his vocabulary in both languages increased exponentially and he started talking like a normal toddler in two languages. After our experience with Max, we knew what to expect with Sarah. She followed roughly the same timeline; she was a month shy of her second birthday when she said her first Vietnamese word to me, her first English word to Jeff.

People outside of our family couldn't get over the fact that they could speak and understand two different languages at such a young age. I didn't speak English to Max and Sarah out in public, either, because I'd heard that, for children of multilingual households, once the parent starts speaking English to them in public, the kids take it as a greenlight to also speak English back at home.

Jeff and I always spoke English to each other in front of the kids, but I only spoke Vietnamese to them. When the kids spoke to me in English, I always replied in Vietnamese, "I don't understand what you're saying" and they had to switch to Vietnamese.

The effectiveness of my diligence in the matter was made clear one evening at dinner, when Max, who was seven at the time, put his fork down and looked at Jeff.

"Dad?" he said. "Sarah and I were wondering something." He cast a glance in my direction before continuing to address Jeff. "How come when we speak English to Mom she doesn't understand, but when *you* speak English to her, she does?"

"Yeah," Sarah said. "It doesn't make sense. How does that happen?"

I didn't say anything, curious as to what Jeff's reply might be. Having not anticipated a question like this, we hadn't talked about what a good answer might be.

"That's a great question," he said after a moment. He looked at me, barely able to conceal his smile. "And you know what,

I'm afraid I don't have a good answer. Why do you think that's the case?"

The kids looked at me with confusion. And in Vietnamese, Sarah said, "That's so weird. I'm still not sure why that is."

They both went back to eating their dinner, and continued to speak only Vietnamese to me and English to Jeff.

* * *

It was around that time that Max and Sarah began to learn more about their Jewish heritage as well. We sent them to the synagogue twice a week so they could begin to learn to read Hebrew and start their Jewish education. At first, it was a new experience and they didn't mind going. But I began to notice some resistance when it was time to go—they would rather stay home so they could play with the other neighborhood kids, or they were tired after a day at school, or they just simply didn't feel like going. Their reasons varied, but Jeff and I always responded in the same way: *Even when you don't like it, or it's not exactly what you want to be doing, it's what we have to do, because that's what we do as Jews.*

* * *

When Max and Sarah were old enough—thirteen and twelve respectively—it was time for their coming of age ceremony— Bar Mitzvah, for boys, and Bat Mitzvah, for girls. Because they were doing it together, it was known as B'nei Mitzvah. For this special occasion, Jeff and I decided to fly the family to Israel. My own personal experience had taught me that information is assimilated more easily and more deeply when you're able to directly immerse yourself in it. So we arranged for a tour specializing in Bar and Bat Mitzvah.

In preparation for the special event, the kids had to get special bar/bat mitzvah tutoring from our cantor for nine months. Wanting to learn, I sat in the room every week while Cantor Martin Goldstein taught Max and Sarah how to chant parts of the Torah and Haftorah. I told them I wanted to learn with them. Though I was present, I had promised the kids I would not chime in or read along with them. It was such a special moment for me, and the kids loved and "hated" me for it. They loved how engaging I was, and hated the fact that whenever they did not do all their homework, I was able to tell them that they only practiced a quarter of their homework since I attended the tutoring and could read the Hebrew portion that the cantor expected them to learn.

I was amazed watching the cantor teach the kids how to perform when delivering their speeches, similar to what one would learn in Toastmasters. But they were only twelve and thirteen, learning how to speak in front of a crowd, when I knew many adults in their position would be terrified. At that moment, I wished I had that type of tutoring prior to delivering my valedictorian speech many years earlier.

After the tutoring period, Max and Sarah had a small ceremony at our synagogue prior to us leaving for Israel. They read their Torah and Haftorah passages in Hebrew and delivered their speeches in English to the whole congregation.

We then left for Israel days later. My dear friend Lora, a long-time African American friend, went with us, and we spent a few days in Tel Aviv, to give everyone a chance to recover from jet lag and get acclimated to our new surroundings. A few other friends also were flying to Israel for the ceremony. Lora was a great addition to our trip since she is always cheery and funny and her laughter is contagious, which makes everyone love being around her. We were laughing about our small group being representative of the diversity of the United States in Israel: White, Asian, Black, and "combo-meal-kids." Tel Aviv is a bustling, vibrant coastal city, renowned for its colorful Bauhaus architecture and its lively nightlife. Initially, I had been expecting a reception similar to what Jeff and I had received in Tam Ky or Ashland, Kentucky—the judgmental, often mean-spirited looks. But I was in for quite the pleasant surprise! Everybody was very friendly and accepting of our mixed race family who had come together in the Jewish faith. Of course, greeting them in Hebrew might have had something to do with that.

After a few days in Tel Aviv, we began our journey to Jerusalem. We stopped at the Tower of David, an ancient citadel near the Jaffa Gate, which was the main entrance to the Old City. We stood on the observation deck and had a stunning view of the Old City. We also spent some time exploring the Museum of the History of Jerusalem, which was located within the Citadel.

From there, it was through the Jaffa Gate and straight into the Old City. Not even half a square mile in size, the city's parameters were constructed of stone walls built in the sixteenth century. It was divided into four distinct neighborhoods: The Christian Quarter, the Jewish Quarter, the Muslim Quarter, and the Armenian Quarter. No matter what religious belief you ascribed to, the Old City was an area steeped in history.

Just walking along the narrow cobblestone alleys was incredible—they were over two thousand years old! Had even one of those cobblestones been in America, it would have been preserved and put on display in some museum, yet here in the Old City, we walked right over them, as people had been doing for thousands of years.

We spent some of our time exploring the many different *shuks* or markets in the four different quarters. The sidewalks were lined with the various wares the vendors were hawking and it reminded me of some of the markets in Vietnam I used to go to as a child. You could find anything at those markets, it seemed, so long as you were willing to look for it. Jewelry, tapestries, vintage clothes, art of all sorts . . . I was in my element. That market reminded me of my childhood experience, especially at Cho Lon market when I followed my cigarette dealer. Jeff, Lora, and the kids had the best time watching me bargain when buying things such as purses, Jewish gifts like Shabbat candles, and scarves. There was a camel purse I particularly liked, though not for the asking price of three hundred dollars. With a smile, I asked the merchant if he would sell it for fifty.

He scoffed. "*Two* fifty," he retorted and looked at me as if I was from a different planet. "It's a quality camel purse. Let me burn the leather to show you that it's real leather. Very nice."

"It is," I agreed. "But your price is way more than I want to spend on a purse. I could do sixty."

Jeff, Lora, and the kids stood just a few feet off to the side, their eyes going back and forth between the merchant and me, as if they were watching a competitive sport, which, in a way, I suppose they were.

I kept a smile on my face the whole time and joked around, and in the end, got the purse for eighty dollars. After I handed the merchant the money, he looked at Jeff, shaking his head. "Who is this woman?"

Jeff grinned. "That's my wife!"

"Our mom!" Max and Sarah chimed in.

The merchant returned their smiles. "She's a hard woman—just like my wife!"

The kids, particularly Max, were very interested in how it was I had managed to get a three-hundred-dollar purse for eighty dollars. "When did your bargaining skills get so good?" he asked.

"I learned young," I told him. "That's how I survived on the streets of Saigon when I was a kid—we needed money for food and I had to learn fast how to bargain and be a good negotiator."

He had a similar look of awe on his face that the merchant did. "I want to learn how to do that," he said.

"To start off, the key to a successful negotiation is that both parties walk away feeling content, and not mad," I said, giving Max and Sarah their first lesson in bargaining.

While in the Old City, we visited the Jewish Quarter, which was located in the southeastern section of the city. Its borders consisted of the Zion Gate to its south, the Armenian Quarter to its west, the Temple Mount in the east, and the Street of the Chain to the north, which extended all the way to the Western Wall. Before we visited the Western Wall, we explored the Roman Cardo marketplace. Magnificent stone columns lined the streets and we passed beautiful murals and mosaics depicting religious scenes, and the sense of history was almost palpable in the air. For thousands of years, Jewish people had walked these narrow streets. And I was there, enjoying the experience with my family.

We then made our way to the Western Wall, which is considered Judaism's holiest site. The ancient limestone wall is a place that Jews have come to visit for centuries, to pray, mourn, and celebrate. As its name implies, the Western Wall is located to the west of Temple Mount, which is a holy site for Jews, Christians, and Muslims.

Over the next several days, we explored much of Israel. We visited Yad Vashem, the country's national memorial to the victims of the Holocaust, which housed, among other things, the Hall of Names and the Avenue of the Righteous Among Nations. The kids had a great time getting to dig for artifacts at the Tel Maresha Dig, located at Beit Guvrin, though they might have enjoyed themselves even more when we were able to spend some time with Bedouins, nomadic people whose name means "desert dwellers." We learned all about their culture and customs and even got to go for a camel ride in the Negev, which was great fun though my legs started to ache after we'd gone quite some distance.

We concluded the day at the Dead Sea, where we floated in the salty water and took a jeep ride up a mountain that was made entirely of salt. It was easily one of the most unbelievable things I had ever seen, and when we stopped, I got out, went over, and licked the wall of the mountain, just to see. Yes, it was salt. And because it was made up almost entirely of salt, no vegetation could grow. Jeff broke off a big piece and handed it to me.

But the main reason for our trip to Israel occurred the following day, December 28—Max and Sarah's B'nai Mitzvah.

The family woke up early, while it was still dark, to begin the drive to Masada, where the ceremony would be held.

Masada is an ancient fortress that sat atop a high plateau in the Judean Desert. The rugged fortress had been constructed by King Herod in the year 30 BCE. Masada would eventually become the last holdout for Jews living in Judea; when the Romans finally succeeded with their siege in April of 73 AD, all but seven of them—two women and five children—took their own lives, rather than surrender and become Roman slaves.

For centuries, Masada was uninhabited. Around the middle of the twentieth century, Israeli scientists and researchers began to excavate the site. In 1966, the Israel Nature and Parks Authority made the area a national park, and about a decade later, a cable car was built that would take visitors right to the top of the mountain.

And it was there, at that place steeped in history, that Max and Sarah would have their B'nai Mitzvah ceremony. We wanted the kids to experience Israel firsthand and learn some of the history of the country. Their ceremony would be small—just myself, Jeff, Lora, and a few others who flew in from Denver—in contrast to the large celebrations that often occurred in America. But it would be just as, if not more, special, because of the historic location.

Though people traditionally dressed up quite fancy for a Bar or Bat Mitzvah, we dressed down for the day, since we would be at the top of Masada, and would explore the rugged area afterward. Still, we were dressed nicely; white button-down shirts paired with slacks for Max and Jeff; Sarah wore a white blouse and a black skirt. For my own outfit, I had chosen black pants and strappy sandals, an off-white shirt over which I wore a purple and blue shawl. Jeff wore a fringed Jewish prayer shawl, called a *tallit*, accented with the same shades of purple and blue. Jeff's parents had given Max and Sarah their own *tallitot* as a gift to celebrate their B'nai Mitzvah.

We took the Masada cableway, which carried us over the low peaks and valleys and the winding switchback that the more adventurous could hike up or down. The cable car was equipped with large windows on all four sides, which gave us an incredible view, and as we ascended, we saw a stunning panorama view of the Dead Sea. While the kids enjoyed the stunning view, I could tell they were both nervous and excited. Their Jewish education had been preparing them for that moment, and it had finally arrived.

The rabbi conducted the service as the sun was rising over the desert. I stood next to Jeff and watched first Max, and then Sarah, read from the Torah scroll in Hebrew, atop a mountain at that holy, historic site, as they crossed the threshold to become adults in the eyes of Jewish law. To witness that as a parent was awe-inspiring and my heart swelled with pride for my children. There might have been times when they argued about going to Hebrew school, but clearly, they had been paying attention. And as I stood there, I couldn't help but also be aware of all the moments that had led us there, that had made that unforgettable moment possible.

CHAPTER NINETEEN
OUR FAMILY GROWS . . . AGAIN!

In the winter of 2016, our family was going to expand again. No, I wasn't pregnant—my brother, Fourth, and his family were finally coming to live with us. The paperwork we had started over a decade ago had finally, thirteen years later, cleared all the hurdles and red tape that was required. Fourth and Koi's children, who were young the last time we saw them in Vietnam, were teenagers. Our family went from four members to nine.

But it could not have been a more joyous occasion.

Though it had taken far longer than anyone expected, it felt as if an emptiness I wasn't even aware of had been filled. To once again live under the same roof with my brother, after all that time, was like a salve to my soul.

And it wasn't just me either—Jeff and the kids welcomed Fourth and his family with open arms. Max and Sarah learned what it meant to love unconditionally. Max shared a room with his cousin Nguyen, and Sarah shared a room with Khanh, who was her age. It was common to pass by their room at night and hear them talking or giggling softly about something.

"Grandma said America was the greatest country in the world," I overheard Khanh confide in Sarah. "And she's right!" I smiled, imagining my mother telling her grandkids the same thing she used to say to my siblings and me when we were kids.

To make sure that my brother and his family would not face the same struggles I had upon my arrival in America, Jeff and I provided them everything they needed—our family's long-time nanny Kim (whose job had pivoted to that of my assistant since the kids were older) helped Fourth and Koi with cooking and cleaning, and Kim and I would split driving duties, since neither my brother nor his wife had their driver's licenses yet. I helped them fill out the necessary paperwork to obtain Social Security numbers and health insurance, as well as registering the kids for school. Eventually, we would give Fourth and Koi driving lessons so they could get their licenses, though a driver's license isn't much use if you don't have a car. I helped them buy a car so they would have the freedom to go out as a family and not have to feel they needed to ask permission first.

There was so much love and harmony in our big family, and Jeff acted like a saint. Not every spouse would be up for the task of taking family in—after all, this wasn't a vacation they'd be departing from in a week. They were there in the morning before Jeff left for work, and there in the evening when he returned home. Some people would grow tired of it, but not Jeff. Every evening when he got home, he walked in the door with a huge smile on his face, eager to hear from everyone about their day. Even when it was just the two of us lying in bed at night, when he would have been free to vent whatever feelings or frustrations he had, he never once complained about taking care of a huge family. To see him open his heart in the way he did just deepened my love for him.

"It makes me so happy to see you getting to make up for lost time with your family," he told me one night as we lay next to each other in bed, the other members of our family asleep in their rooms down the hall. "Just seeing you happy gives me so much joy."

"I'm so glad we were able to get Fourth and his family over here and be able to provide them the support they need." I would occasionally reflect on my own arrival in the United States, staying with Sister Second, who did her best, but who just wasn't equipped to look after a little sister. My early days in America had not been full of familial love and unification, and it filled me with immense gratitude that Jeff and I were able to provide a different experience for my brother and his family.

"You know," Jeff said, "I bet Fourth would excel at running his own business. Do you think he'd be interested in doing something like that?"

"I don't see why not. Maybe we should talk to him about it." Fourth, after all, had been successful as the manager at the ice cream company, where he'd had five hundred employees working under him. I lay there, looking up at the ceiling, feeling Jeff's warmth next to me. It brought a smile to my face just thinking about the amazing opportunities my brother could have. That was the thing about America, as Mother had said—anyone could make something of themselves. I couldn't wait to see all the great things my brother was going to do. But many times, things don't turn out the way we want, especially when it comes to family.

* * *

Fourth, as it turned out, did not have any interest in exploring business ventures in Colorado. After they'd been with us for about three months, they came to talk to us one night after the kids had gone to bed.

"First, we want you to know how thankful we are for what you've done for our family," my brother started. "You have all been so loving and generous, it is more than we ever expected." Koi sat next to him on the couch, her smile looking a little nervous. It was then I got a little feeling, right in the middle of my chest, the sort of discomfort you think you might be able to get rid of if you shifted positions. What it sounded like to me was that my brother was about to follow it up with a *but*—

"But," Fourth said, glancing at Koi and then back to Jeff and me, "we would like to move out and have our own place."

A smile broke out onto my face, and that little feeling of anxiety dissipated. Yes, I'd grown accustomed to our big house, with people coming and going constantly, but I also completely understood Fourth and Koi's desire to have their own home— just them and their kids.

"Well, you know you're welcome to stay with us for as long as you want," I said. "But I get that you'd also want to live on your own."

"We'd be happy to let you stay at one of our rental properties," Jeff said. "That way, you'll have your own place, but still be close by. The best of both worlds."

Fourth and Koi exchanged glances. "Actually . . . " The feeling of unease slammed back into me. "We want to move to California."

In that moment, it felt like everything stopped.

No one said anything for several seconds. I didn't want to believe my ears, yet I had heard my brother's words with perfect clarity.

We want to move to California.

Which meant they would no longer be here. Never mind in our house—not even the same state! My throat ached, and my eyes filled with tears.

"Please don't take it personally!" Koi said. "None of this would have been possible without you, and we are so thankful. But my dad is in California, and I miss him so much. I need to be closer to him."

I could hear in her voice that their minds were made up; nothing Jeff or I could say would change it. Realizing that made me cry harder. Jeff wasn't crying, but I could see from the shocked expression on his face that he was just as floored by the news as I was.

They were going to leave. My family, who had only arrived a few months ago, was going to leave. Hadn't they been happy with us? I understood that Koi wanted to be closer to her father, but it hadn't been her father who had sponsored them. Such a thought was unfair—there were many reasons why her father had not done so—and just because Jeff and I had been able to did not mean they owed us something.

"But if that's so," I said, my mind desperate for something that might convince them to change their minds, "if your father, Koi, could really support you guys, wouldn't he have done so before this? What if his feelings change after you move closer to him?"

Koi shook her head. "He won't," she said. "Your feelings didn't change, did they?"

Well, they had—I'd fallen in love with the fact that I had some of my biological family members as a daily part of my life again. But they were going to be leaving. There was nothing Jeff and I could say to change their minds—they were adamant about the move.

The pain of the news burrowed into my core and stayed there. I tried my best to put on a brave face when telling the kids and Kim that our big, happy family was about to be fractured.

"Leaving?" Max and Sarah both said, nearly in unison. "Like on vacation?"

"Not like vacation," I said, trying to hold back tears. I'd already cried about it so much, it seemed impossible that I would even have any tears left, but I could feel them building in the corners of my eyes. "They're going to be moving to California. We'll still see them, but they want to be closer to Aunt Koi's father in California."

"It can be hard when you have family all over the place," Jeff said. "It's not that they don't like being here—they do."

"They just want to be in California more. What did we do wrong? We were so kind to them. Sarah and I shared everything with them. We never fought with them," Max said sadly. Sarah was quiet, fighting back tears.

"Sometimes, people don't feel the way we want," I hugged Sarah. "And that's okay. They have to do what's right for their family." It was the right thing to say, even though inside, my initial sadness had shifted to include anger, too—they were rejecting our love and our willingness to provide them with whatever it was they needed to ensure they had the best start.

When I shared the news with our nanny, Kim, she was also upset. She opened her mouth but then closed it. A heavy silence filled the air. "But we were so good to them. We even taught Koi how to drive so that she could get her license. You gave them so much. How can they just leave like this? We fell in love with them. This is terrible news."

I looked at Jeff, whose expression mirrored how I felt inside. Yet what could we do? I wanted to think that there was a reason for this, that there was some logical explanation as to why things would be going so well, all of us living here together, only for my brother to decide to upend that and move to California.

* * *

Still, there was a part of me that hoped they might change their minds. And also, I wasn't fully sure they understood the reality of the situation—perhaps they thought being provided with someone to cook, clean, and assist with errands was something all families in America had.

"I know you said you want to move to California," I told them one afternoon. "And Jeff and I signed sponsorship paperwork that said we are financially responsible for you. The thing is: we can't take care of you in another state."

"We understand," Fourth said. "Nhi, you've already done so much for our family."

I paused, not sure how my next point might be taken, or how it might come off sounding. Like I was trying to keep them here with promises of a cook and an assistant? I knew it could be construed as such, but life was hard enough already—especially when you were starting out somewhere new. Wouldn't they want to have access to things that could make it easier? "A lot of people in America don't have assistants," I said. "And I know Kim has really enjoyed working with you guys and help-ing you out. She'd be more than happy to continue to do so."

"You've done more than I ever hoped for," Koi said. "And we're still family. We might be moving to another state, but we're so much closer than if we were in Vietnam. We will come back and visit. And you can come visit us." Her expression was somber, but I could hear the excitement in her voice. She wanted to get to California. She wanted to be with her dad.

I tried to accept their decision. Refusing to accept it was not going to change the outcome, and regardless of where they lived, they were family. If they were going to start over again in California, I wanted them to be as prepared as possible.

A few days before they left, I went down into our basement to try and find some of the kitchen items we had duplicates of—I knew there was a new coffee maker and a teapot that had only been used a few times, and likely several other things they might want—yet instead of finding those things, I came across several large cardboard boxes, still sealed with packing tape. Their names were scrawled on the top and the sides. The boxes had never been opened, and I realized that my brother and his family had never intended to live with us for the long term. Had it been their plan all along?

I returned from the basement feeling like I'd been punched. I didn't want to think that my brother had used us just to get to America, yet everything suggested that was exactly what had happened.

The day after their kids finished school, Jeff and I watched them pack their van up with the unopened boxes from the base-ment and the many gifts we gave them for their future home. I was watching it happen with my own two eyes, yet at the same time, I couldn't believe it was really happening. I kept expecting it to be a nightmare I'd awaken from, and then we could all go back to how it had been.

And it did feel like a dream, it did feel surreal, to hug each of them and say goodbye. The children cried. I cried. Jeff fought back tears. We were surprised to see Koi crying—isn't leaving what she wanted? I tried to tell myself it wasn't the last time I was going to see them, yet their abrupt departure was dredging up old memories, dragging me right back to my childhood and having to say goodbye to my mom, not knowing if I'd ever see her again. But instead of just concern for myself, my heart was breaking for my children, who had never experienced that sort of loss before. They had welcomed their cousins and their aunt and uncle with open arms and open hearts. They loved them unconditionally. And though I knew nothing had to stop them from loving them, the distance that was now going to be between us meant we would not be able to continue as one big happy family, as I had hoped.

* * *

It's difficult to fully explain the impact Fourth and his family leaving had on me, and my own family. The truth of it was that they were still much closer to us in California than they ever had been in Vietnam. Yet my heart was broken. I felt used. I felt like my loved ones took advantage of me and my life.

It was a difficult time. And not just for me but the kids, as well. Jeff tried to remain positive, but I knew it was hard on him to see how it was affecting me, and feeling like there was nothing he could do to help.

I still got up and went to work and went through the motions, but inside, I felt destroyed. When I returned from work, I would cry, out of sadness but also just from the exhaustion of trying to keep it together all day. Jeff had never seen me cry so much.

"Is there anything I can do?" he asked one night as I sobbed in bed. I could hear the desperation in his voice, the frustration that there was nothing he could do.

"Your brother loves you," he said. Hearing Jeff's voice soothed me and I took a ragged breath, the flow of tears slowing. "I know he does. But think about him for a second. He's older than you. You're his little sister. For a guy . . . well, not every guy would be comfortable with being supported by their little sister. Fourth grew up under communism. He had to keep quiet about anything he was planning to do or possibly face prison."

It made sense, everything Jeff was saying. And I knew Fourth loved me. But I still felt so cheated and unloved.

We only shared the details of the situation with our close friends and family. We told other people that the weather in Colorado was too cold for Fourth and his family, so they decided to move to California. Every time I told someone this, it felt like my heart was breaking all over again.

The people in our lives who knew the truth were so wonderful during that time. Mary Lou would call me regularly just to check in and tell me that she loved me.

"I just wasn't expecting to still feel like this," I said one afternoon when she called. "It's been over a month now, and I still feel as awful about it as when they first left. I don't want to always feel like this."

"You won't. It takes time to get over something like this. And Nhi, I just want you to know—even though I didn't give birth to you, you are my daughter, and part of the family, and we will always be here for you. We love you so much and don't want to see you in pain."

My father-in-law, Richard, would regularly call and echo Mary Lou's sentiments. So would my sister-in-law, Amy, and they made it abundantly clear that they were there for me—"If you need to call and yell, cry, scream—we're here for you, Nhi. You are family and we love you."

I talked with Nanny Kim quite a bit, and felt that, in her, I had someone who really understood how I felt. When I would get home from work, Kim would have a pot of tea ready and we would stand in the kitchen talking. The kids would be with friends or doing their homework, and Kim and I would commiserate.

"They have no idea how hard life in America is," Kim said. "You and Jeff helped them so much, but what they don't realize is that it's not going to be like that everywhere." She sighed. "I miss them."

It compounded my own pain to see how much it hurt Kim, too. "I wish they realized how much hurt they have caused everyone," I said.

"It was a stupid move. They shouldn't have done it. But I guess they'll have to learn the hard way."

* * *

Even though I wasn't feeling like myself during that time, I wanted to be forthright with the kids. They were still hurting too, and trying, in their own ways, to come to terms with what had happened. No parent wants to see their children in pain,

[I overheard Sarah crying in her room one night and I went over and knocked on the door, which was slightly ajar. I heard her sniffling and then saying, "Come in." I stepped into the room, thinking back to all those evenings when Sarah and her cousin were in here, chit chatting and laughing together.]

"I'm so sad, Mom," Sarah said. I sat on the edge of her bed. "I miss them, especially Khanh."

"I know you do," I said. "I do, too. And I know how you feel because I was so sad when they left. I'm still sad. But you know what?"

"What?"

"I'm so proud of you and your brother. Just seeing the way you guys opened your hearts to your cousins, to your aunt and uncle. I don't want you to be afraid to love like that in the future. And I want you to know that you didn't do anything wrong. That's not why they left. You know that, right?"

Sarah sniffled again. "Right," she said, her voice quavering. "But it hurts how much I miss them. I just want it to stop. I want them to come back."

She was verbalizing everything I was feeling inside. "I do, too," I said. "But they have to do what's right for their family, and that meant moving to California. I just want to make sure you know that you should never be afraid to love, and that loving someone is one of the greatest gifts a person can give to someone else. Even though sometimes it can cause you pain, too."

"I'll always love them," Sarah said.

I gave her a hug, wanting nothing more than to take her pain away, even though I wasn't sure how much more I could endure myself.

* * *

Unlike Sarah, Max did not want to talk about his cousins, or that his aunt and uncle had decided to move the family to California. I knew his silence did not mean he was unaffected, but Jeff and I wanted to give him the space to grieve in his own way. We made sure he knew that we were there for him whenever he felt ready to talk about it.

I also needed to talk, and not just to my family or friends who knew the situation. I went to see our therapist Todd, who had coached Jeff and me through many things over the years, but after Fourth left, I was going to see him one on one.

Only three months earlier, at seeing my jubilance over my family's arrival, Todd had said, "Your life has come in full circle, finding lost love."

But there I was, sitting in his office, barely able to maintain my composure as I told him they had left.

"Oh, no," he said, and the surprise in his voice was genuine. "That is not what I was expecting to hear. Nhi, I'm so sorry."

"I don't think they ever planned to stay with us," I said. I told him about the unpacked boxes. The undecorated bedroom. "It would be easier to accept if they had been forthright from the beginning, but they weren't. I feel like they used us just to get over here. I don't believe it was their intention, but I was so hurt after everything we did for them! We gave them everything we could to help them get on their feet. Jeff and I had just been talking about helping Fourth find a business he could get into. And they just decide to leave!"

Todd sat and listened while I let it all out. And when I was finished, he shook his head. "I'm so sorry that you are in this situation. I understand why you are heartbroken and it makes me sad to hear this."

"I was so happy when they finally got here after thirteen years."

"I know you were. And now they've moved, and you're left to deal with the fallout. How are the kids?"

"They're hurt, too. They didn't understand why their cousins had to leave like that. Those three months they were with us—we were all so happy! Like one big, happy family. I know that sounds like a cliché, but it's true, we were. It made me fall in love with Jeff even more, to see the way he'd come home from work, just so happy to see everyone. And he's been so strong and supportive, but he's not used to seeing me cry all the time. He doesn't know what to do. *I* don't know what to do."

Todd had helped us so much in the past, but the way I felt at that point, I wasn't sure if there was anything he'd be able to do.

"Nhi," he said, "you are going to get through this. But it will take time, and you've got to be patient with yourself and give yourself the time to go through the grieving process. There will be different stages. You'll be sad, angry, enraged, frustrated. Maybe all at once. And it might seem like you'll always feel this way, but you won't. It's important to remember that as you go through this process."

When I left my appointment that day, I didn't feel much different, but I kept Todd's words at the forefront of my mind. *This is a process. There are different stages.*

I would continue to see Todd on a weekly basis during that time. For a while, it didn't seem his initial assessment had been correct—that I wouldn't always feel that way—but slowly, the heartbreak I felt began to subside.

One day, I got a call from my sister Second, who still lived in Kentucky. "Have you talked to our brother?" she asked.

"No," I said. "They haven't bothered to keep in touch as they promised."

"Well, you're not going to believe it, then," she said. My sister proceeded to tell me that their move to California had not been as smooth as they hoped; Koi's father was not able to provide much in the way of help. They'd only been living there a few months, apparently, when Koi's cousin in Texas suggested they move to Dallas, because they were in a better position to provide support.

"So they moved," Sister Second said.

My jaw dropped. "They're in Texas? With Koi's cousin?"

"Well, not really. Yes, they're in Texas, but Koi's cousin wasn't able to take care of them either. Fourth didn't give me many details. But he did say they're planning to stay in Dallas. He was a fool to leave Colorado! I told him so."

It was hard to wrap my mind around the news my sister had shared. I found no joy in being correct that Koi's father would not be able to help them, but it felt like reopening wounds that had barely started to heal, realizing that they would rather stay in Texas than reach out to Jeff and me.

"You can only help people who want to be helped," Todd told me at one of our appointments. "You cannot force help upon someone who doesn't want it. You and I both know that your brother and his family would have had many more opportunities if they had stayed with you. But that isn't the choice they made."

I tried not to think about why they didn't call us after they knew California wasn't going to work out. Todd was right—you couldn't force help upon someone who didn't want it, even if it would've been the best thing for them.

About a year after my brother and his family left, I began to feel more like myself again. Several days would go by and I would realize I hadn't cried; then it was a full week. I felt as if a fog was lifting, and I knew it was thanks to Todd and the love and support from my family and friends.

And as I began to emerge from the haze of my depression, I had a realization that would again change the trajectory of my life.

CHAPTER TWENTY
LIFE TODAY

I realized I had been neglecting myself.

Most of my childhood had been focused on survival; my young adulthood on playing catch up and being successful; and then tending to both a family and a thriving career. Self-care had never really been a factor.

In the years before Fourth's arrival, Jeff and I had met with our financial advisor to put together a plan that made sense and would sustain us for the rest of our lives, while also setting aside funds to help take care of my brother and his family.

But they were gone, and so was our responsibility to care for their family of five. And one day, Jeff came to me with an idea. "We are in a fortunate position that we no longer need your income for survival. Why don't you retire early?" he said. "We're in a good place financially. You can take some time for yourself, do something you've always wanted to do but never had the time for."

"I don't even know what I'd do." I had cut my hours back at work after Fourth and his family arrived because I wanted to be available to help them as much as I could, but since they were gone, I wasn't sure what I'd do with myself if I didn't have work.

"You don't have to know just yet," Jeff said. "You've had a hard year and I think you deserve some time to take care of yourself. However that looks."

When I brought it up to Todd the next time I saw him, he echoed Jeff's sentiments. "It surprises people sometimes, to realize that they have to learn how to take care of themselves. You're so good at taking care of your family, but how good are you at taking care of yourself?"

"Not good," I said.

He smiled. "I know. And I think it's a good time now for you to learn to take care of *you*. It's okay to be selfish sometimes and enjoy living now because you've been working since you were five when most kids in this country don't work until they are sixteen. You would not be able to give and pay it forward until you truly take care of yourself."

And so, on January 1, 2017, at forty-one years old, I stopped working and officially "retired" and let Jeff take over the business. It was a true blessing for a Vietnamese woman who on more than one occasion nearly lost her life trying to find her way to the United States, never mind surviving and prospering in her new home. Though my life has not been free from challenges, I am grateful every day for the multitude of opportunities I have had in America.

* * *

I took Todd's advice to heart. And during that first year, I loved my "retirement." I enjoyed going to the gym, playing tennis, and going out to lunch with friends. During school vacation, the family would travel all over the country—we visited family in Virginia, went to the Grand Canyon, Las Vegas, Florida, Manhattan, and most of New England. It was great to be able to spend so much time with my family, and it was also gratifying to be able to give my children experiences that I did not have growing up.

But the novelty of retirement wore off after that first year. With a school break approaching, both Max and Sarah came to me, asking that we please stay home because they didn't want to travel so much.

"Of course!" I told them. "We don't have to go anywhere." Yet inside I was wondering what I was supposed to do.

What is my new purpose in life?

It began to feel like the walls were closing in. My days started to feel pointless, and all the same—*gym, tennis, lunch with so and so.* Sarah and Max were busy with school, Jeff had work. I no longer woke up excited to start each day; I felt rather listless. I was not going in the direction I wanted to; that listlessness was not the point of early retirement.

We had heard some of the horror stories about people who achieve their dream of retiring early only to find themselves in retirement hell. They lose their sense of worth and sometimes struggle with depression, frustration, and anxiety. It can also spill over into their relationship with their spouse; after all, their spouse is still moving forward full steam ahead. I didn't want to be one of those retirees that sat at home wondering what to do next, and then pick my husband and kids apart for the little things simply because I needed the interaction. Yet everything I had ever dreamed of as a child came true, so there were seemingly no more dreams, no more goals, and no more walls to scale. Sometimes that can be harder than failure.

What's going to get me up on the morning? How am I going to feel relevant, productive, and positive?

What can I do to make a difference in the community and the world?

It became clear I needed to figure out my WHY. I started looking into various organizations and volunteer opportunities. I didn't commit to anything, but looked at it as a testing-the-waters phase. I would know when I came across the right thing, I felt, it was just a matter of finding it.

I also asked my family and friends what they thought might be a good fit. "What do you think is something I would be good at doing, enjoy doing it, and would make a difference in people's lives?"

Three different friends suggested mediation, which was something I had no clue about. But they all said the same thing: *Based on your personality and negotiation skill, you should be a mediator.*

When you have three different people, at three different times, tell you that you would be perfect for something, it's at least worth looking into based on my intuition. So I went online and signed up for mediation training.

* * *

Today, I spend my time as a mediator helping people resolve their conflicts, and occasionally work as a Vietnamese interpreter for those who need medical help. Being the liaison between a patient who needs care yet is unable to communicate with his or her doctor because of a language barrier really has brought me full circle—I can easily recall myself as a girl, stuck in a Thai hospital, with no way to talk to the doctors and nurses who were helping me.

I'm grateful I've been able to help. Because that's what it's really all about, isn't it? Being able to help each other out as much as we can. Everyone we encounter in our lives plays a role in some way or another, and every person I've encountered along the way has played a critical role, both good and bad, in the story of my life.

I've had plenty of moments wondering if there was something bigger than myself, than us, at work, some unseen force setting events in motion. There are so many variables, so many times I was dependent on the kindness of those around me. Is there a reason certain people end up in our lives?

I still sometimes think back to that question Jeff asked, when we went out on that dinner cruise so many years ago now. *Do you believe in soul mates?* At the time, I had scoffed and called it bullshit. But now, married for twenty-plus wonderful years, I have to amend my original answer and say *Yes*. Not because I'm now an expert in soul mates, but because Jeff has shown me how transformative loving acceptance and respect can be. His feelings mirror my own, and because of this, my love for him has continued to grow—though this doesn't mean we don't irritate each other from time to time! I have so much gratitude that Jeff has brought his wonderful family into my life. The wish I had made when I was in the refugee camp years ago about having a family to love and cherish has become a reality, many times over, in ways I only could have dreamed of then. The humanity and love I've experienced have transcended me into who I am today.

* * *

Let me finish my book by sharing with you a little story about a gift, my favorite gift, given to me by Jeff. It wasn't fancy jewelry or an expensive car—no, it was a toilet.

That's right, a toilet.

But not just any old toilet. This toilet came with every feature imaginable—and probably a few you wouldn't think a toilet would be able to do. It could wash you, dry you, spray you, and even keep you warm on a cold winter's night. It had a sensor to automatically lift the lid when you entered the bathroom and then close it when you left. It's amused friends, frightened unsuspecting children, and been a fun dinner conversation topic with guests. A few guests have jokingly inquired as to why I don't just have our toilet turned into 24k gold. Yes, it's a toilet, but it's the best birthday present I ever got.

Not just for its many conveniences, though. This gift from my husband is symbolic of my life's journey. From a gaping, foul-smelling hole in the ground to the pinnacle of comfort and ease, I made my way from the depths of poverty and oppression to the joy of a full, rewarding life. It might sound strange to have a toilet represent your life's arc, but for me, it's a reminder to live each day with gratitude for every circumstance.

Because chances are, I wouldn't be where I am right now had I not lived through each and every experience—from fleeing my homeland to getting stranded on a deserted island; surviving the refugee camp and making my way to America; being adopted into Mary Lou's family and taking a delayed flight to Denver—today, it feels as if my life has come full circle. It's sort of like the story of Job. The family, love, and even the nanny I lost in the first part of my life were replaced tenfold with everything and everybody I have today.

To have come so far from where I started makes me sometimes wonder if it was fate or divine intervention that brought
me together with Jeff, and with my adopted family. Was it the
universe or some higher power guiding me to follow my heart,
instructing me to trust my intuition to grasp the opportunities
being presented to me? It's one of those questions that will
probably never be fully answered, yet I do believe it was more
than just chance or randomness.

The adversities and misfortunes in my life have taught me
to be grateful every day; I've always grasped the opportunities
that presented themselves and even during the lowest points in
my life, I never gave up. My resilience and indomitable spirit
helped me push on even at my lowest points and gave me the
strength to work hard and find my way to success and prosper-
ity. What I've learned is that it doesn't matter what religion we
belong to or what we had to overcome in life, so long as we radiate kindness, generosity, and are willing to help out the people
we meet along the way.

My hope is to encourage everyone who reads my book to
never give up, never give in, and always stay positive.

AFTERWORD

It was Jeff, the kids, family, and close friends who encouraged me to write this book. After writing the first draft, I interviewed several editors and decided to work with the one I found online (even though she lives in Massachusetts) to give the manuscript a second set of eyes. While reading my initial manuscript (which had full names of each character), Erica made an incredible discovery: She lived in the same neighborhood as Bridget, my guardian angel who shepherded me to the safety of the Minors Center. For years, I had tried to locate Bridget online, but had been unsuccessful, as she did not appear to have any social media accounts, and she had moved away after my last contact. I have since been able to reconnect with her, an opportunity that wouldn't have been possible had I not chosen to work with this particular editor, which wouldn't have been necessary if my family had not talked me into writing this book.

Some people might write it off as coincidence or good luck, but to me, it's just one more example that makes me believe the things that happen, the people that come into our lives, have a purpose, and for that reason, we should embrace each day with as much gratitude as we can.

ACKNOWLEDGMENTS

A huge thank you to all the people who helped me bring this book to publication:

My literary manager Sharlene Martin for believing that my story is worth sharing to the world.

My editor Caroline Russomanno and the team at Skyhorse Publishing for your dedication to launching this book.

My dear friends, Marisol Konczal and Rob Simon, for advising me to get help when I had writer's block and could not write certain scenes that were too difficult for me emotionally.

My husband Jeff Aronheim for always believing in me, accepting me for who I am—the good, the bad, and the ugly—and encouraging me to reach my full potential. There would be no book if I did not have you by my side.

My children Max and Sarah for asking me to write down the story about my journey so that you would know more about my background and your heritage.

My Vietnamese mother Vo Thi Dao for teaching me how to survive in the toughest environment and for sending me away hoping that I would be able to find the American Dream.

My adoptive mother Mary Lou Hearn, brothers Tom, Alan, and Bryan, and Uncle Richard Hearn for accepting me as your own family member regardless of my race. You taught me a great lesson about humanity, diversity, tolerance, and unconditional love.

My parents-in-law Richard and Gloria Aronheim and sisters-in-law Amy Fradkin and Marnie Aronheim for your continuous love and support, and for embracing my "uniqueness" from the very beginning.

My dearest friend Lora Wilson for your friendship over the years and for listening to me when I got discouraged and frustrated with my writing progress.

My friend Angela Bartley Pahley for pushing me to call Jeff. Without your encouragement, there would be no second part of this book.

My friends Kevin Skeeters and Chris Jordan for always being there for me. Your friendship means the world to me.

Dr. Clarence Wyatt for making my first family reunion in Vietnam possible.

Dale and Jim Roggenkamp and Caroll and Walter Gander for many wonderful dinners and weekends at your home when I had nothing to offer you, except my friendship.

To all the wonderful friends and teachers in Kentucky who came into my life and lifted me up when I needed help the most. I am sorry that I could not share about my painful past with you until now. After some crying in the middle of the night while recalling my experiences and writing down some of the most difficult scenes, this book is from the bottom of my heart to yours. Your support and unconditional love transformed me to who I am today and with that I am thankful.

In loving memory of my brother, Nguyen Dinh Cu, and my adoptive father Lewis Hearn.